ExamKrackers MCAT

ORGANIC CHEMISTRY

6TH EDITION

OSOTE
PUBLISHING

ISBN 1-893858-39-1 (Volume 3)
ISBN 1-893858-42-1 (5 Volume Set)

6th Edition

To purchase additional copies of this book or the rest of the 5 volume set,
call 1-888-572-2536 or fax orders to 1-859-255-0109.

examkrackers.com

osote.com

audioosmosis.com

Inside layout design: Saucy Enterprizes (www.saucyenterprizes.com)
Cover design: Scott Wolfe, Visible Theory 626-795-1885
Inside front cover design consultant: Fenwick Design Inc. (212) 246-9722; (201) 944-4337
Illustrations by the ExamKrackers staff.

Printed and bound in China

Acknowledgements

Although I am the author, the hard work and expertise of many individuals contributed to this book. The idea of writing in two voices, a science voice and an MCAT voice, was the creative brainchild of my imaginative friend Jordan Zaretsky. I would like to thank Scott Calvin and Jerry Johnson for lending their exceptional science talent and pedagogic skills to this project. I would like to thank Alex Merkulov for his contributions to the lecture questions. I also must thank 8 years worth of ExamKrackers students for doggedly questioning every explanation, every sentence, every diagram, and every punctuation mark in the book, and for providing the creative inspiration that helped me find new ways to approach and teach organic chemistry. Finally, I wish to thank my wife, Silvia, for her support during the difficult times in the past and those that lie ahead.

Jonathan Orsay

READ THIS SECTION FIRST!

This manual contains all the organic chemistry tested on the MCAT and more. It contains more organic chemistry than is tested on the MCAT because a deeper understanding of basic scientific principles is often gained through more advanced study. In addition, the MCAT often presents passages with imposing topics that may intimidate the test-taker. Although the questions don't require knowledge of these topics, some familiarity will increase the confidence of the test-taker.

In order to answer questions quickly and efficiently, the test-taker must understand what is, and is not, tested directly by the MCAT. To assist the test-taker in gaining this knowledge, this manual will use the following conventions. Any term or concept that is tested directly by the MCAT will be written in bold and underlined. To ensure a perfect score on the MCAT, you should thoroughly understand all terms and concepts that are in bold and underlined in this manual. Sometimes it is not necessary to memorize the name of a concept, but it is necessary to understand the concept itself. These concepts will also be in bold and underlined. It is important to note that the converse of the above is not true: just because a topic is not in **bold and underlined** does not mean that it is not important.

If a topic is discussed purely as background knowledge, it will be written in *italics*. If a topic is written in italics, it is not likely to be required knowledge for the MCAT but may be discussed in an MCAT passage. Do not ignore items in italics, but recognize them as less important than other items. Answers to questions that directly test knowledge of italicized topics are likely to be found in an MCAT passage.

 Text written in this font is me, Salty the Kracker. I will remind you what is and is not an absolute must for MCAT. I will help you develop your MCAT intuition. In addition, I will offer mnemonics, simple methods of viewing a complex concept, and occasionally some comic relief. Don't ignore me, even if you think I am not funny, because my comedy is designed to help you understand and remember. If you think I am funny, tell the boss. I could use a raise.

Each chapter in this manual should be read three times: twice before the class lecture, and once immediately following the lecture. During the first reading, you should not write in the book. Instead, read purely for enjoyment. During the second reading, you should both highlight and take notes in the margins. The third reading should be slow and thorough.

The 24 questions in each lecture should be worked during the second reading before coming to class. The in-class exams in the back of the book are to be done in class after the lecture. Do not look at them before class.

Warning: Just attending the class will not raise your score. You must do the work. Not attending class will obstruct dramatic score increases. If you have Audio Osmosis, then listen to the appropriate lecture before and after you read a lecture.

If you are studying independently, read the lecture twice before doing the in-class exam and then once after doing the in-class exam. If you have Audio Osmosis, listen to Audio Osmosis before taking the in-class exam and then as many times as necessary after taking the exam.

A scaled score conversion chart is provided on the answer page. This is not meant to be an accurate representation of your MCAT score. Do not become demoralized by a poor performance on these exams; they are not accurate reflections of your performance on the real MCAT. The thirty-minute exams have been designed to educate. They are similar to an MCAT but with most of the easy questions removed. We believe that you can answer most of the easy questions without too much help from us, so the best way to raise your score is to focus on the more difficult questions. This method is one of the reasons for the rapid and celebrated success of the Examkrackers prep course and products.

If you find yourself struggling with the science or just needing more practice materials, use the Examkrackers 1001 Questions series. These books are designed specifically to teach the science. If you are already scoring 10s or better, these books are probably not for you.

You should take advantage of the bulletin board at www.examkrackers.com. The bulletin board allows you to discuss any question in this book with an MCAT expert at Examkrackers. All discussions are kept on file so you have a bank of discussions to which you can refer for any question in this book.

Although we are very careful to be accurate, errata is an occupational hazard of any science book, especially those that are updated regularly as is this one. We maintain that our books have fewer errata than any other prep book. Often what a student is certain is error is the student's error and not an error in the book. So that you can be certain, any errata in this book will be listed as they are discovered at www.examkrackers.com on the bulletin board. Check this site initially and periodically. If you discover what you believe to be an error, please post it on this board and we will verify it promptly. We understand that this system calls attention to the very few errata that may be in our books, but we feel that this is the best system to ensure that you have accurate information for your exam. Again, we stress that we have fewer errata than any other prep book on the market. The difference is that we provide a public list of our errata for your benefit.

Study diligently, trust this book to guide you, and you will reach your MCAT goals.

TABLE OF CONTENTS

BIOLOGICAL SCIENCES

DIRECTIONS. Most questions in the Biological Sciences test are organized into groups, each preceded by a descriptive passage. After studying the passage, select the one best answer to each question in the group. Some questions are not based on a descriptive passage and are also independent of each other. You must also select the one best answer to these questions. If you are not certain of an answer, eliminate the alternatives that you know to be incorrect and then select an answer from the remaining alternatives. Indicate your selection by blackening the corresponding oval on your answer document. A periodic table is provided for your use. You may consult it whenever you wish.

PERIODIC TABLE OF THE ELEMENTS

1 H 1.0																	2 He 4.0
3 Li 6.9	4 Be 9.0											5 B 10.8	6 C 12.0	7 N 14.0	8 O 16.0	9 F 19.0	10 Ne 20.2
11 Na 23.0	12 Mg 24.3											13 Al 27.0	14 Si 28.1	15 P 31.0	16 S 32.1	17 Cl 35.5	18 Ar 39.9
19 K 39.1	20 Ca 40.1	21 Sc 45.0	22 Ti 47.9	23 V 50.9	24 Cr 52.0	25 Mn 54.9	26 Fe 55.8	27 Co 58.9	28 Ni 58.7	29 Cu 63.5	30 Zn 65.4	31 Ga 69.7	32 Ge 72.6	33 As 74.9	34 Se 79.0	35 Br 79.9	36 Kr 83.8
37 Rb 85.5	38 Sr 87.6	39 Y 88.9	40 Zr 91.2	41 Nb 92.9	42 Mo 95.9	43 Tc (98)	44 Ru 101.1	45 Rh 102.9	46 Pd 106.4	47 Ag 107.9	48 Cd 112.4	49 In 114.8	50 Sn 118.7	51 Sb 121.8	52 Te 127.6	53 I 126.9	54 Xe 131.3
55 Cs 132.9	56 Ba 137.3	57 La* 138.9	72 Hf 178.5	73 Ta 180.9	74 W 183.9	75 Re 186.2	76 Os 190.2	77 Ir 192.2	78 Pt 195.1	79 Au 197.0	80 Hg 200.6	81 Tl 204.4	82 Pb 207.2	83 Bi 209.0	84 Po (209)	85 At (210)	86 Rn (222)
87 Fr (223)	88 Ra 226.0	89 Ac† 227.0	104 Unq (261)	105 Unp (262)	106 Unh (263)	107 Uns (262)	108 Uno (265)	109 Une (267)									

	58 Ce 140.1	59 Pr 140.9	60 Nd 144.2	61 Pm (145)	62 Sm 150.4	63 Eu 152.0	64 Gd 157.3	65 Tb 158.9	66 Dy 162.5	67 Ho 164.9	68 Er 167.3	69 Tm 168.9	70 Yb 173.0	71 Lu 175.0
†	90 Th 232.0	91 Pa (231)	92 U 238.0	93 Np (237)	94 Pu (244)	95 Am (243)	96 Cm (247)	97 Bk (247)	98 Cf (251)	99 Es (252)	100 Fm (257)	101 Md (258)	102 No (259)	103 Lr (260)

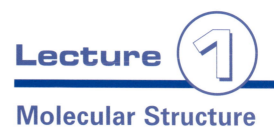

Lecture 1

Molecular Structure

Organic chemistry is probably the most feared topic on the MCAT. Few MCAT test-takers feel confident about their organic chemistry skills. If you feel confident about organic chemistry, it is probably either because you have a PhD, or because you have only taken first-year organic chemistry and haven't yet learned that organic chemistry is far more complex than your first-year textbook led you to believe.

Attempting to master advanced organic chemistry concepts in order to improve your MCAT score is not *just* a futile waste of time; it is likely to lower your MCAT score. The writers of the MCAT neither test nor claim to test any organic chemistry beyond "content typically covered in undergraduate introductory science courses". In fact, they go to great lengths to ensure that the test does not require knowledge beyond "content typically covered in undergraduate introductory science courses". If you *think* that MCAT might test more, and you look for more in an MCAT organic chemistry question, you are likely to overlook the obvious answer, which is based upon "content typically covered in undergraduate introductory science courses". You are also likely to spend more time on each question because you are choosing the answer from a larger pool of knowledge; more answer choices will *seem* possible within your larger, but inaccurate, context.

Any and all organic chemistry required to answer any question on the MCAT will be covered in this book. For the reasons stated in the preceding paragraph, it is possible that using other organic chemistry MCAT prep books to supplement this book could alter your perception of what is tested by the MCAT thereby lowering your score. We suggest against it.

You should expect questions to look complex and to *appear* that they require in-depth knowledge of organic chemistry. When answering such questions, consider only the simplest organic chemistry concepts and answer the questions accordingly.

1-1

Introduction

Structural formulae are representations of molecules on paper. The MCAT may use any or all of the various formulae so you should be familiar with all of them. The most basic form of structural formula is the **Lewis dot structure**.

1-2

Structural Formula

1-3

Lewis Dot Structures

There are three rules for forming Lewis dot structures.

1.   Find the total number of valence electrons for all atoms in the molecule.

2.   Use one pair of electrons to form one bond between each atom.

3.   Arrange the remaining electrons around the atoms to satisfy the duet rule for hydrogen and the octet rule for other atoms.

Exceptions: Sometimes atoms break the octet rule. Molecules with such atoms include molecules with an odd number of electrons, molecules with an atom having less than an octet, and molecules with an atom having more than an octet. Compounds containing boron and beryllium may contain less than an octet. Molecules with an atom containing more than an octet must contain an atom from the third period or greater in the periodic table because only these atoms have vacant *d* orbitals available for hybridization.

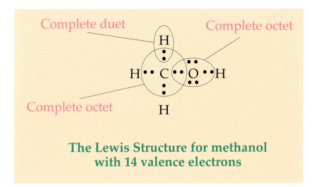

The Lewis Structure for methanol with 14 valence electrons

When writing Lewis structures, don't worry about which electrons come from which atoms. Simply count the number of total electrons and distribute them to complete the valence shells. It is useful to know the atom's **valence** (the number of bonds it usually forms). Some important valences for common atoms in organic chemistry are as follows: carbon is tetravalent; nitrogen is trivalent; oxygen is divalent; hydrogens and halogens are monovalent. (Halogens other than fluorine are capable of making more than one bond.)

It is also useful to know the **formal charge** of an atom. The formal charge is the number of electrons in the isolated atom, minus the number of electrons assigned to the atom in the Lewis structure. For instance, in the cyanide ion carbon has a pair of nonbonding electrons and one electron from each bond in the triple bond for a total of five electrons.

$$[:C \equiv N:]^-$$

cyanide ion

A neutral carbon atom has only four electrons, so the formal charge on carbon in the cyanide ion is minus one. It is important to know that, although the sum of the formal charges for each atom in a molecule or ion represents the total charge on that molecule or ion, the formal charge on a given atom does not represent a real charge on that atom. The actual charge distribution requires consideration of electronegativity differences among all the atoms in the molecule.

The **dash formula** shows the bonds between atoms, but does not show the three dimensional structure of the molecule.

The **condensed formula** does not show bonds. Central atoms are usually followed by the atoms that bond to them even though this is not the bonding order. For instance, the three hydrogens following the carbon in CH_3NH_2 do not bond to the nitrogen.

1-4
Other Structures

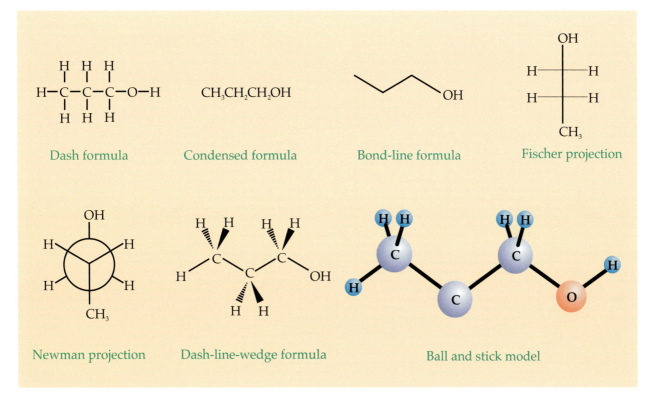

Dash formula   Condensed formula   Bond-line formula   Fischer projection

Newman projection   Dash-line-wedge formula   Ball and stick model

The **bond-line formula** is likely to be the most prevalent on the MCAT. In the bond-line formula, line intersections, corners, and endings represent a carbon atom unless some other atom is drawn in. The hydrogen atoms that are attached to the carbons are not usually drawn but are assumed to be present.

The **Fischer projection** is also important on the MCAT. In Fischer projections the vertical lines are assumed to be oriented into the page. The horizontal lines are assumed to be oriented out of the page.

The **Newman projection** is a view straight down the axis of one of the σ-bonds. Both the intersecting lines and the large circle are assumed to be carbon atoms.

In the **dash-line-wedge formula** the black wedge is assumed to be coming out of the page, the dashed wedge is assumed to be going into the page, and the lines are assumed to be in the plane of the page.

Unless otherwise indicated, in all **ball and stick models** in this manual covalently bonded atoms will be drawn to scale using comparisons of their atomic radii as single atoms. Although the sum of the atomic radii is a reasonable approximation of bond length, in the ball and stick models shown in this manual the bond length is drawn to approximately twice this length so that the atoms are clearly visible.

1-5
Index of Hydrogen Deficiency

The **index of hydrogen deficiency** indicates the number of pairs of hydrogens a compound requires in order to become a saturated alkane. Since a saturated alkane contains $2n + 2$ hydrogens (where n is the number of carbons), in order to find the index of deficiency of any compound, subtract the compound's total number of hydrogens from the number of hydrogens on a corresponding saturated alkane and divide by two. For this procedure count halogens as hydrogens, ignore oxygen atoms, and count nitrogen atoms as one half of a hydrogen atom. Of course, the index of hydrogen deficiency for any saturated alkane will be zero.

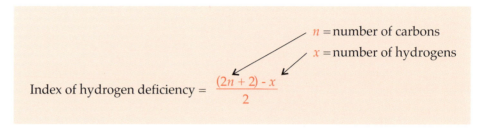

n = number of carbons
x = number of hydrogens

$$\text{Index of hydrogen deficiency} = \frac{(2n + 2) - x}{2}$$

1-6
Functional Groups

The first step in solving any organic chemistry problem on the MCAT is to recognize which functional groups are involved in the reaction. The MCAT tests only reactions involving the basic functional groups. Many of the molecules on the MCAT are likely to be large and unfamiliar; however, in order to solve an MCAT problem, it is only important to be familiar with the attached functional groups and how they react.

Functional groups are reactive, non-alkaline portions of molecules. The following two lists display functional groups. Memorization of List #1 is absolutely vital to success on the MCAT. List #2 is less important, but should still be memorized.

You must know these groups for MCAT Orgo! Stop now and memorize List #1.

List #1

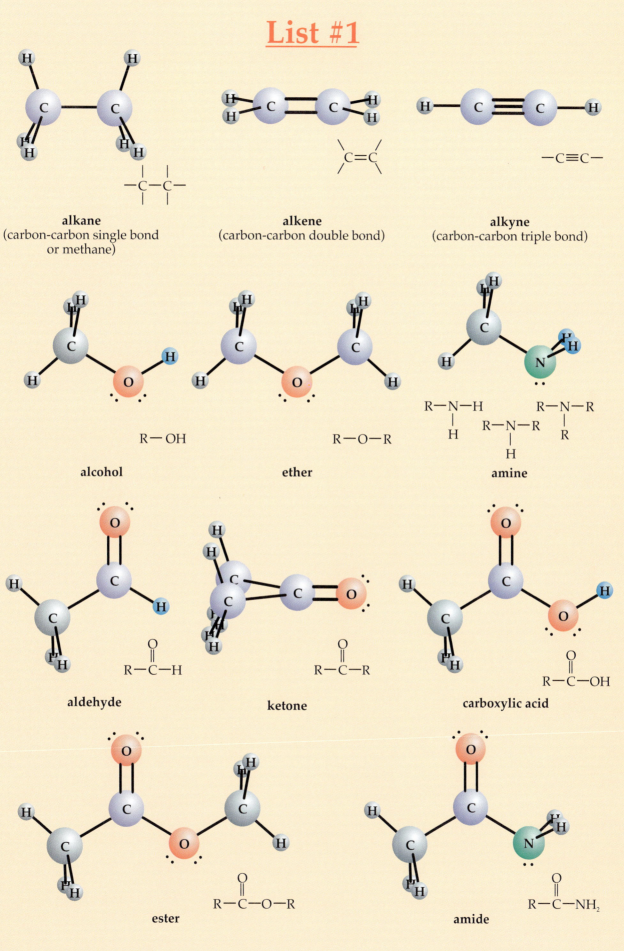

alkane
(carbon-carbon single bond
or methane)

alkene
(carbon-carbon double bond)

alkyne
(carbon-carbon triple bond)

R—OH

alcohol

R—O—R

ether

R—N—H
|
H

R—N—R
|
H

R—N—R
|
R

amine

$$R-\overset{O}{\overset{\|}{C}}-H$$

aldehyde

$$R-\overset{O}{\overset{\|}{C}}-R$$

ketone

$$R-\overset{O}{\overset{\|}{C}}-OH$$

carboxylic acid

$$R-\overset{O}{\overset{\|}{C}}-O-R$$

ester

$$R-\overset{O}{\overset{\|}{C}}-NH_2$$

amide

List #2

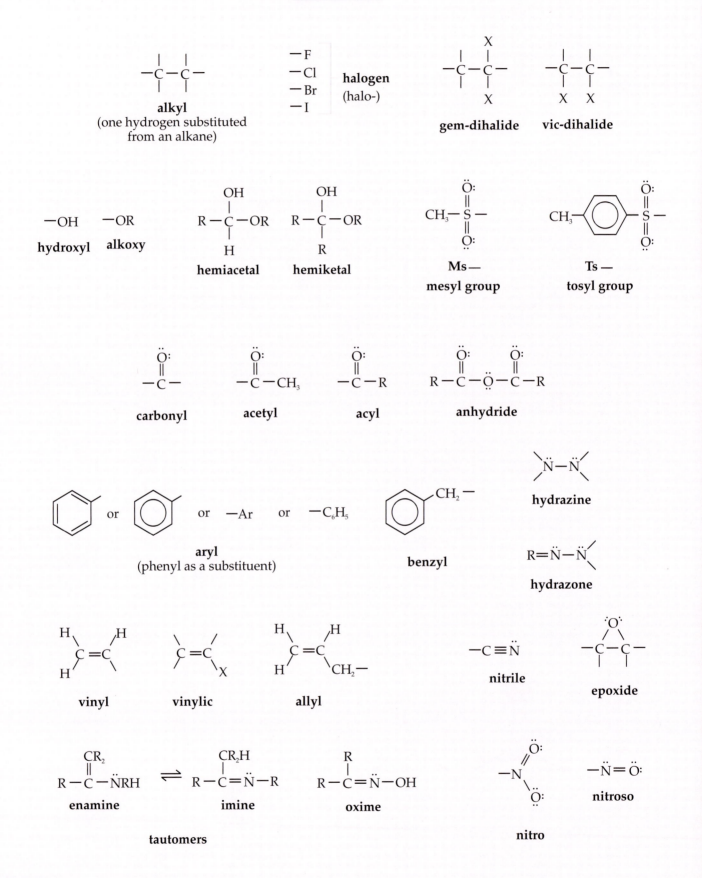

The MCAT requires knowledge of basic organic chemistry nomenclature. For alkanes you must memorize the following:

prefix	number of carbons
meth-	1
eth-	2
prop-	3
but-	4
pent-	5
hex-	6
hept-	7
oct-	8
non-	9
dec-	10

In addition you should be able to recognize the following structures drawn in any orientation:

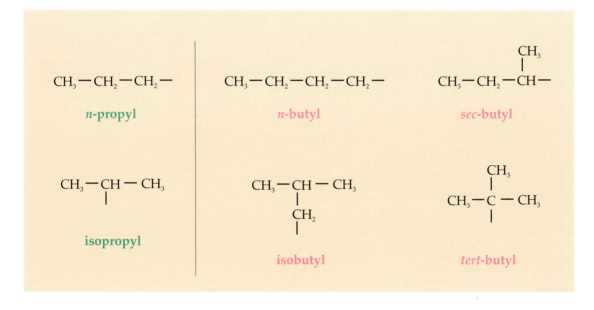

The following are the IUPAC rules for nomenclature:

- The longest carbon chain with the most substituents determines the base name.

- The end carbon closest to a carbon with a substituent is always the first carbon. In the case of a tie, look to the next substituent.

- Any substituent is given the same number as its carbon.

- If the same substituent is used more than once, use the prefixes di-, tri-, tetra, and so on.

- Order the substituents alphabetically.

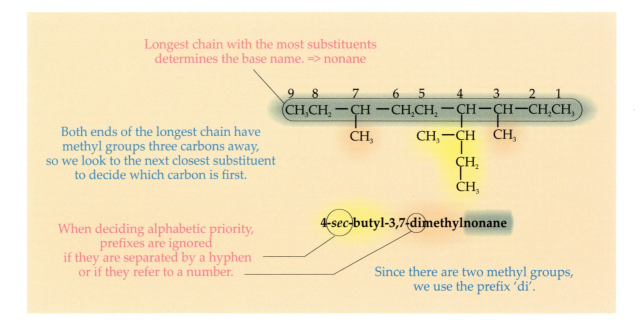

Longest chain with the most substituents determines the base name. => nonane

Both ends of the longest chain have methyl groups three carbons away, so we look to the next closest substituent to decide which carbon is first.

When deciding alphabetic priority, prefixes are ignored if they are separated by a hyphen or if they refer to a number.

4-*sec*-butyl-3,7-dimethylnonane

Since there are two methyl groups, we use the prefix 'di'.

1. β-D-(+)-glucose is reacted with methanol and dry hydrogen chloride. The product of this reaction is then treated with methyl sulfate and sodium hydroxide yielding methyl β-2,3,4,6-tetra-O-methyl-D-glucoside. Which of the following molecules is this product?

A.

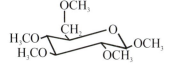

B.

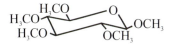

C.

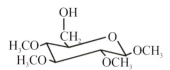

D.

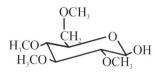

2. Benzoyl chloride reacts with ammonia to form benzamide. Which of the following molecules is the correct structure for benzamide?

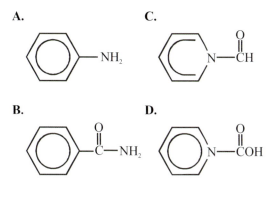

3. Of the bonds listed in the table below, the most stable bond is between:

Bond	Energy
$C_2H_5 - Cl$	339
$C_2H_5 - CH_3$	356
$H_2C = CH - Cl$	352
$H_2C = CH - CH_3$	385
$C_6H_5 - Cl$	360
$C_6H_5 - CH_3$	389

*bond energies given in kJ/mol

A. a saturated alkyl group and a halogen.
B. a saturated alkyl group and a methyl group.
C. an unsaturated alkyl group and a halogen.
D. an unsaturated alkyl group and a methyl group.

4. An α-hydroxy acid is heated to form the compound shown below. What functional group is created in this reaction?

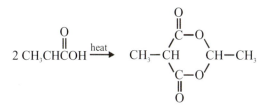

A. ether
B. aldehyde
C. ester
D. ketone

5. How many amide groups are there in the molecule of guanosine shown below?

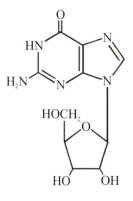

A. 0
B. 1
C. 3
D. 5

6. Just as ammonia, NH_3, is a weak Lewis base, there is a large group of nitrogen-containing organic compounds that behaves like weak bases and is known as:

A. amides
B. amines
C. ethanol alcohols
D. ethers

7. Which of the following functional groups are found in phenylalanine?

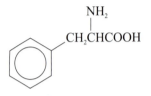

Phenylalanine

A. alkyl, double bond and aromatic ring
B. amine, carboxylic acid and aromatic ring
C. double bond, amide, and alcohol
D. aromatic ring, halide and ketone

8. Which of the following is the IUPAC name for this non-polar alkane?

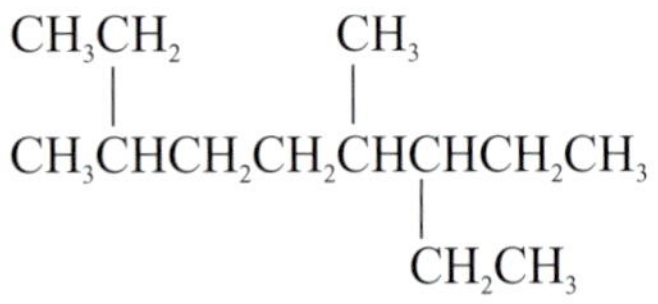

$$CH_3CH_2 \qquad CH_3$$
$$\overset{|}{CH_3CHCH_2CH_2CHCHCH_2CH_3}$$
$$\underset{CH_2CH_3}{|}$$

A. 3-Ethyl-4-methylheptane
B. 3-Ethyl-4, 7-dimethylnonane
C. 3-Methyl-7-ethyldecane
D. 3,4-Diethyl-5, 7-dimethylnonane

STOP.

MCAT organic chemistry is about tracking electrons through reactions of carbon compounds. If we can keep track of the electrons we can understand the reactions and we can master MCAT organic chemistry.

Electrons are negatively charged. They are attracted to positively charged nuclei. It is the **electrostatic force** between the electrons and the nuclei that creates all molecular bonds. Both nuclei tug on both electrons, and the result is a bond between the two nuclei.

Electrons are transitory passengers on their respective nuclei. They are in constant search of ways to unload some of their energy and will do so whenever possible. They are at their lowest energy state when they are nearest to a positive charge and farthest from a negative charge. Because negative charge in proximity to electrons raises their energy level, electrons will share an orbital with, at most, only one other electron. The only thing which prevents an electron from releasing all its energy and crashing into the positively charged nucleus is the quantization of energy. The electron must give up a minimum quantum of energy. This minimum amount is greater than the amount that would be released if the electron collided with the nucleus.

A bond is formed when a pair of electrons can lower their energy level by positioning themselves between two nuclei in such a way as to take advantage of the positive charge of both nuclei.

Two electrons are required to form a bond. Each of the bonded nuclei can donate a single electron to the bond, or, in a **coordinate covalent bond**, one nucleus can donate both electrons.

A **σ-bond** (sigma-bond) forms when the bonding pair of electrons are *localized* directly between the two bonding atoms. Since the electrons in a σ-bond are as close as possible to the two sources of positive charge (the two nuclei), a σ-bond has the lowest energy and is the most stable form of covalent bond. Thus σ-bonds are strong. A σ-bond is always the first type of covalent bond to be formed between any two atoms; a single bond must be a σ-bond.

If additional bonds form between two σ-bonded atoms, the new bonds are called **π-bonds** (π-bonds). Because the σ-bond leaves no room for other electron orbitals directly between the atoms, the orbital of the first π-bond forms above and below the σ-bonding electrons. A double bond now exists between the two atoms. If still another π-bond is formed, the new orbital is formed on either side of the σ-bond. A triple bond now exists between the two atoms. Double and triple bonds are always made of one σ-bond and one or two π-bonds.

Although a π-bond is weaker than a σ-bond(less energy is required to break the bond), π-bonds are always added to an existing σ-bond, and thus strengthen the overall bond between the atoms. Since bond strength is inversely related to bond length, the additional π-bonds shorten the overall bond. The bond energy of a double bond is greater than that of a single bond. Bond energy can be thought of as the energy necessary to break a bond.

The electrons in a π-bond are further from the nuclei than the electrons of a σ-bond, and therefore at a higher energy level, less stable, and form a weaker bond. This is important because less stability means π-bonds are more reactive. Third row elements form weaker π-bonds than second row elements. Double and triple bonds are rare for all atoms except carbon, nitrogen, oxygen, and sulfur.

1-8
Bonding

You should know that it takes two electrons to form a bond. When the force between two objects is attractive and decreases with distance, the lowest potential energy level for those objects is when they are the closest to each other. Electrons are at their lowest energy level when they form a bond because they have minimized their distance from both nuclei.

1-9
σ and π Bonds

Any single bond is a sigma bond, and any double or triple bond contains one sigma bond.

Double and triple bonds are made by adding π-bonds to a sigma bond. Each additional bond shortens the distance between the bonding atoms.

Pi bonds are more reactive than sigma bonds. Carbon, nitrogen, oxygen and sulfur are the only atoms that commonly form π-bonds. Phosphorous forms π-bonds with oxygen in nucleotide phosphates such as ATP.

Pi bonds prevent rotation.

Another important point about π-bonds is their effect on spatial arrangement. The atoms bonded by a single σ-bond are free to rotate about the bonding axis but a π-bond locks its atoms into one spatial orientation preventing rotation.

1-10
Hybridization

If we examine the electrons of a lone carbon atom in its ground state we would see that its four valence electrons are in their expected **atomic orbitals**, two in the orbital of the s subshell and two in orbitals of the p subshell. The p electrons are at a higher energy state than the s electrons.

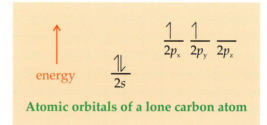

Atomic orbitals of a lone carbon atom

However, if we examine a carbon with four σ-bonds, we find that the four bonds are indistinguishable. Since the bonds are indistinguishable, the orbitals which form them must be equivalent. In order to form four σ-bonds, the electrons form four new orbitals. The new orbitals are hybrids of the old s and p orbitals and are equivalent to each other in shape and energy.

Atomic orbitals of a carbon atom with four σ-bonds

When one of these **hybrid orbitals** overlaps an orbital of another atom, a σ-bond is formed in the area where the orbitals coincide. π-bonds are formed by the overlap of pure p orbitals.

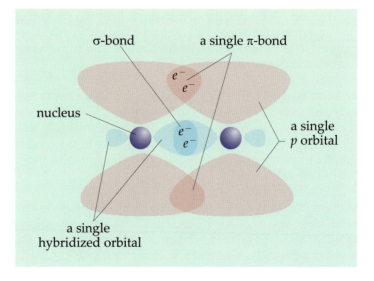

There are several types of hybrid orbitals: _sp; sp²; sp³; dsp³; d²sp³;_ etc. In order to figure out the type of hybrid orbital formed by an atom on the MCAT, simply count the number of sigma bonds and lone pairs of electrons on that atom. Match this number to the sum of the superscripts in a hybrid name (letters without superscripts are as-sumed to have the superscript '1'). Remember, there are one orbital in the _s_ subshell that must be formed first, three orbitals in the _p_ subshell that must be formed next, and five orbitals in the _d_ subshell to be formed only after the _s_ and _p_ or-bitals are formed. For example, water makes two sigma bonds and has two lone pairs of electrons. Thus the sum of the superscripts in the name of the hybrid must add up to four. The oxygen in water must be sp³ hybridized.

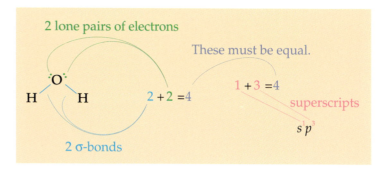

A hybrid orbital resembles in shape and energy the _s_ and _p_ orbitals from which it is formed to the same extent that _s_ or _p_ orbitals are used to form it. This extent is re-ferred to as **character**. The superscripts indicate the character as follows: an _sp²_ orbital is formed from one _s_ and two _p_ orbitals and thus has 33.3% _s_ character and 66.7% _p_ character; an _sp_ orbital is formed from one _s_ and one _p_ orbital and has a 50% _s_ character and 50% _p_ character; and so on. The more _s_ character a bond has, the more stable, the stronger, and the shorter it becomes.

When molecules are formed, s and p atomic orbitals hybridize to form new shapes and energy levels.

The electrons in an orbital seek to minimize their energy by moving as far away from other electron pairs as possible, thus lessening repulsive forces. This leads to specific bond angles and molecular shape for different numbers and combinations of σ-bonds and lone pair electrons.

HYBRIDIZATION	BOND ANGLES	SHAPE
_sp_	180°	Linear
sp²	120°	Trigonal planar
sp³	109.5°	Tetrahedral, Pyramidal, or Bent
dsp³	90°, 120°	Trigonal-bypyramidal, Seesaw, T-shaped, Linear
d²sp³	90°	Octahedral, Square pyramidal, Square planar

Where more than one possible shape exists, the shape depends upon the number and position of lone pairs. Lone pairs, π electrons, and ring strain can distort the predicted bond angles. Lone pairs and π electrons require more room than bonding pairs. For example, the lone pairs on water make the bond angle 104.5°.

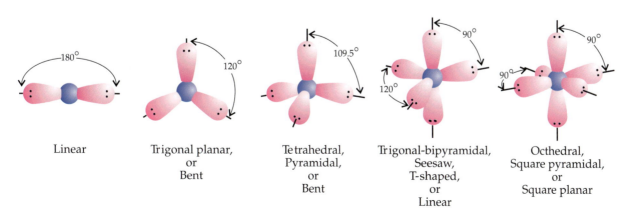

Linear   Trigonal planar, or Bent   Tetrahedral, Pyramidal, or Bent   Trigonal-bipyramidal, Seesaw, T-shaped, or Linear   Octhedral, Square pyramidal, or Square planar

1-11

Electron Delocalization

Sometimes bonding electrons are spread out over three or more atoms. These electrons are called *delocalized electrons*. For MCAT purposes delocalized electrons only result from π-bonds. Molecules containing delocalized electrons can be represented by a combination of two or more Lewis structures called **resonance structures**. The weighted average of these Lewis structures most accurately represents the real molecule. The real molecule must be at a lower energy than any single Lewis structure representing it since otherwise it would simply retain that structure. The difference between the energy of the real molecule and the energy of the most stable Lewis structure is called the *resonance energy*. Remember, the real molecule does not resonate between these structures but is a stable weighted average of all contributing structures.

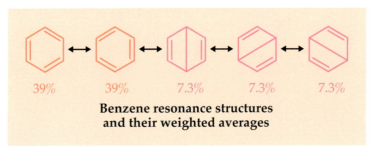

Benzene resonance structures and their weighted averages

The following are **four rules for writing resonance structures**:

For all resonance structures:

- **Atoms must not be moved.** Move electrons not atoms.

- **Number of unpaired electrons must remain constant.**

- **Resonance atoms must lie in the same plane.**

- **Only proper Lewis structures allowed.**

The contribution made to the actual molecule by any given structure is roughly proportional to that structure's stability; the most stable structures make the greatest contribution and equivalent structures make equal contributions. In general, the more covalent the bonds, the more stable the structure. Separation of charges within a molecule decreases stability.

For MCAT purposes, two conditions must exist for resonance to occur: 1) a species must contain an atom either with a *p* orbital or an unshared pair of electrons; 2) that atom must be single bonded to an atom that possesses a double or triple bond. Such species are called *conjugated unsaturated systems*. The adjacent *p* orbital in a conjugated system may contain zero, one, or two electrons (as in another π-bond). The *p* orbital allows the adjacent π-bond to extend and encompass more than two nuclei.

The above two conditions are required but not always sufficient for resonance. Ring structures must also satisfy *Huckel's rule*, which states: planar monocyclic rings with $4n + 2$ π-electrons (where *n* is any integer, including zero) should be **aromatic** (display resonance).

A **dipole moment** occurs when the center of positive charge on a molecule or bond does not coincide with the center of negative charge. A dipole moment can occur in a bond or a molecule. The concept of center of charge is analogous to the concept of the center of mass. All the positive charge in a molecule comes from the protons of the nuclei. All the negative charge comes from the electrons. In chemistry the dipole moment is represented by an arrow pointing from the center of positive charge to the center of negative charge. The arrow is crossed at the center of positive charge. The dipole moment is measured in units of the *debye*, D, and given by the equation:

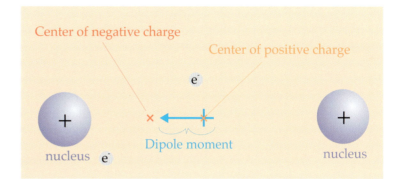

1-12
Dipole Moment

$$\mu = qd$$

where q is the magnitude of charge of either end of the dipole, and d is the distance between the centers of charge.

A molecule or bond which has a dipole moment is referred to as polar; a molecule or bond without a dipole moment is referred to as nonpolar.

A polar bond results from the difference in electronegativity of its atoms. Atoms with greater electronegativities attract the electrons in a bond more strongly, pulling the center of negative charge toward themselves, and thus creating a dipole moment.

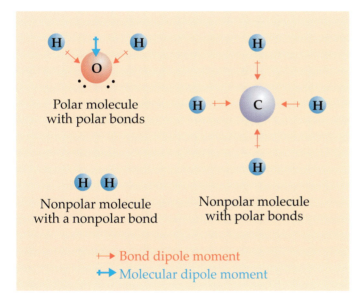

A molecule with polar bonds may or may not have a dipole moment. Since a dipole moment is a vector, it is possible for the sum of the dipole moments in the polar bonds of a molecule to equal zero, leaving the molecule without a dipole moment.

A dipole moment can be momentarily induced in an otherwise nonpolar molecule or bond by a polar molecule, ion, or electric field. The polar molecule or ion creates an electric field, which pushes the electrons and nuclei in opposite directions, separating the centers of positive and negative charge. Such dipole moments are called **induced dipoles**. Induced dipoles are common in nature and are generally weaker than permanent dipoles.

An **instantaneous dipole moment** can exist in an otherwise nonpolar molecule. Instantaneous dipoles arise because the electrons in a bond move about the orbital, and at any given moment may not be distributed exactly between the two bonding atoms even when the atoms are identical. Although instantaneous dipoles are generally very short lived and weaker than induced dipoles, they can act to induce a dipole in a neighboring atom.

Intermolecular attractions (attractions between separate molecules) occur solely due to dipole moments. The partial negatively charged side of one molecule is attracted to the partial positively charged side of another molecule. Dipole forces are much weaker than covalent forces, generally about 1% as strong. The attraction between two molecules is roughly proportional to their dipole moments.

When hydrogen is attached to a highly electronegative atom, such as nitrogen, oxygen, or fluorine, a large dipole moment is formed leaving hydrogen with a strong partial positive charge. When the hydrogen approaches a nitrogen, oxygen, or fluorine on another atom, the intermolecular bond formed is called a **hydrogen bond**. This is the strongest type of dipole-dipole interaction. It is hydrogen bonding that is responsible for the high boiling point of water.

The weakest dipole-dipole force is between two instantaneous dipoles. These dipole-dipole bonds are called **London Dispersion Forces**. Although London Dispersion Forces are very weak, they are responsible for the phase changes of nonpolar molecules.

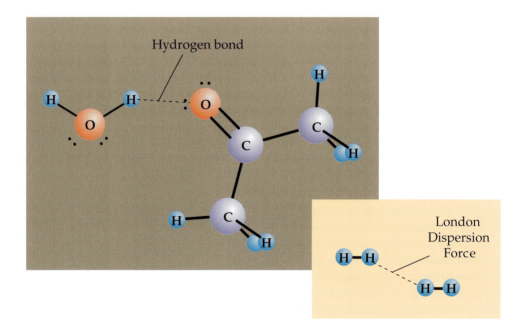

For this section, you should understand what hybridization is, and be able to identify *sp*, *sp²*, and *sp³* orbitals. Also, you must be able to recognize resonance structures. Learn the rules for resonance. Most of the bonding stuff is review from inorganic, but it is important. Understand that intermolecular and intramolecular forces are electrostatic. Make the connection between energy level of electrons and position relative to positive charge. In other words, as electrons move closer to positive charge they lower their energy level. Remember this by realizing that it would require energy input to separate opposite charges. Nature likes to spread the energy around. A system with low energy is a stable system. Thus, a bond is formed when electron energy level is the lowest.

Just a reminder: bond energy is closely related to bond dissociation energy and in many cases, it is the same thing. Bond energy is the average energy required to break a bond. Thus, high bond energy indicates a bond with electrons at very low energy, and is a stable bond. Recall from inorganic chemistry that this is because the high energy bond is really a high negative energy bond.

Questions 9 through 16 are **NOT** based on a descriptive passage.

9. Pyrrole, shown below, exhibits resonance stabilization.

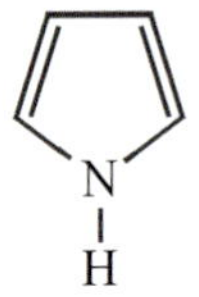

pyrrole

Which of the following is a valid resonance structure of pyrrole?

A.

C.

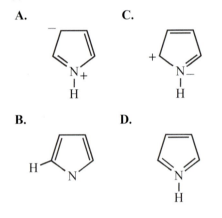

B.

D.

10. In the Wittig reaction a phosphorous ylide reacts with a ketone to yield an alkene.

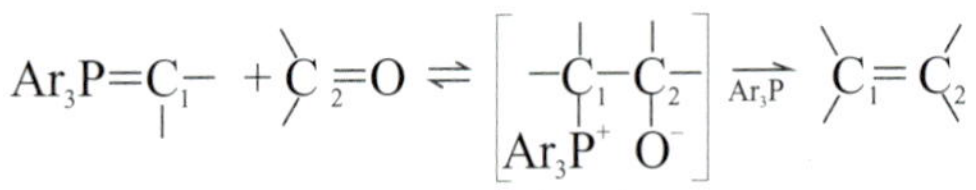

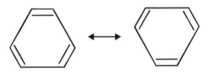

betaine
intermediate

What is the hybridization of carbon 2 in the ketone, the betaine, and the alkene, respectively?

A. sp^3; sp^2; sp^3
B. sp^2; sp^2; sp^3
C. sp^2; sp^3; sp^2
D. sp^3; sp^4; sp^3

11. Benzene exhibits resonance. The carbon-carbon bonds of benzene are:

A. shorter and stronger than the double bond of an alkene.
B. longer and weaker than the double bond of an alkene.
C. longer and stronger than the carbon-carbon bond of an alkane.
D. longer and weaker than the carbon-carbon bond of an alkane.

12. The electron pair in the π-bond of an alkene have:

A. 33% p character and are at a lower energy level than the electron pair in the σ-bond.
B. 50% p character and are at a higher energy level than the electron pair in the σ-bond.
C. 100% p character and are at a lower energy level than the electron pair in the σ-bond.
D. 100% p character and are at a higher energy level than the electron pair in the σ-bond.

13. The structures below are 1,3,5-cyclohexatriene. Although double bonds are shorter than single bonds, the structures below could not qualify as proper resonance contributors for benzene because:

A. 1,3,5-cyclohexatriene is a higher energy molecule than benzene.
B. benzene is more stable than 1,3,5-cyclohexatriene.
C. benzene actually resonates between these two structures.
D. the positions of the atoms are different in the two structures.

14. When dealing with organic compound hybridization, which angle is associated with the strongest bond formation?

A. 109°
B. 120°
C. 180°
D. 360°

15. All of the following compounds have a dipole moment EXCEPT:

A. CH_3Cl
B. H_2O
C. Benzene
D. $H_2C=N=N$

16. Natural gas consists of chiefly methane, but also contains ethane, propane, butane and isobutene. Which of the following compounds is NOT found in natural gas?

A. sec-butane
B. 2-methylbutane
C. olefin (CH_2CH_2)
D. cyclopropane

18

STOP.

There is relatively little to know about stereochemistry on the MCAT. The concepts are not difficult to understand and can be easily memorized. The difficult aspect of stereochemistry on the MCAT is mentally manipulating three-dimensional molecular structures. The only way to become better at manipulating molecular structures is to practice. It is best to acquire a molecular model set and actually build some of the replica molecules with your own hands.

1-13
Stereochemistry

Isomers are unique molecules with the same molecular formula. "Iso" is a Greek prefix meaning "the same" or "equal". A lone molecule cannot be an isomer by itself. It must be an isomer to another molecule. Two molecules are isomers if they have the same molecular formula but are different compounds.

1-14
Isomerism

Conformational isomers or **conformers** are not true isomers. Conformers are different spatial orientations of the same molecule. At room temperature, atoms rotate rapidly about their σ-bonds resulting in a mix of conformers at any given moment. Because of the difference in energy levels between eclipsed and staggered conformers, staggered conformers can sometimes be isolated at low temperatures. The simplest way to distinguish between conformers is with **Newman projections**. The diagram below shows the Newman projections of the conformers of butane and their relative energy levels.

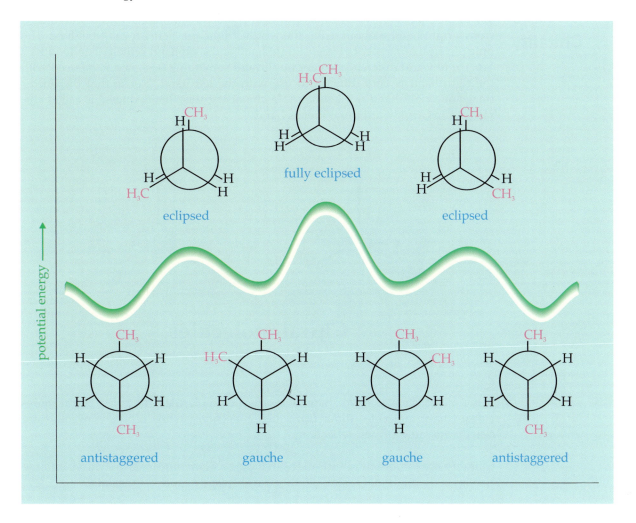

The simplest form of isomer is a **structural isomer**. Structural isomers have the same molecular formula but different bond-to-bond connectivity.

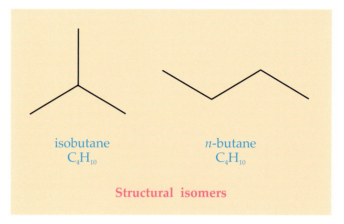

isobutane
C_4H_{10}

n-butane
C_4H_{10}

Structural isomers

If two unique molecules have the same molecular formula and the same bond-to-bond connectivity, they are stereoisomers. In order to distinguish stereoisomers we must first understand chirality.

1-15

Chirality

Try to describe a left hand by its physical characteristics alone, and distinguish it from a right hand without using the words "right" or "left". It can't be done. The only physical difference between a right hand and a left hand is their "handedness". Yet, the physical difference is very important. Something designed to be used with the right hand is very difficult to use with the left hand. Notice that the mirror image of a right hand is a left hand. In chemistry, this "handedness" is called **chirality**. The Greek word *chiros* means hand.

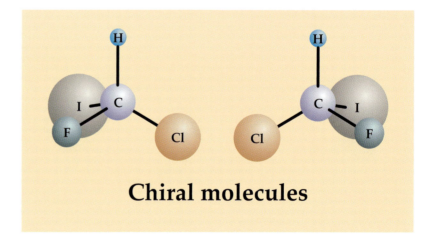

Chiral molecules

Some molecules also have "handedness". Such molecules are called **chiral molecules**. Chiral molecules differ from their reflections, while achiral molecules are exactly the same as their reflections.

Chirality has important ramifications in biology. Many nutrients are chiral, and the human body might not assimilate the mirror image of such a nutrient.

Chirality on the MCAT will mainly be concerned with carbon. Any carbon is chiral when it is bonded to **four different substituents**.

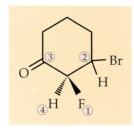

There is only one way to physically describe the orientation of atoms about a chiral center such as a chiral carbon. That is by **absolute configuration**. Since there are two possible configurations, the molecule and its mirror image, absolute configuration is given as **R** (*rectus*: the Latin word for *right*) or **S** (*sinister*: the Latin word for *left*). In order to determine the configuration of a given molecule, the atoms attached to the chiral center are numbered from highest to lowest *priority*. The largest atomic weights are given the highest priority. If two of the atoms are the same element, then their substituents are sequentially compared in order of decreasing priority until one of the substituents is found to have a greater priority than the corresponding substituent on the other atom. Substituents on double and triple bonds are counted two and three times respectively. In the molecule shown above, the carbon marked 2 has a higher priority than the carbon marked 3 because bromine has a higher priority than oxygen. The carbon marked 3 is considered to have two oxygens for priority purposes. Once priorities have been assigned, the chiral molecule is rotated about one of the σ-bonds as shown below so that the lowest priority group faces away. In this orientation a circle is drawn in the direction from highest to lowest priority for the remaining three substituents. The circle will point clockwise or counterclockwise. A clockwise circle indicates an absolute configuration of R and a counterclockwise circle indicates an absolute configuration of S. The mirror image of a chiral molecule always has the opposite absolute configuration.

1-16
Absolute Configuration

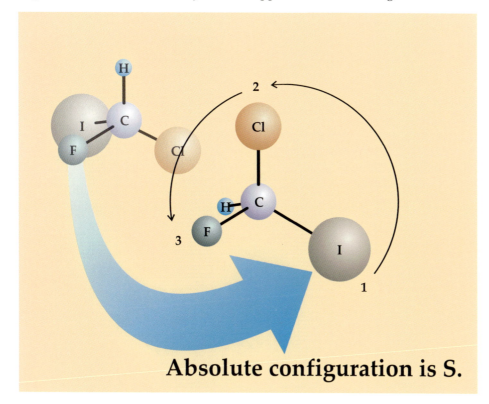

Absolute configuration is S.

The absolute configuration of a molecule does <u>not</u> give information concerning the direction in which a compound rotates plane-polarized light.

1-17

Relative Configuration

Relative configuration is not related to absolute configuration. Two molecules have the same relative configuration about a carbon if they differ by only one substituent and the other substituents are oriented identically about the carbon. In an S_N2 reaction, it is the relative configuration that is inverted.

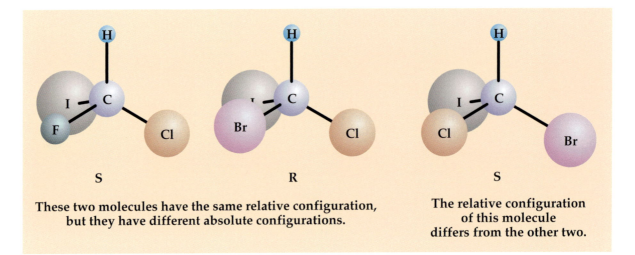

S	R

These two molecules have the same relative configuration, but they have different absolute configurations.

S

The relative configuration of this molecule differs from the other two.

1-18

Observed Rotation

The direction and the degree to which a compound rotates plane-polarized light is given by its **observed rotation**.

Light is made up of electromagnetic waves. A single photon can be described by a changing electric field and its corresponding changing magnetic field, both fields being perpendicular to each other and to the direction of propagation. For simplicity, the magnetic field is often ignored and only the direction of the electric field is considered. A typical light source releases millions of photons whose fields are oriented in random directions. A **polarimeter** screens out photons with all but one orientation of electric field. The resulting light consists of photons with their electric fields oriented in the same direction. This light is called **plane-polarized light**.

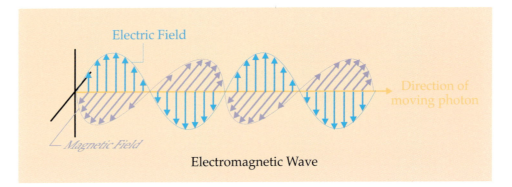

Electric Field

Direction of moving photon

Magnetic Field

Electromagnetic Wave

When a photon reflects off any molecule, the orientation of the electric field produced by that photon is rotated. The mirror image of that molecule will rotate the electric field to the same degree but in the opposite direction. In a typical compound where a photon is just as likely to collide with either mirror image, there are so many millions of molecules producing so many collisions that the photon is most likely to leave the compound with the same electric field orientation with which it entered the compound. No single molecular orientation is favored and so the net result is no rotation of the plane of the electric field. Such compounds are **optically inactive**. Optically inactive compounds may be compounds with no chiral centers, or they may be chiral compounds containing equal amounts of both stereoisomers. The latter is called a **racemic mixture**.

Chiral molecules can be separated from their mirror images by chemical, and in rare cases physical, means. The result of such a separation is a compound containing molecules with no mirror image existing in the compound. When plane-polarized light is projected through such a compound, the orientation of its electric field is rotated. Such a compound is **optically active**. If the compound rotates plane-polarized light clockwise it is designated with a **'+' or 'd'** for *dextrotorary*. If it rotates plane-polarized light counterclockwise it is designated with a **'–' or 'l'** for *levorotary* (Latin: *dexter*; right: *laevus*; left).

The direction and number of degrees that the electric field in plane-polarized light rotates when it passes through a compound is called the compound's **observed rotation**. **Specific rotation** is simply a standardized form of observed rotation that is arrived at through calculations using observed rotation and experimental parameters. For instance, the degree of rotation to which polarized light is rotated depends upon the length of the polarimeter, the concentration of the solution, the temperature, and the type of wavelength of light used. Specific rotation is equal to the observed rotation after these adjustments have been made.

If you understand observed rotation, you won't have any trouble with specific rotation should it come up in a passage on the MCAT.

1-19
Stereoisomers

Two molecules with the same molecular formula and the same bond-to-bond connectivity that are not the same compound are called **stereoisomers**. Unless they are geometric isomers, stereoisomers must each contain at least one chiral center in the same location. There are two types of stereoisomers: enantiomers and diastereomers.

1-20
Enantiomers

Enantiomers have the same molecular formula, have the same bond-to-bond connectivity, are mirror images of each other, but are not the same molecule. Enantiomers must have opposite absolute configurations at each chiral carbon.

When placed separately into a polarimeter, enantiomers rotate plane-polarized light in opposite directions to an equal degree. For example, the specific rotation of (R)-2-Butanol is –13.52° while its enantiomer, (S)-2-Butanol, has a specific rotation of +13.52°.

Except for reactions with plane-polarized light and with other chiral compounds, enantiomers have the same physical and chemical properties.

When enantiomers are mixed together in equal concentrations, the resulting mixture is called a **racemic mixture**. Since the mirror image of all orientations of each molecule exist in a racemic mixture with equal probability, racemic mixtures do not rotate plane-polarized light. Unequal concentrations of enantiomers rotate plane-polarized light. In unequal concentrations, the light is rotated in the same direction as a pure sample of the excess enantiomer would rotate it but only to a fraction of the degree, the same fraction that exists as excess enantiomer. The ratio of actual

Enantiomers must have opposite absolute configurations at each and every chiral carbon.

What's this?
An-ant-in-a-mirror!

Enantiomers are mirror images of each other.

rotation to the rotation of pure sample is called *optical purity*; the ratio of pure enantiomer to racemic mixture is called *enantiomeric purity*. Optical purity equals enantiomeric purity for any mixture of enantiomers. The separation of enantiomers is called **resolution**.

For enantiomers, you must know that they have the same chemical and physical characteristics except for two cases: 1. reactions with other chiral compounds; 2. reactions with polarized light.

1-21
Diastereomers

Diastereomers have the same molecular formula, have the same bond-to-bond connectivity, are <u>not</u> mirror images to each other, and are not the same compound.

One special type of diastereomer is called a **geometric isomer**. Geometric isomers exist due to hindered rotation about a bond. Rotation may be hindered due to a ring structure or a double or triple bond. Since rotation is hindered, similar substituents on opposing carbons may exist on the same-side or opposite sides of the hindered bond. Molecules with same side substituents are called **cis-isomers**; those with opposite-side substituents are called **trans-isomers** (Latin: *cis*: on the same side; *trans*: on the other side).

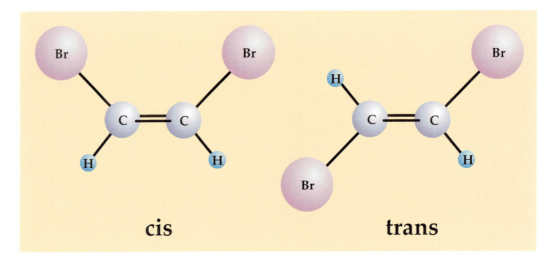

cis   trans

Geometric isomers have **different physical properties**. For the MCAT, it is important to know that cis molecules have a dipole moment while trans molecules do not. As a rule of thumb, the following predictions can be made concerning the melting and boiling points of geometric isomers: due to their dipole moment, cis molecules have stronger intermolecular forces leading to higher boiling points; due to their lower symmetry, however, cis molecules do not form crystals as readily, and thus have lower melting points.

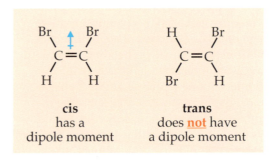

The substituent groups in the cis position may crowd each other; a condition known as **steric hindrance**. Steric hindrance in cis molecules produces higher energy levels resulting in higher heats of combustion.

For tri and tetrasubstituted alkenes or ring structures, the terms cis and trans may be ambiguous or simply meaningless. The following system may be used to describe all geometric isomers unambiguously. First, the two substituents on each carbon are prioritized using atomic weight, similar to the system in absolute configuration. If the higher priority substituent for each carbon exists on the opposite sides, the molecule is labeled **E** for *entgegen;* if on the same side, then **Z** for *zusammen* (German: entgegen: opposite; zusammen: together).

Diastereomers have different physical properties (i.e. rotation of plane-polarized light, melting points, boiling points, solubilities, etc...). Their chemical properties also differ.

The maximum number of optically active isomers that a single compound can have is related to the number of its chiral centers by the following formula:

maximum number of optically active isomers = 2^n

where n is the number of chiral centers.

Two chiral centers in a single molecule may offset each other creating an optically inactive molecule. Such compounds are called **meso compounds**. Meso compounds have a plane of symmetry through their centers which divides them into two halves that are mirror images to each other. Meso compounds are achiral and therefore optically inactive.

Diastereomers that differ at only one chiral carbon are called **epimers**. If a ring closure occurs at the epimeric carbon, two possible diastereomers may be formed. These new diastereomers are called **anomers**. The chiral carbon of an anomer is called the **anomeric carbon**. Anomers are distinguished by the orientation of their substituents. Glucose forms anomers. When the hydroxyl group on the anomeric carbon on glucose is oriented in the opposite direction to the methyl group, the anomer is labeled α; when in the same direction, the anomer is β.

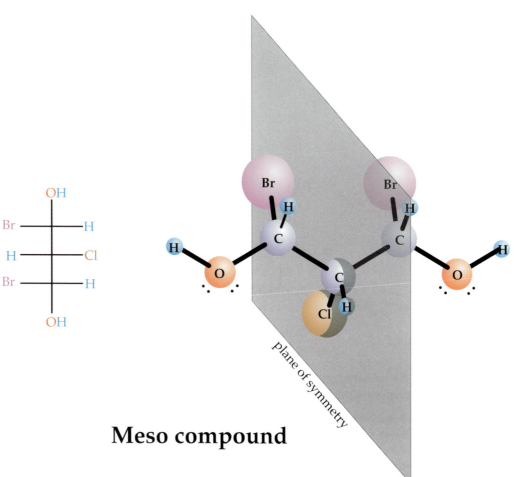

Meso compound

17. Which of the following compounds can exist as either a cis or trans isomer?

A. $CH_3CH_2CCl=CClH$

B. 2-methyl-2-butene

C.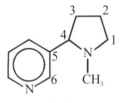

D.

18. (–)-nicotine shown below is an alkaloid found in tobacco.

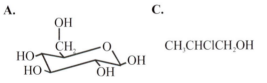

nicotine

At which of the following carbons does the structure of (+)-nicotine differ from (–)-nicotine?

A. carbons 1,4, and 6 only
B. carbons 4 and 5 only
C. carbon 4 only
D. carbon 5 only

19. All of the following compounds are optically active EXCEPT:

A.

C. $CH_3CHClCH_2OH$

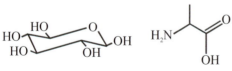

B.

D.

20. Which one of the following properly named compounds could exist in enantiomeric form?

A. 3-chloro-1-propene
B. 3-chloro-1,4-dichlorocyclohexane
C. *trans*-1,4-dichlorocyclohexane
D. 4-chloro-1-cyclohexene

21. Which of the following compounds is not optically active?

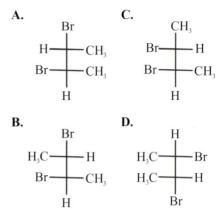

22. Which of the following characteristics correctly describe differences between structural (constitutional) isomers?

I. these compounds may have different carbon skeletons
II. chemical properties are altered due to differences in functional groups
III. functional groups may occupy different positions on the carbon skeleton

A. I only
B. II and III only
C. I and III only
D. I, II and III

23. When described using rectus or sinister, the spatial arrangement of substituents around a chiral atom is called:

A. achirality
B. absolute configuration
C. observed rotation
D. enantiomeric purity

24. Which of the following stereoisomers is a mirror image of itself?

A. anomer
B. epimer
C. meso compound
D. geometric isomer

26

STOP.

Hydrocarbons, Alcohols, and Substitutions

Methane and compounds whose major functional group contains only carbon-carbon single bonds are <u>alkanes</u>. Carbons in alkanes are referred to as <u>methyl, primary, secondary, and tertiary</u>, depending upon how many other alkyl groups are attached to them. Methyl carbons have no attached alkyl groups, primary carbons have one, secondary have two, and tertiary have three.

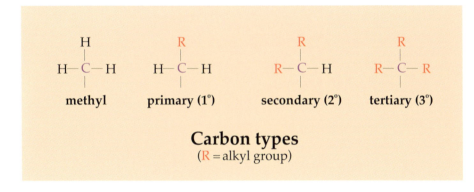

Carbon types
(R = alkyl group)

The <u>physical properties</u> of alkanes follow certain general trends. Boiling point is governed by intermolecular forces. As carbons are added in a single chain and molecular weight increases, the intermolecular forces increase and, thus, the boiling point of the alkane increases. Branching, however, significantly lowers the boiling point. Melting points of unbranched alkanes also tend to increase with increasing molecular weight, though not as smoothly. This is because intermolecular forces within a crystal depend upon shape as well as size.

Alkanes have the lowest density of all groups of organic compounds. Density increases with molecular weight.

Alkanes are almost totally insoluble in water. They are soluble in benzene, carbon tetrachloride, chloroform, and other hydrocarbons. If an alkane contains a polar functional group, the polarity of the entire molecule, and thus its solubility, decreases as the carbon chain is lengthened.

To remember that alkanes have low density, think of an oil spill where alkanes float on water.

There is a lot to memorize with physical properties of alkanes. The most important things to remember are that molecular weight increases boiling point and melting point, and branching decreases boiling point but increases melting point. The first four alkanes are gases at room temperature.

$\uparrow$M.W. => $\uparrow$B.P. => $\uparrow$M.P.

$\uparrow$Branching => $\downarrow$B.P. => $\uparrow$M.P.

2-3 Cycloalkanes

Cycloalkanes are alkane rings. For the MCAT, remember that some ring structures put strain on the carbon-carbon bonds because they bend them away from the normal 109.5° angle of the sp^3 carbon and cause crowding. **Ring strain** is zero for cyclohexane and increases as rings become larger or smaller. The trend continues up to a nine-carbon ring structure, after which ring strain decreases to zero as more carbons are added to the ring. Less ring strain means lower energy and more stability.

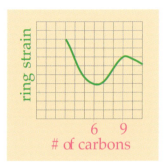

Cyclohexane exists as three conformers: the **chair**; the *twist*; and the **boat**. All three conformers exist at room temperature; however, the chair predominates almost completely because it is at the lowest energy. Although the boat configuration is often discussed, the twist-boat is usually intended.

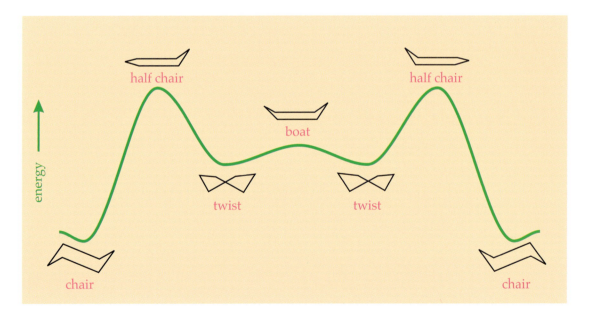

Each carbon on cyclohexane has two hydrogens. In the chair conformation, the two hydrogens are oriented in different directions. The hydrogens projecting outward from the center of the ring are called **equatorial hydrogens**; the hydrogens projecting upward or downward are called **axial hydrogens**. When the ring reverses its conformation, all the hydrogens reverse their conformation. Neither axial nor equatorial hydrogens are energetically favored. However, when the ring has substituent groups attached, crowding occurs most often between groups in the axial position. Crowding causes instability and raises the energy level of the ring. Thus most substituent groups are favored in the equatorial position.

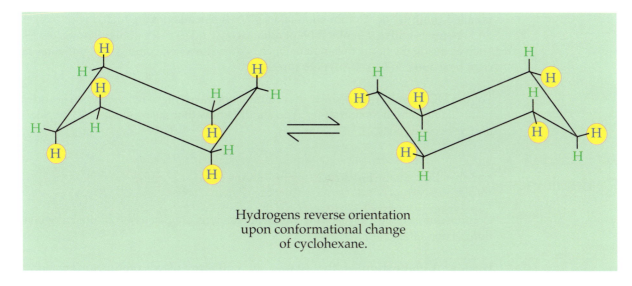

Hydrogens reverse orientation
upon conformational change
of cyclohexane.

Since the carbons in a ring cannot rotate about the σ-bonds, cis and trans isomerism is possible in a ring structure without a double bond. Ring structure cis and trans isomers have different physical properties, but the trends are not as predictable as alkene cis and trans isomers. However, like other cis molecules, ring structures with cis groups on adjacent carbons may experience steric hindrance resulting in a higher energy level for the entire molecule. Notice that for five-carbon rings and less, the cis isomers are meso compounds. The chair conformation of cis-1,2-dichlorocyclohexane (also for 1,3 and 1,4 isomers and higher carbon rings) exists in equilibrium with its own mirror image and thus is optically inactive as well.

The main things to know about ring structures are in terms of energy. For instance, for small rings, ring strain is lowest in cyclohexane, so it is the most stable ring structure. Also, large substituents in the axial position require more energy and create less stability.

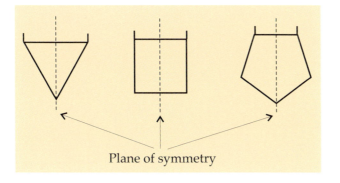

Plane of symmetry

2-4
Combustion

Alkanes were originally called paraffins (Latin: *parum affinis*: low inclination) because they are not inclined to react with other molecules. They do not react with strong acids or bases or with most other reagents. However, with a sufficiently large energy of activation, they are capable of violent reactions with oxygen. This reaction is called **combustion**. Combustion takes place when alkanes are mixed with oxygen and energy is added. Combustion of alkanes only takes place at high temperatures, such as inside the flame of a match. Once begun, however, combustion generates its own heat and can be self-perpetuating.

For the MCAT you should know that combustion takes place when oxygen is added to an alkane at high temperatures. You should know that the products are CO_2, H_2O, and, especially, heat.

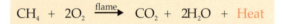

$$CH_4 + 2O_2 \xrightarrow{\text{flame}} CO_2 + 2H_2O + \text{Heat}$$

Combustion is a **radical reaction**. (Radical reactions are discussed in the halogenation section later.)

Heat of Combustion is the change in enthalpy of a combustion reaction. Combustion of isomeric hydrocarbons requires equal amounts of O_2 and produces equal amounts of CO_2 and H_2O. Therefore heats of combustion can be used to compare relative stabilities of isomers. The higher the heat of combustion, the higher the energy level of the molecule, the less stable the molecule. For cycloalkanes, comparisons can be made of different size rings on a "per CH_2" basis to reveal relative stabilities. Although the molar heat of combustion for cyclohexane is nearly twice that of cyclopropane, the "per CH_2" group heat of combustion is greater for cyclopropane due to ring strain.

Alkanes will react with halogens (F, Cl, and Br, but not I) in the presence of heat or light to form a **free radical**. Energy from light or heat homolytically cleaves the diatomic halogen. In homolytic cleavage each atom in the bond retains one electron from the broken bond. The result is two highly reactive species each with an unpaired electron and each called a free radical. The free radicals are the active, reacting species in the halogenation of the alkane.

Halogenation is a chain reaction with at least three steps. You must know all three steps for the MCAT.

1. **initiation:** The halogen starts as a diatomic molecule. The molecule is homolytically cleaved x by heat or by UV light, resulting in a free radicals.

2. **propagation:** The halogen radical removes a hydrogen from the alkane resulting in an alkyl radical. The alkyl radical may now react with a diatomic halogen molecule creating an alkyl halide and a new halogen radical. Propagation can continue indefinitely. Or:

3. **termination:** Either two radicals bond or a radical bonds to the wall of the container to end the chain reaction or propagation.

2-5 Halogenation

In halogenation, most of the product is formed during propagation, NOT during termination.

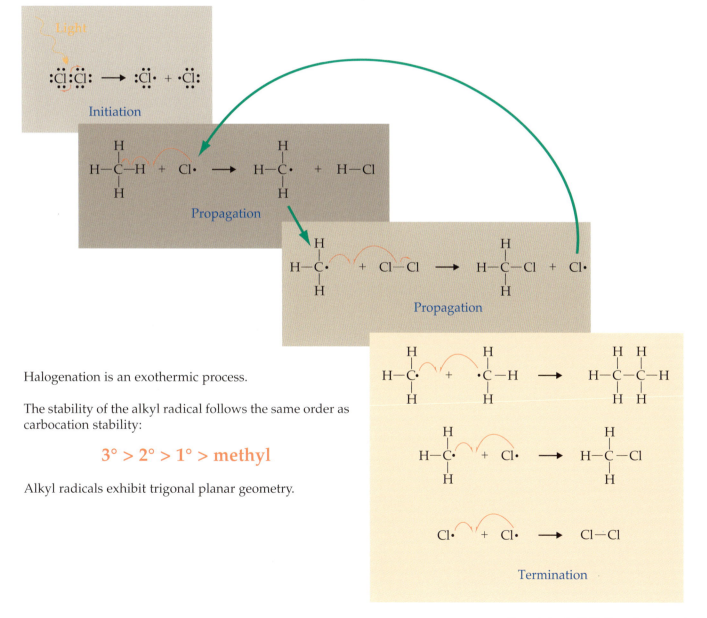

Halogenation is an exothermic process.

The stability of the alkyl radical follows the same order as carbocation stability:

3° > 2° > 1° > methyl

Alkyl radicals exhibit trigonal planar geometry.

The reactivity of halogens from most reactive to least is as follows: F, Cl, Br, I. Fluorine is so reactive that it can be explosive, whereas bromine requires heat to react and iodine won't react at all. *Selectivity* of the halogens follows exactly the opposite order. (Selectivity is how selective a halogen radical is when choosing a position on an alkane.) Even though we know the order of selectivity, we must be careful when predicting products. For instance, since chlorine is somewhat selective, we might suppose that the primary product of 2-methylbutane and chlorine reacting at 300°C would be 2-chloro-2-methyl butane, the tertiary alkyl halide. This would be wrong. Although chlorine is five times more likely to react with the single hydrogen on the tertiary carbon to produce the more stable tertiary radical, there are nine hydrogens attached to primary carbons and two hydrogens attached to the secondary carbon which can also react. Thus, on 2-methylbutane, a chlorine free radical will collide with a primary hydrogen nine times as often as it will collide with the tertiary. As a rough rule of thumb, assume the order of reactivity for chlorine with tertiary, secondary, and primary hydrogens will follow a 5:4:1 ratio. In other words, a primary hydrogen will require five times as many collisions to react as a tertiary and so on.

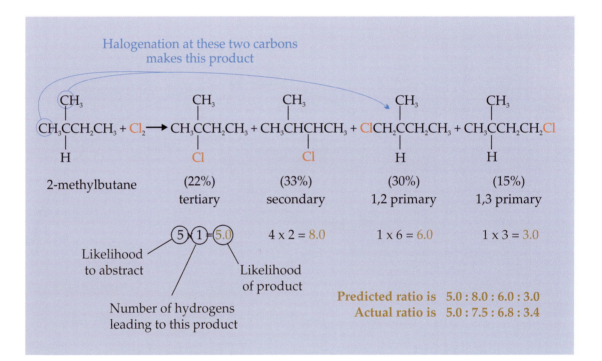

This example demonstrates that the rule of thumb is an estimate at best. Most importantly, it is a reminder that the tertiary product will not necessarily be the primary product. Bromine is more selective than chlorine and substituting bromine for chlorine in the same reaction will result in predominately 2-bromo-2-methylbutane. Fluorine, on the other hand, is so reactive that the primary product would predominate.

Another concern in halogenation is multi-halogenated products. Increased concentration of the halogen will result in the di-, tri-, and tetra-halogenated products, while dilute solutions will yield only monohalogenated products. This is because in a dilute solution the halogen radical is more likely to collide with an alkane than an alkyl halide.

25. Which of the following compounds contains the fewest tertiary carbons?

    A. $(CH_3)_3C(CH_2)_2CH_3$
    B. 4-isobutylheptane

    C.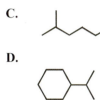

    D.

26. Which of the following halogens will give the greatest percent yield of tertiary alkyl halide when reacted with isobutane in the presence of heat and light?

    A. F_2
    B. Cl_2
    C. Br_2
    D. Isobutane will not yield a tertiary product.

27. Which of the following compounds produces the most heat per mole of compound when reacted with oxygen?

    A. CH_4
    B. C_2H_6
    C. cyclohexane
    D. cycloheptane

28. In a sample of *cis*-1,2-dichlorocyclohexane at room temperature, the chlorines will:

    A. both be equatorial whenever the molecule is in the chair conformation.
    B. both be axial whenever the molecule is in the chair conformation.
    C. alternate between both equatorial and both axial whenever the molecule is in the chair conformation.
    D. both alternate between equatorial and axial but will never exist both axial or both equatorial at the same time.

29. In an alkane halogenation reaction, which of the following steps will never produce a radical?

    A. initiation
    B. propagation
    C. conjugation
    D. termination

30. Cycloalkanes are a group of cyclic saturated hydrocarbons with a general formula of C_nH_{2n}. Which of the following compounds will display the LEAST amount of free rotation around a C—C single bond?

    A. alkanes, which are relatively inert chemically
    B. alkanes, which are able to form numerous types of isomers
    C. cycloalkanes, which are limited by geometric constraints
    D. cycloalkanes, which are polar and water soluble

31.
$$CH_3CHCH_2CCH_3$$
with CH_3, CH_3 groups on the second and fourth carbons and a CH_3 group below the fourth carbon

In the above compound, how many hydrogen atoms can be identified as primary?

    A. 3
    B. 15
    C. 17
    D. 18

32. General reaction mechanism:

$$A—B + C—D \rightarrow A—C + B—D$$

What reaction type is being demonstrated by the equation above?

    A. addition
    B. elimination
    C. substitution
    D. rearrangement

STOP.

2-6
Alkenes

We are, of course, aware that the topic of alkenes has been removed from the list of topics tested by the MCAT. We suggest that this section will be helpful anyway.

If a carbon chain contains a carbon-carbon double bond, it is an **alkene**. Alkenes have π-bonds. π-bonds are less stable than σ-bonds; thus, alkenes are more reactive than alkanes. When dealing with alkenes, remember that π-bonds are electron-hungry. This explains why alkenes are more acidic than alkanes. When a proton is removed, the π-bond of the alkene absorbs some of the negative charge stabilizing the conjugate base. However, at the same time remember that the π-bond is a large area of negative charge and is thus attractive to electrophiles.

The more highly substituted the alkene, the more thermodynamically stable.

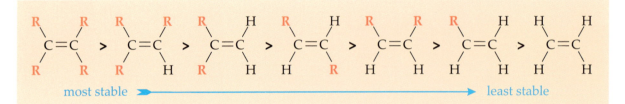

The diagram above refers to thermodynamic stability. When we discuss addition reactions you will see that the most stable alkene when mixed with an electrophile is the most reactive according to this diagram. This paradox is due to the intermediate, usually a carbocation. Since a tertiary carbocation is more stable, the energy of activation is lowered and a reaction with a tertiary intermediate proceeds more quickly. In general, to predict the alkene product, use the above diagram as a reference, but to predict the most reactive alkene to an electrophile, the order is based on cation formation and is nearly reversed.

2-7
Physical Properties

Alkenes follow the same trends as alkanes. An increase in molecular weight leads to an increase in boiling point. Branching decreases boiling point. Alkenes are very slightly soluble in water and have a lower density than water. They are more acidic than alkanes.

Alkynes, carbon chains containing a carbon-carbon triple bond, have similar physical property trends to alkanes and alkenes. They are only slightly more polar than alkenes and only slightly more soluble in water.

2-8
Synthesis of Alkenes

Synthesis of an alkene occurs via an **elimination** reaction. One or two functional groups are eliminated or removed to form a double bond. **Dehydration of an alcohol** is an E1 reaction where an alcohol forms an alkene in the presence of hot concentrated acid. E1 means that the rate depends upon the concentration of only one species. In this case, the rate depends upon the concentration of the alcohol. In the first step, the acid protonates the hydroxyl group producing the good leaving group, water. In the next and slowest step (the rate-determining step), the water drops off, forming a carbocation. As always, when a carbocation is formed, rearrangement may occur. **Carbocation stability** follows the same trend as radical stability. From most stable to least stable the order is: **3°, 2°, 1°, methyl**. Rearrangement will only occur if a more stable carbocation can be formed. In the final step, a water molecule deprotonates the carbocation and an alkene is formed. Notice that the major product is the most stable, most substituted alkene. The **Saytzeff rule** states that the major product of elimination will be the most substituted alkene.

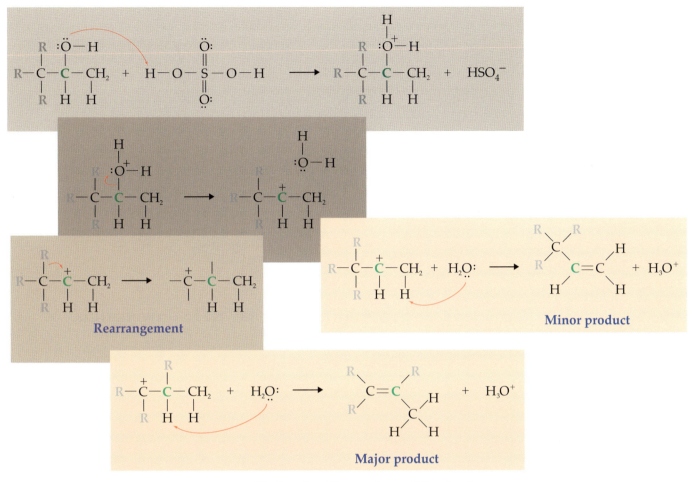

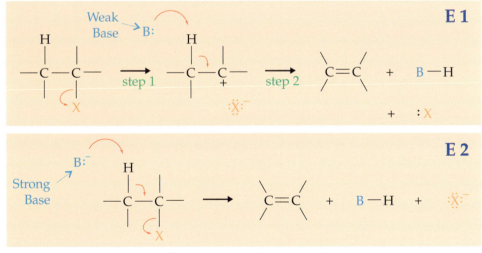

Dehydration of an Alcohol

Dehydrohalogenation may proceed either by an E1 mechanism (absence of a strong base) or by an E2 mechanism (a high concentration of a strong, bulky base). In the E1 reaction, the halogen drops off in the first step and a hydrogen is removed in the second step. In the E2 reaction, the base removes a proton from the carbon next to the halogen-containing carbon and the halogen drops off, leaving an alkene. The E2 reaction is one step. The bulky base prevents an S_N2 reaction, but, if the base is too bulky, the Saytzeff rule is violated, leaving the least substituted alkene.

Notice that in elimination, the base abstracts a hydrogen. This is a different behavior than that of a nucleophile in a substitution reaction. In a substitution reaction, the nucleophile attacks the carbon.

Dehydrohalogenation

2-9
Catalytic Hydrogenation

Hydrogenation is an example of an addition reaction. In order for hydrogenation to occur at an appreciable rate, a *heterogeneous* catalyst is employed. A heterogeneous catalyst is a catalyst that exists in a different phase (i.e. gas, liquid, solid, aqueous, etc.) than the reactants or products. Normally tiny shavings of metal act as the catalyst to promote **syn-addition** (same side addition).

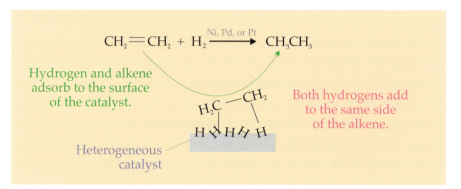

Syn Addition in catalytic hydrogenation

Hydrogenation is an exothermic reaction with a high energy of activation. Heats of hydrogenation can be used to measure relative stabilities of alkenes. The lower the heat of hydrogenation, the more stable the alkene.

Syn addition of alkynes creates a cis alkene.

2-10
Oxidation of Alkenes

Oxidation of alkenes may produce glycols (hydroxyl groups on adjacent carbons) or oxidation may cleave the alkene at the double bond as in *ozonolysis*.

Ozone contains reactive elctron pairs with a high charge density, so it is very reactive; it breaks right through alkenes and alkynes.

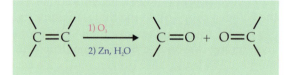

Ozonolysis of an alkene

Alkynes produce carboxylic acids when undergoing ozonolysis.

2-11
Electrophilic Addition

Electrophilic addition is an important reaction for alkenes. When you see an alkene on the MCAT, check for electrophilic addition. An **electrophile** is an electron-loving species, so it will have at least a partially positive charge, even if it is only from a momentary dipole. The double bond of an alkene is an electron-rich environment and will attract electrophiles.

When hydrogen halides (HF, HCl, HBr, and HI) are added to alkenes, they follow **Markovnikov's rule** unless otherwise specified on the MCAT. Markovnikov's rule says "the hydrogen will add to the least substituted carbon of the double bond". The reaction takes place in two steps. First, the hydrogen halide, a Bronsted-Lowry acid, creates a positively charged proton, which acts as the electrophile. Second, the newly formed carbocation picks up the negatively charged halide ion. The first step is the slow step and determines the rate.

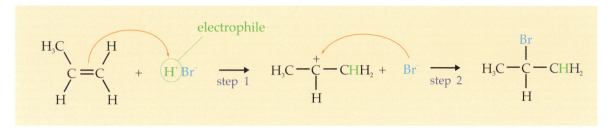

Electrophilic addition
via Markovnikov's rule
forming the most stable carbocation

The reaction follows Markovnikov's rule because the rule dictates the formation of the more stable carbocation. You should be aware that if peroxides (ROOR) are present, the *bromine*, not the hydrogen, will add to the least substituted carbon. This is called an **anti-Markovnikov addition**. The other halogens will still follow Markovnikov's rule even in the presence of peroxides.

The most reactive alkenes in electrophilic addition are the most thermodynamically stable. This is because they also have the lowest activation energy when forming carbocations. Hydrogen halides add to alkynes in nearly the same way they add to alkenes.

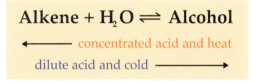

Hydration of an alkene also follows Markovnikov's rule. Hydration takes place when water is added to an alkene in the presence of an acid. This reaction is the reverse of dehydration of an alcohol. Low temperatures and dilute acid drive this reaction toward alcohol formation; high temperatures and concentrated acid drive the reaction toward alkene formation.

Another reaction which creates an alcohol from an alkene is *oxymercuration/demercuration* (shown on the next page). This is a two-step process which also follows Markovnikov's rule but rarely results in rearrangement of the carbocation. A two-step theory has the mercury-containing reagent partially dissociate to $^+Hg(OAc)$. The $^+Hg(OAc)$ acts as an electrophile creating a *mercurinium ion*. Water attacks the mercurinium ion to form the *organomercurial alcohol* in an **anti-addition** (addition from opposite sides of the double bond). The second step is demercuration to form the alcohol by addition of a reducing agent and base.

What's important here is not to memorize the mechanism, but to realize that in organometallic compounds the metal likes to lose electrons and take on a full or partial positive charge.

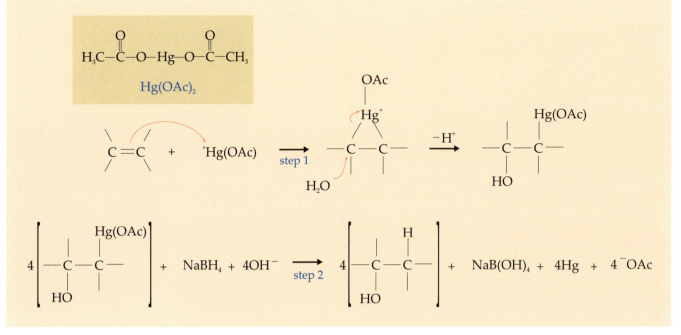

Oxymercuration/Demercuration

If an alcohol is used instead of water, the corresponding ether is produced. This is called an *alkoxymercuration/demercuration* reaction.

Hydroboration provides yet another mechanism to produce an alcohol from an alkene. This is an anti-Markovnikov and a syn addition.

Notice that this reaction is in the presence of peroxide. This should help you remember that it is anti-Markovnikov. You may see hydroboration on the MCAT, but you probably won't have to know anything about it to answer the questions.

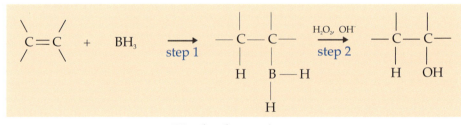

Hydroboration

Halogens are much more reactive toward alkenes than toward alkanes. Br_2 and Cl_2 add to alkenes readily via anti-addition to form *vic-dihalides* (two halogens connected to adjacent carbons).

You should know halogenation of an alkene for the MCAT. Notice that alkanes will not react with halogens without light or heat, but alkenes will. Alkynes behave just like alkenes when exposed to halogens.

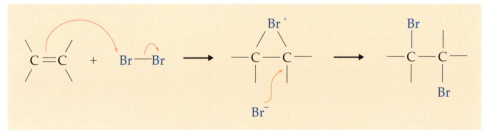

Halogenation of an Alkene

When this reaction takes place with water, a *halohydrin* is formed and Markovnikov's rule is followed where the electrophile adds to the least substituted carbon. Water acts as the nucleophile in the second step instead of the bromide ion. (A halohydrin is a hydroxyl group and a halogen attached to adjacent carbons.)

Benzene undergoes **substitution NOT addition**. If a functional group were added to benzene, it would disrupt the resonance and the compound would no longer be aromatic.

From stereochemistry, we know that resonance atoms must be in the same plane, so benzene is a **flat molecule**. Benzene is stabilized by **resonance** and its carbon-carbon bonds have partial double bond character. Although benzene is normally drawn without its six hydrogens, don't forget that they exist. If a benzene ring contains one substituent, the remaining 5 positions are labeled **ortho, meta, or para** as shown below.

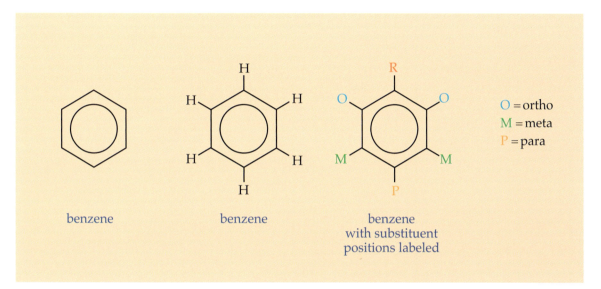

benzene   benzene   benzene
                                              with substituent
                                              positions labeled

O = ortho
M = meta
P = para

Don't let ring structures intimidate you. Since benzene only undergoes substitution, benzene presents little challenge on the MCAT. AAMC has announced that they will not ask questions on benzene starting in 2003. Nevertheless, it won't hurt to learn the names of the substituted positions: ortho, meta, para.

When an **electron withdrawing group** is in the R position, it deactivates the ring and directs any new substituents to the meta position. **Electron donating groups** activate the ring and direct any new substituents to ortho and para positions. **Halogens are an exception** to the rule. They are electron withdrawing and deactivate the ring as expected. However, they are ortho-para directors. (To deactivate the ring simply means to make it less reactive.) Knowing whether a functional group is electron withdrawing or donating can be very helpful in all of organic chemistry.

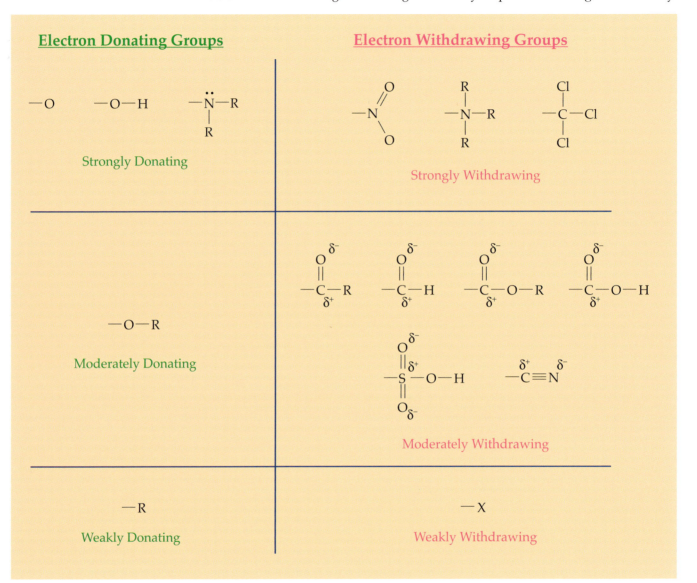

The groups are labeled in relation to the electron withdrawing-donating tendencies of a lone hydrogen atom. Hydrogen is considered neither electron withdrawing nor electron donating. Benzene, itself, is an ortho-para director and ring activator; however, for reasons that are well beyond the MCAT, it is best to consider benzene as electron withdrawing in most other situations.

It may help to familiarize yourself with the names of the following benzene compounds, but it is unlikely that a correct MCAT answer will require this knowledge.

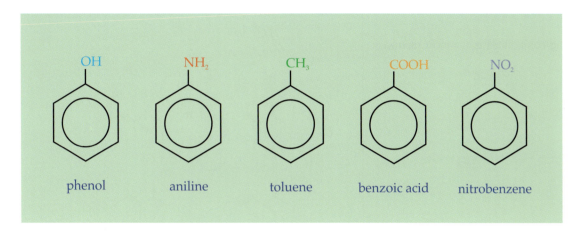

Don't memorize too many reactions. So far, you should thoroughly understand:

1. combustion;

2. halogenation of an alkane;

3. dehydration of an alcohol and the reverse reaction, hydration of an alkene;

4. electrophilic addition (via Comrade Markovnikov); and

5. halogenation of an alkene. Assume that alkynes behave like alkenes.

Rather than memorizing other reactions, be familiar with the behavior of functional groups. For instance, the double bond of alkenes makes a large electron cloud that is attractive to an electrophile, but alkenes withdraw electrons through their bonds, making them stabilized by electron donating groups, and making them more acidic than alkanes; benzene hates addition; etc. A strong start toward understanding functional groups is memorizing their electron withdrawing and donating natures. We will come back to electron withdrawing and donating properties time and again. Remember, the MCAT is not going to require that you have an obscure reaction committed to memory; much more likely, the MCAT will show you a reaction that you have never seen and ask you "why?" The answer will be because the functional group involved normally behaves that way. Know your functional groups.

33. Which of the following compounds is the most thermo-dynamically stable?

   A. $CH_3CH_2CH=CH_2$

   B. $CH_3CH=CH_2$

   C.

   D.

34. Which of the following compounds will be the most reactive with HBr?

   A. $CH_3CH_2CH=CH_2$

   B. $CH_3CH=CH_2$

   C.

   D.

35. What is the product of the following oxidation reaction?

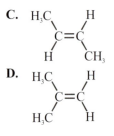

   1) O_3
   2) Zn, H_2O

A.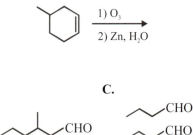

B.

C.

D.

36. What is the major product of the following reaction?

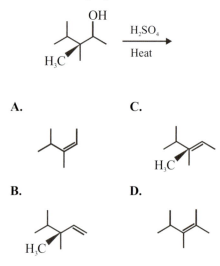

H_2SO_4 / Heat

A.

C.

B.

D.

37. When 2,4-dimethyl-2-pentene is hydrated with cold dilute acid, the major product is:

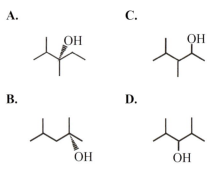

A.

C.

B.

D.

38. Anthracene is an aromatic compound described by which of the following characteristics?

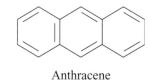

Anthracene

   I. cyclic
   II. planar
   III. satisfies Huckel's rule
   IV. has an even number of š electrons

   A. I and II only
   B. II, III and IV only
   C. I, III and IV only
   D. I, II, III and IV

39. Which of the following statements is true regarding the two reaction mechanisms and the deuterium (D) effect?

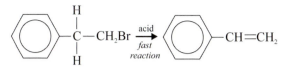

[1-Bromo-2-phenylethane]

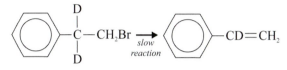

[1-Bromo-2,2-dideuterio
-2-phenylethane]

A. Deuterium (D) isotope is identical to hydrogen in every way.

B. C—H or C—D bond is broken in the reaction rate limiting step.

C. 1-Bromo-2-phenylethane reactant undergoes a one step substitution reaction.

D. Carbon hydrogen bond is stronger than the corresponding carbon deuterium bond.

40. Natural rubber is a diene polymer known as isoprene. What is the most likely explanation for isoprene's ability to stretch?

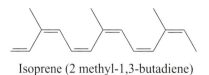

Isoprene (2 methyl-1,3-butadiene)

A. Isoprene undergoes vulcanization, which induces cross-linking between carbon atoms in nearby rubber chains.

B. Double bonds induce shape irregularities, which prevent neighboring chains from nestling together.

C. Alkane polymer chains orient along the direction of pull by sliding over each other.

D. Isoprene is able to undergo rapid hydration/dehydration reaction.

2-13
Substitutions

<u>Substitution</u> reactions occur when one functional group replaces another. Two important types of substitution reactions are <u>S_N1</u> and <u>S_N2</u>. These are substitution, nucleophilic, unimolecular and bimolecular. The numbers represent the order of the rate law and NOT the number of steps.

2-14
S_N1

An S_N1 reaction has 2 steps and has a rate that is dependent on only one of the reactants. The first step is the formation of the carbocation. This is the **slow step** and thus the **rate-determining step**. Since this step has nothing to do with the nucleophile, the rate is independent of the concentration of the nucleophile and is directly proportional to the concentration of the **substrate** (The substrate is the electrophile or the molecule being attacked by the nucleophile.). In an S_N1 reaction the **leaving group** (the group being replaced) simply breaks away on its own to leave a carbocation behind. The second step happens very quickly. The nucleophile attacks the carbocation.

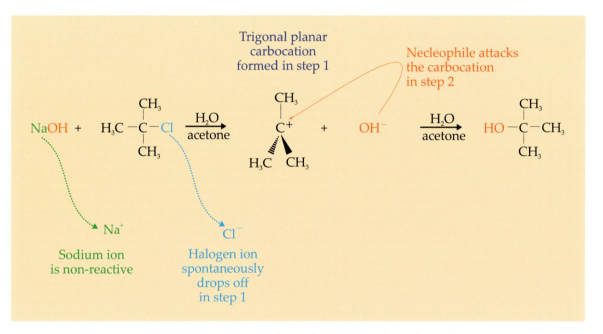

Substitution, Nucleophilic, Unimolecular

Notice that if the carbocation carbon began and ended an S_N1 reaction as a chiral carbon, both enantiomers would be produced. The intermediate carbocation is planar and the nucleophile is able to attack it from either side. Carbon skeleton rearrangement may occur if the carbocation can rearrange to a more stable form. Elimination (E1) often accompanies S_N1 reactions because the nucleophile may act as a base to abstract a proton from the carbocation, forming a carbon-carbon double bond.

Since the carbocation must be formed spontaneously in an S_N1 reaction, a tertiary substrate is more likely to undergo an S_N1 reaction than is a primary or secondary substrate. On the MCAT, probably only tertiary substrates will undergo S_N1. The rate of an S_N1 reaction is determined solely by the concentration of the substrate.

S_N2 reactions occur in a single step. The rate is dependent on the concentration of the nucleophile and the substrate. In an S_N2 reaction a nucleophile attacks the intact substrate from behind the leaving group and knocks the leaving group free while bonding to the substrate.

2-15

S_N2

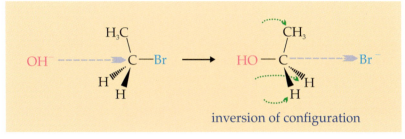

inversion of configuration

Substitution, Nucleophilic, Bimolecular

Notice the **inversion of configuration** on the carbon being attacked by the nucleophile. If the carbon were chiral, the relative configuration would be changed but the absolute configuration might or might not be changed. Notice also that a tertiary carbon would **sterically hinder** the nucleophile in this reaction. The rate of S_N2 reactions decreases from methyl to secondary substrates. S_N2 reactions don't typically occur with tertiary substrates. If the nucleophile is a strong base and the substrate is too hindered, an elimination (E2) reaction may occur. In an E2 reaction, the nucleophile acts as a base abstracting a proton and, in the same step, the halogen leaves the substrate forming a carbon-carbon double bond. Bulky nucleophiles also hinder S_N2 reactions.

The strength of the nucleophile is unimportant for an S_N1 reaction but important for an S_N2 reaction. A base is always a stronger nucleophile than its conjugate acid, but basicity is not the same thing as nucleophilicity. If a nucleophile behaves as a base, elimination results. To avoid this, we use a less bulky nucleophile. A negative charge and polarizability add to nucleophilicity. Electronegativity reduces nucleophilicity. In general, nucleophilicity decreases going up and to the right on the periodic table.

2-16

Nucleophilicity

Polar protic solvents (polar solvents that can hydrogen bond) stabilize the nucleophile and any carbocation that may form. A stable nucleophile slows S_N2 reactions, while a stable carbocation increases the rate of S_N1 reactions. Thus polar protic solvents increase the rate of S_N1 and decrease the rate of S_N2. *Polar aprotic solvents* (polar solvents that can't form hydrogen bonds) do not form strong bonds with ions and thus increase the rate of S_N2 reactions while inhibiting S_N1 reactions. In S_N1 reactions, the solvent is often heated to reflux (boiled) in order to provide energy for the formation of the carbocation.

2-17

Solvents

In *solvolysis* the solvent acts as the nucleophile.

2-18
Leaving Groups

The best leaving groups are those that are stable when they leave. Generally speaking, the weaker the base, the better the leaving group. Electron withdrawing effects and polarizability also make for a good leaving group. The leaving group will always be more stable than the nucleophile.

2-19
S_N1 vs. S_N2

There are six things to remember about S_N1 vs. S_N2. Remember the six things as "The nucleophile and the five Ss": 1) Substrate; 2) Solvent; 3) Speed; 4) Stereochemistry; and 5) Skeleton rearrangement.

The nucleophile: S_N2 requires a strong nucleophile, while nucleophilic strength doesn't affect S_N1.

1st S: S_N2 reactions don't occur with a sterically hindered Substrate. S_N2 requires a methyl, primary, or secondary substrate, while S_N1 requires a secondary or tertiary substrate.

2nd S: A highly polar Solvent increases the reaction rate of S_N1 by stabilizing the carbocation, but slows down S_N2 reactions by stabilizing the nucleophile.

3rd S: The Speed of an S_N2 reaction depends upon the concentration of the substrate and the nucleophile, while the speed of an S_N1 depends only on the substrate.

4th S: S_N2 inverts Stereochemistry about the chiral center, while S_N1 creates a racemic mixture.

5th S: S_N1 may be accompanied by carbon Skeleton rearrangement, but S_N2 never rearranges the carbon skeleton.

Also remember that elimination reactions can accompany both S_N1 and S_N2 reactions. Elimination occurs when the nucleophile behaves as a base rather than a nucleophile; it abstracts a proton rather than attacking a carbon. Elimination reactions always result in a carbon-carbon double bond. E1 and E2 kinetics are similar to S_N1 and S_N2 respectively.

2-20
Physical Properties of Alcohols

Alcohols follow trends similar to hydrocarbons, but alcohols hydrogen bond, giving them considerably higher boiling points and water solubilities than similar-weight hydrocarbons.

Alcohols follow the same general trends as alkanes. The boiling point goes up with molecular weight and down with branching. The melting point trend is not as reliable but still exists. Melting point also goes up with molecular weight. Branching generally lowers boiling point and has a less clear effect on melting. Although alcohols follow the same trend as alkanes, their boiling and melting points are much higher than alkanes due to **hydrogen bonding**. The hydrogen bonding increases the intermolecular forces, which must be overcome to change phase.

Alcohols are more soluble in water than alkanes and alkenes. The hydroxyl group increases polarity and allows for hydrogen bonding with water. The longer the carbon chain, the less soluble the alcohol.

Alcohol   Water

Since an alcohol can lose a proton, it can act like an acid. However, alcohols are less acidic than water. The order of acidity for alcohols from strongest to weakest is: methyl; 1°; 2°; 3°. If we examine the conjugate base of each alcohol, the most stable conjugate base will be the conjugate of the strongest acid. Since excess charge is an instability, the most stable conjugate base will have the weakest negative charge. Methyl groups are electron donating compared to hydrogens, thus they act to prevent the carbon from absorbing some of the excess negative charge of the conjugate. Because a tertiary alcohol has the most methyl groups, a tertiary carbon can absorb the least amount of negative charge; the conjugate base of a tertiary alcohol is the least stable; and a tertiary alcohol is the least acidic.

2-21
Alcohols as Acids

Acid	pK_a
hydrochloric acid	−2.2
acetic acid	4.8
phenol	10
water	15.7
ethanol	15.9
t-butyl alcohol	18

Electron donation and withdrawal helps to explain many of the reactions in MCAT organic chemistry. For instance, placing an electron withdrawing group on the alcohol increases its acidity by reducing the negative charge on the conjugate base.

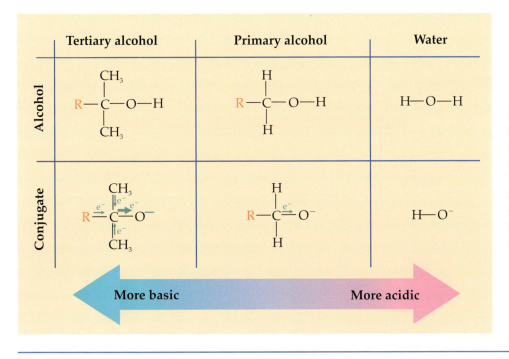

We've already looked at several alcohol synthesis reactions: hydration of an alkene, oxymercuration/demercuration, hydroboration, and nucleophilic substitution. Another method of synthesizing an alcohol is with an organometallic compound. Organometallic reagents possess a highly polarized carbon-metal bond. The carbon is more electronegative than the metal, so the carbon takes on a strong partial negative charge. The poloarized carbon-metal bond and the partial negative charge on the carbon atom makes this carbon a strong nucleophile and base. The most common reaction for organometallic compounds is nucleophilic attack on a carbonyl carbon, which, after an acid bath, produces an alcohol.

2-22
Synthesis of Alcohols

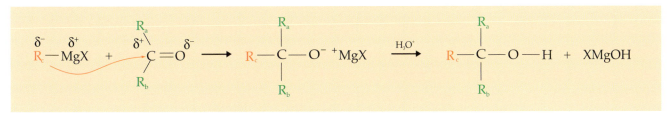

Grignard Synthesis of an Alcohol

Grignard reagents will react in a similar fashion with C=N, C≡N, S=O, N=O. The Grignard is a strong enough base to deprotonate the following species: O—H, N—H, S—H, —C≡C–H. Grignard reagents are made in ether, and are incompatible with water and acids stronger than water.

In a nucleophilic attack mechanism similar to Grignard synthesis of an alcohol, hydrides (H^-) will react with carbonyls to form alcohols. Unlike Grignard synthesis of an alcohol, the use of hydrides does not extend the carbon skeleton.

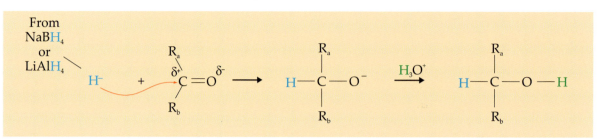

Reduction Synthesis of an Alcohol

Question: Why is it more difficult to reduce esters and acetates than ketones and aldehydes?

Answer: Because the group attached to the carbonyl of the ester or acetate is a stronger electron donor than an alkyl group or hydrogen. By donating electrons more strongly, it reduces the positive charge on the carbonyl carbon making it less attractive to the nucleophile.

In reduction synthesis, both $NaBH_4$ and $LiAlH_4$ will reduce aldehydes and ketones, but only $LiAlH_4$ is strong enough to reduce esters and acetates.

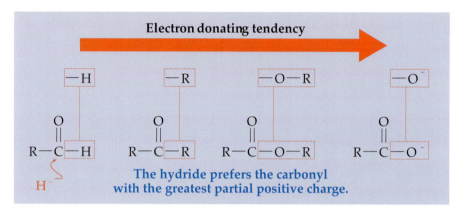

2-23

Reactions with Alcohols

We've already seen dehydration of an alcohol. Most of the time on the MCAT, if an alcohol is a reactant, it will be acting as a nucleophile. The two lone pairs of electrons on the oxygen are pushed out by the bent shape, and they search for a positive charge. The oxygen will find and connect to the substrate and the positively charged proton will drop off into solution.

Alcohols like to be nucleophiles.

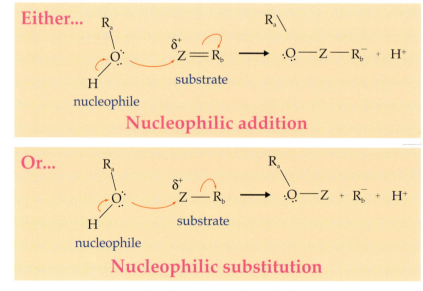

Alcohols as nucleophiles

Primary and secondary alcohols can be oxidized. Tertiary alcohols cannot be oxidized on the MCAT. In organic chemistry, you can use the following rule to determine if a compound has been oxidized or reduced:

2-24
Oxidation of Alcohols

Oxidation: loss of H_2; addition of O or O_2; addition of X_2 (X = halogens)

Reduction: addition of H_2 (or H^-); loss of O or O_2; loss of X_2

Neither Oxidation nor reduction: addition or loss of H^+, H_2O, HX, etc.

Primary alcohols oxidize to aldehydes, which, in turn, oxidize to carboxylic acids. Secondary alcohols oxidize to ketones. In each case, the reverse process is called **reduction**.

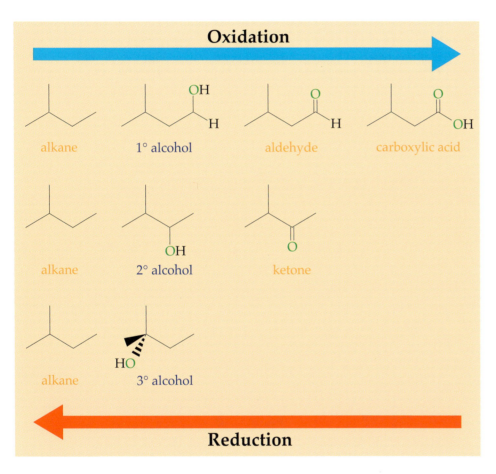

A simple way to think of oxidation for any compound in organic chemistry is to consider the oxygen-to-hydrogen ratio of a molecule. If this ratio increases, then the molecule has been oxidized. If this ratio decreases, then the molecule has been reduced. This rule doesn't cover all situations, but it works well for many.

Generally speaking, *oxidizing agents* will have lots of oxygen and *reducing agents* will have lots of hydrogen. Below is a table of common oxidizing and reducing agents.

Oxidizing agents	Reducing agents
$K_2Cr_2O_7$	$LiAlH_4$
$KMnO_4$	$NaBH_4$
H_2CrO_4	H_2 + pressure
O_2	
Br_2	

2-25
Alkyl Halides from Alcohols

We saw in the S_N2 reaction that the halogen ion, as a weak base, is a good leaving group, and the hydroxyl group, as a strong base, is a good nucleophile. However, if the hydroxyl group is protonated by an acid, it becomes water, an excellent leaving group. The halide ion is an unusual nucleophile in that it is a very weak base and does not become protonated in acidic solution.

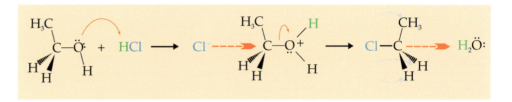

This reaction can occur as S_N1 with a tertiary alcohol or S_N2 with other alcohols.

Notice that this reaction breaks the C—O bond rather than the O—H bond. When the C—O bond is broken, alcohol is behaving as an electrophile. When the O—H bond is broken, it is a nucleophile. Alcohols are very weak electrophiles because the hydroxyl group is such a weak leaving group. Protonating the hydroxyl group makes the good leaving group water. However, protonating an alcohol requires a strong acid. Strong acids react with most good nucleophiles, destroying their nucleophilicity.

Alcohols can also be converted to alkyl halides by phosphorus halides such as PCl_3, PBr_3, and PI_3, via an S_N2 mechanism resulting in poor yields with tertiary alcohols. Another reagent for producing alkyl halides from alcohols is thionyl chloride, $SOCl_2$, resulting in sulfur dioxide and hydrochloric acid.

2-26
Preparation of Mesylates and Tosylates

Alcohols form esters called sulfonates. The __formation of the sulfonates__ shown below is a nucleophilic substitution, where alcohol acts as the nucleohile. The reaction proceeds with retention of configuration, so if the carbon atom bearing the hydroxyl group is stereogenic, it is NOT inverted as it would be in an S_N2 reaction.

__Tosylates and mesylates__ are commonly used sulfonates that you need to know for the MCAT. The sulfonate ions are very weak bases and excellent leaving groups. When tosylates and mesylates are leaving groups, the reaction may proceed via an S_N1 or S_N2 mechanism.

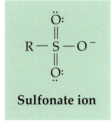

Sulfonate ion

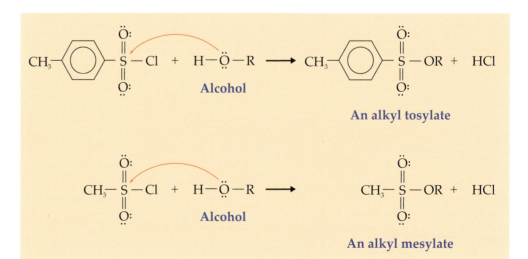

The **pinacol rearrangement** is a dehydration of an alcohol that results in an unexpected product. When hot sulfuric acid is added to an alcohol, the expected product of dehydration is an alkene. However, if the alcohol is a vicinal diol, the product will be a ketone or aldehyde. The reaction follows the mechanism shown below. The first hydroxyl group is protonated and removed by the acid to form a carbocation in an expected dehydration step. Now, a methyl group may move to form an even more stable carbocation. This new carbocation exhibits resonance as shown. Resonance Structure 2 is favored because all the atoms have an octet of electrons. The water deprotonates Resonance Structure 2, forming pinacolone and regenerating the acid catalyst.

2-27
The Pinacol
Rearrangement

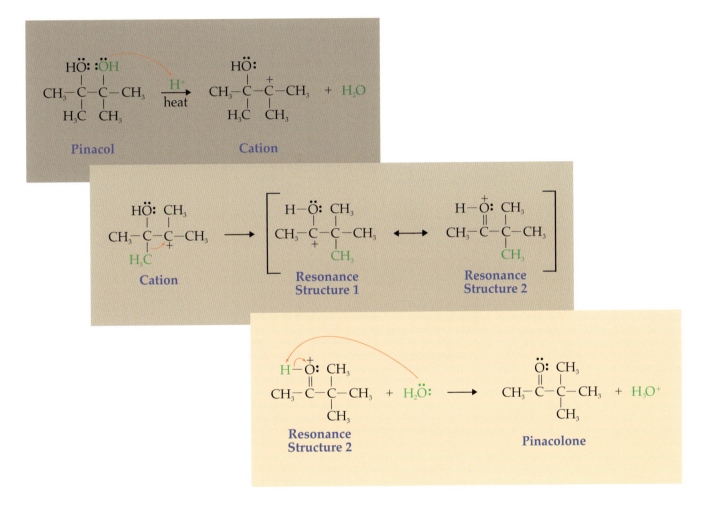

Ethers (other than epoxides) are relatively non-reactive. They are polar. Although they cannot hydrogen bond with themselves, they can hydrogen bond with compounds that contain a hydrogen attached to a N, O, or F atom. Ethers are roughly as soluble in water as alcohols of similar molecular weight, yet organic compounds tend to be much more soluble in ethers than alcohols because no hydrogen bonds need to be broken. These properties make ethers useful solvents.

Since an ether cannot hydrogen bond with itself, it will have a boiling point roughly comparable to that of an alkane with a similar molecular weight. Their relatively low boiling points increase their usefulness as solvents.

2-28
Ethers

Ether is almost always the answer to solvent questions on the MCAT.

For the MCAT, ethers (other than epoxides) undergo one reaction. Ethers are cleaved by the halo-acids HI and HBr to form the corresponding alcohol and alkyl halide. If a large concentration of acid is used, the excess acid will react with the alcohol, as described above, to form another alkyl halide.

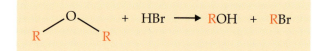

Ethers can also be oxidized to peroxides, but this is unlikely to be on the MCAT.

2-29 Epoxides

Epoxides (also called *oxiranes*) are three-membered cyclic ethers. They are more reactive than typical ethers due to the strain created by the small ring. Epoxides react with water in the presence of an acid catalyst to form diols, commonly called glycols. This is an anti-addition.

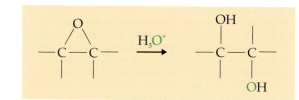

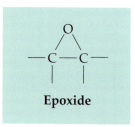

Epoxide

The epoxide oxygen is often protonated to form an alcohol when one of the carbons is attacked by a nucleophile.

An epoxide is an ether but is far more reactive. You don't have to memorize the reactions of epoxides for the MCAT.

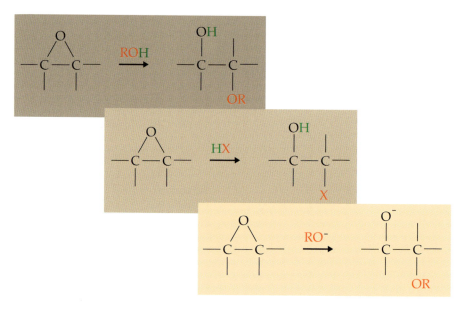

2-30 Acidities of the Functional Groups

Now that you know all about the important functional groups, it is a good idea to know their acidities. From weakest to strongest acids, they are as follows:

$$H_3C-CH_3 < H_2C=CH_2 < H_2 < NH_3 < HC\equiv CH < H_3C-\overset{\overset{\displaystyle O}{\|}}{C}-H$$

$$< H_3C-CH_2-OH < H_2O < H_3C-\overset{\overset{\displaystyle O}{\|}}{C}-OH$$

Acid Strength →

41. A student added NaCl to ethanol in the polar aprotic solvent DMF, and no reaction took place. To the same solution, he then added HCl. A reaction took place resulting in chloroethane. Which of the following best explains the student's results?

A. The addition of HCl increased the chloride ion concentration which increased the rate of the reaction and pushed the equilibrium to the right.
B. The chloride ion is a better nucleophile in a polar protic solvent and the HCl protonated the solvent.
C. The HCl protonated the hydroxyl group on the alcohol making it a better leaving group.
D. The HCl destabilized the chloride ion complex between the chloride ion and the solvent.

42. All of the following will increase the rate of the reaction shown below EXCEPT:

I. increasing the concentration of tertbutyl alcohol
II. increasing the concentration of hydrobromic acid
III. increasing the temperature

A. I only
B. II only
C. III only
D. II and III only

43. The following reaction is one of many steps in the laboratory synthesis of cholesterol. What type of reaction is it?

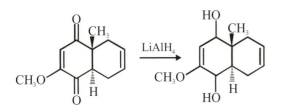

A. reduction reaction
B. oxidation reaction
C. catalytic hydrogenation
D. electrophilic substitution

44. Labetalol is a β-adrenergic antagonist which reduces blood pressure by blocking reflex sympathetic stimulation of the heart.

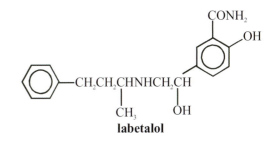

labetalol

Which of the following intermolecular bonds contributes least to the water solubility of labetalol?

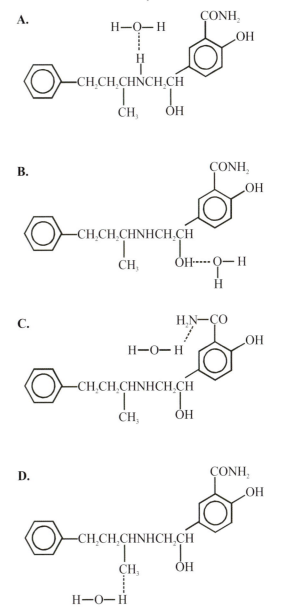

GO ON TO THE NEXT PAGE.

45. The Lucas test distinguishes between the presence of primary, secondary, and tertiary alcohols based upon reactivity with a hydrogen halide. The corresponding alkyl chlorides are insoluble in Lucas reagent and turn the solution cloudy at the same rate that they react with the reagent. The alcohols, A, B, and C, are solvated separately in Lucas reagent made of hydrochloric acid and zinc chloride. If the alcohols are primary, secondary, and tertiary respectively, what is the order of their rates of reaction from fastest to slowest?

   A. A, B, C
   B. B, A, C
   C. C, B, A
   D. B, C, A

46. Reactions 1 and 2 were carried out in the presence of peroxides. Which of the following is the most likely explanation for why Product B fails to form?

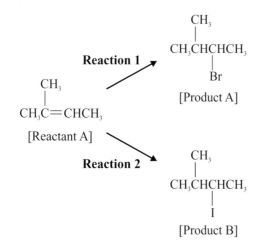

   A. Hydrogen halides always yield products of Markovnikov's addition.
   B. Reactions 1 and 2 show Markovnikov and anti-Markovnikov addition, respectively.
   C. Peroxide dependent anti-Markovnikov addition succeeds only with bromine.
   D. Markovnikov addition reactions 1 and 2 are driven by reagent concentrations.

47. The most common reaction of alcohols is nucleophilic substitution. All of the following correctly describe S_N2 reactions, EXCEPT:

   I. reaction rate = k [S][Nucleophile]
  II. racemic mixture of products results
 III. inversion of configuration occurs

   A. I and II only
   B. II only
   C. III only
   D. I, II and III

48. Which statement is the most likely explanation for why 1-chloro-1, 2-diphenylethane proceeds via S_N1 at a constant rate independent of nucleophilic quality or concentration?

   A. 1-chloro-1, 2-diphenylethane prefers S_N2 mechanism for rapid substitution
   B. S_N1 rate-limiting step determines the overall reaction rate
   C. 1-chloro-1, 2-diphenylethane concentration increase will not cause an increase in product synthesis
   D. reaction product accumulation has a direct effect on the rate-limiting step

 STOP.

Carbonyls and Amines

A **carbonyl** is a carbon double bonded to an oxygen. The double bond is shorter and stronger than the double bond of an alkene. Aldehydes, ketones, carboxylic acids, amides, and esters all contain carbonyls. Whenever you see a carbonyl on the MCAT think about two things: 1) **planar stereochemistry** and; 2) partial negative charge on the oxygen, **partial positive charge on the carbon**. The planar stereochemistry of a carbonyl leaves open space above and below, making it susceptible to chemical attack. The partial positive charge on the carbon means that any attack on the carbonyl carbon will be from a nucleophile. Aldehydes and ketones typically undergo nucleophilic addition, while other carbonyl compounds prefer nucleophilic substitution. The partial negative charge on the oxygen means that it is easily protonated.

3-1
The Carbonyl

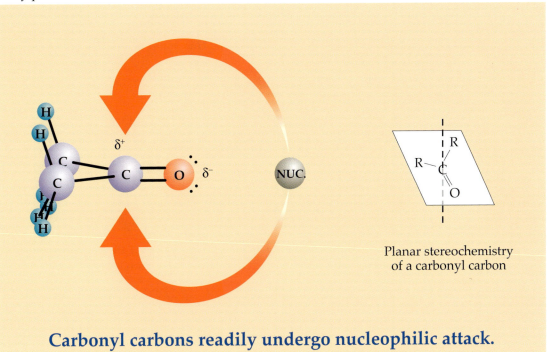

Planar stereochemistry
of a carbonyl carbon

Carbonyl carbons readily undergo nucleophilic attack.

3-2
Aldehydes and Ketones

You should be able to recognize and give the common name for the simple **alde-hydes and ketones** shown below.

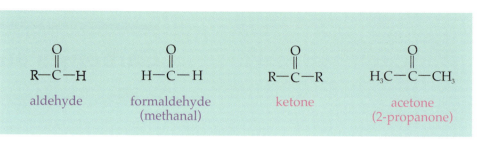

3-3
Physical Properties

Aldehydes and ketones are more polar and have higher boiling points than alkanes and alkenes of similar molecular weight. However, they cannot hydrogen bond with each other, so they have lower boiling points than corresponding alcohols. Aldehydes and ketones do accept hydrogen bonds with water and other compounds that can hydrogen bond. This makes them excellent solvents for these substances. Aldehydes and ketones with up to four carbons are soluble in water.

3-4
Chemical Properties

Most of the time on the MCAT an **aldehyde** or **ketone** will be acting either as the **substrate in nucleophilic addition** or as a Bronsted-Lowry acid by donating one of its **α-hydrogens** (alpha-hydrogens). A carbon that is attached to a carbonyl carbon is in the **alpha position** and is called an **α-carbon**. The next carbon is called a *β-carbon*; the next is the *γ-carbon* and so on down the Greek alphabet. An α-hydrogen is any hydrogen attached to an α-carbon. Normally hydrogens are not easily removed from carbons because carbon anions are very strong bases and unstable. However, α-carbon anions are stabilized by resonance. This anion is called an *enolate ion* (en from alkene and ol from alcohol).

An enolate ion is stabilized by resonance.

When the β-carbon is also a carbonyl (called a β-dicarbonyl), the enol form becomes far more stable due to internal hydrogen bonding and resonance.

The dicarbonyl increases the acidity of the alpha hydrogen between the carbonyls, making it more acidic than water or alcohol.

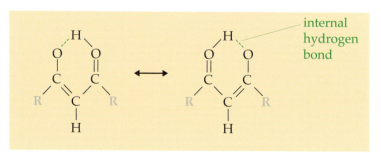

Enol stabilization of β-dicarbonyl

Because alkyl groups are electron donating and a ketone has two alkyl groups attached to the carbonyl, the carbonyl carbon of the conjugate base of the ketone is less able to distribute negative charge and is slightly less stable than that of an aldehyde. Thus aldehydes are slightly more acidic than ketones. This same property makes aldehydes more reactive than ketones. Both aldehydes and ketones are less acidic than alcohols. Any electron withdrawing groups attached to the α-carbon or the carbonyl tend to stabilize the conjugate base and thus increase acidity.

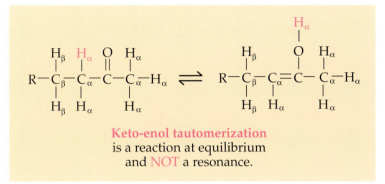

Keto-enol tautomerization
is a reaction at equilibrium
and NOT a resonance.

Due to the properties of the α-hydrogen and carbonyl, ketones and aldehydes exist at room temperature as enol **tautomers**. Tautomerization involves a proton shift, in this case from the α-carbon position to the carbonyl oxygen position. Both tautomers exist at room temperature, but the ketone or aldehyde tautomer is usually favored. Tautomerization is a reaction at equilibrium, not a resonance. (Remember, in resonance structures atoms don't move and neither resonance structure actually exists.)

There are other forms of tautomerization but keto-enol tautomerization is the most likely form to be tested on the MCAT. In order to recognize other forms, simply watch for the proton shift in equilibrium.

Aldehydes and ketones react with alcohols to form *hemiacetals* and *hemiketals*, respectively. In this reaction the alcohols react in typical fashion as the nucleophile. When aldehydes and ketones are attacked by a nucleophile, they undergo addition. Aldehydes and hemiacetals, and ketones and hemiketals, exist in equilibrium when an aldehyde or ketone is dissolved in an alcohol; however, usually the hemiacetal or hemiketal is too unstable to isolate unless it exists as a ring structure. If a second molar equivalent of alcohol is added, an *acetal* is formed from a hemiacetal, or a *ketal* is formed from a hemiketal.

3-5
Formation of Acetals

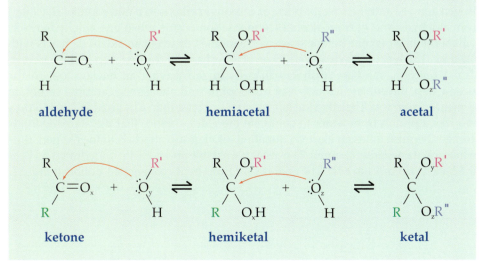

The aldehyde products can be easily distinguished from the ketone products by the lone hydrogen. The hemi products can be distinguished from the acetals and ketals because the hemi products both have alcohols while the full acetals and ketals don't. Hemi formation is catalyzed by acid or base. In formation of acetal and ketal from the hemi forms the hydroxyl group must be protonated to make a good leaving group, thus this part of the reaction is catalyzed by acid only.

Because acetals and ketals are unreactive toward bases, they are often used as *blocking groups*. In other words, a base would typically act as a nucleophile to attack an aldehyde or ketone at the carbonyl carbon, but the aldehyde or ketone can be temporarily changed to an acetal or ketal to prevent it from reacting with a base.

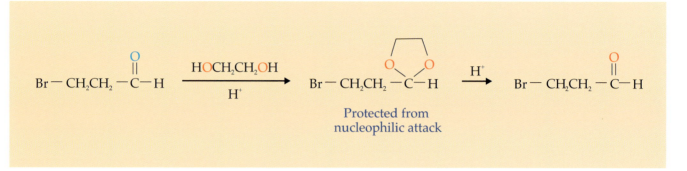

In a similar reaction, when aldehydes or ketones are dissolved in aqueous solution, they establish an equilibrium with their hydrate, a geminal diol.

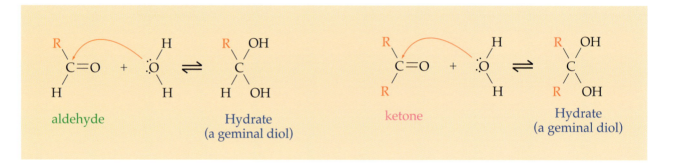

3-6
Aldol Condensation

Aldol condensation is a favorite on the MCAT because it demonstrates both α-hydrogen activity and the susceptibility of carbonyl carbons to a nucleophile. *Aldol* (ald from aldehyde and ol from alcohol) condensation occurs when one aldehyde reacts with another, when one ketone reacts with another, or when an aldehyde reacts with a ketone. The reaction is catalyzed by an acid or base. In the first step of the base-catalyzed reaction, the base abstracts an α-hydrogen leaving an enolate ion. In the second step, the enolate ion acts as a nucleophile and attacks the carbonyl carbon to form an *alkoxide* ion. The alkoxide ion is a stronger base than a hydroxide ion and thus removes a proton from water to complete the aldol. (Notice that the alkoxide ion is stronger because it has an electron donating alkyl group attached to the oxygen, thus increasing its negative charge.) The aldol is unstable and is easily dehydrated by heat or a base to become an *enal*. The enal is stabilized by its conjugated double bonds.

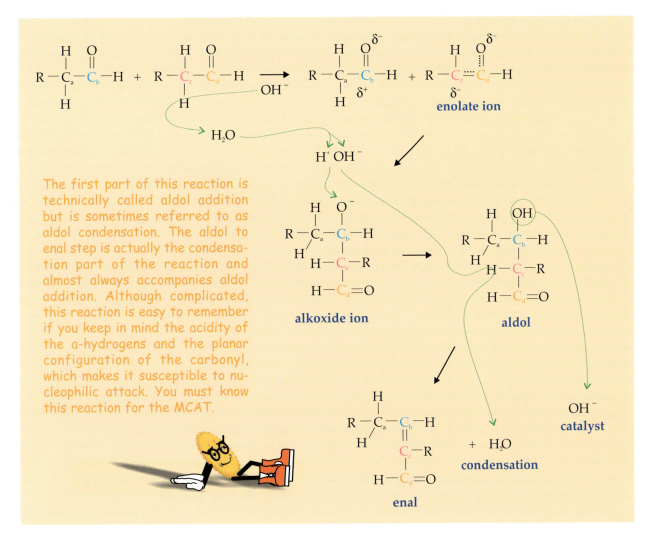

The first part of this reaction is technically called aldol addition but is sometimes referred to as aldol condensation. The aldol to enal step is actually the condensation part of the reaction and almost always accompanies aldol addition. Although complicated, this reaction is easy to remember if you keep in mind the acidity of the α-hydrogens and the planar configuration of the carbonyl, which makes it susceptible to nucleophilic attack. You must know this reaction for the MCAT.

Halogens add to ketones at the alpha carbon in the presence of a base or an acid. When a base is used, it is difficult to prevent halogenation at more than one of the alpha positions. The base is also consumed by the reaction with water as a by-product, whereas the acid acts as a true catalyst and is not consumed.

3-7
Halogenation and the Haloform Reaction

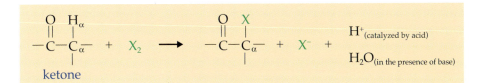

When a base is used with a methyl ketone, the alpha carbon will become completely halogenated. This trihalo product reacts further with the base to produce a carboxylic acid and a haloform (chloroform, $CHCl_3$; bromoform, $CHBr_3$; or iodoform, CHI_3). This is called the Haloform Reaction.

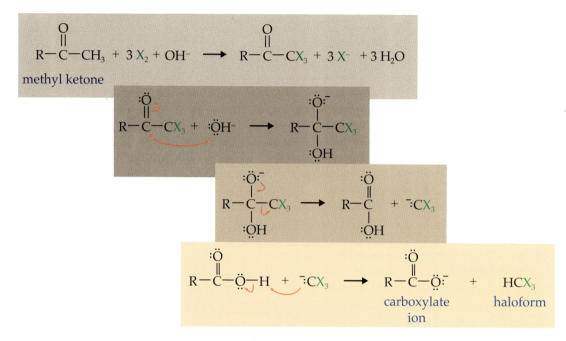

Haloform Reaction

3-8
The Wittig Reaction

The Wittig reaction converts a ketone to an alkene. A phosphorous ylide (pronounced "ill' -id") is used. An ylide is a neutral molecule with a negatively charged carbanion.

The ketone behaves in its normal fashion, first undergoing nucleophilic addition from the ylide to form a betaine (pronounced "bay' -tuh-ene"). However, the betaine is unstable and quickly breaks down to a triphenylphosphine oxide and the alkene. When possible, a mixture of both cis and trans isomers are formed by the Wittig reaction.

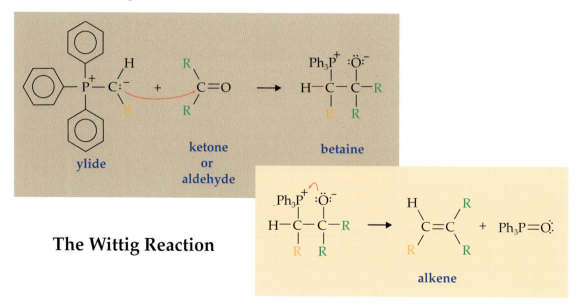

The Wittig Reaction

A carbonyl compound with a double bond between the α and β carbon has some special properties. The carbocation that is produced at the carbonyl carbon when the electrons in the carbonyl double bond shift to the oxygen atom (giving the oxygen a negative charge) is stabilized by resonance. Additionally, the electron withdrawing carbonyl group pulls electrons from the carbon-carbon double bond and makes the β-carbon less susceptible to attack by a nucleophile (electrophilic addition). Thus, rather than the nucleophile adding to the β-carbon, it may sometime add to the oxygen atom, forming the enol-keto tautomers.

Even more strange is the ability of the β-carbon to undergo nucleophilic addition directly. This is sometimes called *conjugate addition*.

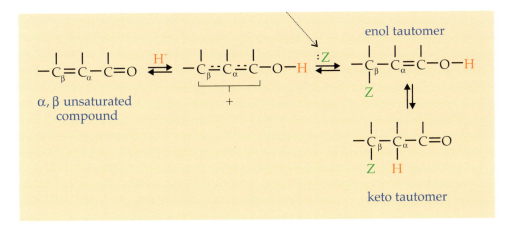

Of course, we know that aldehydes and ketones undergo nucleophilic addition at the carbonyl, and for many nucleophiles this carbonyl addition is still the major product in the above reaction.

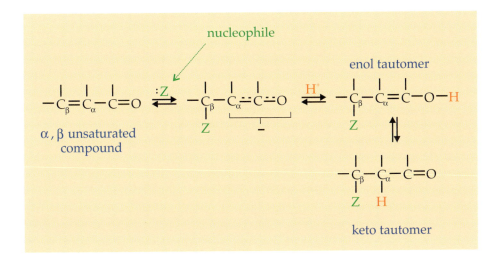

Questions 49 through 56 are **NOT** based on a descriptive passage.

49. What is the major product of the crossed aldol reaction shown below?

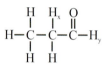

$$C_6H_5\overset{O}{\overset{\|}{C}}H \;+\; CH_3CH_2\overset{O}{\overset{\|}{C}}H \;\xrightarrow[10\,^\circ C]{OH^-}$$

A.

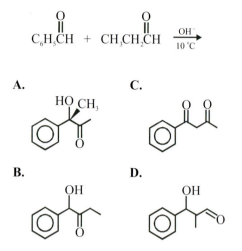

C.

B.

D.

50. Which of the following statements are true concerning the molecule shown below?

$$H-\underset{\underset{H}{|}}{\overset{\overset{H}{|}}{C}}-\underset{\underset{H}{|}}{\overset{\overset{H_x}{|}}{C}}-\overset{\overset{O}{\|}}{C}-H_y$$

   I. H_x is more acidic than H_y.
   II. H_y is more acidic than H_x.
   III. This molecule typically undergoes nucleophilic substitution.

   A. I only
   B. II only
   C. I and III only
   D. II and III only

51. Which of the following is the product of an aldehyde reduction reaction?

A.

C.

B.

D.

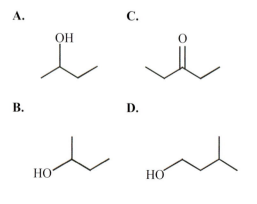

52. If the first step were omitted in the following set of reactions, what would be the final product?

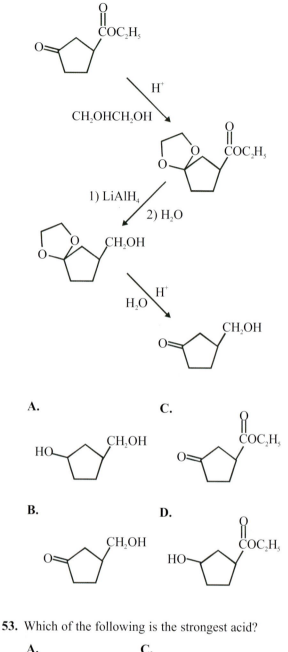

A.

C.

B.

D.

53. Which of the following is the strongest acid?

   A.   **C.**

   B.   **D.**

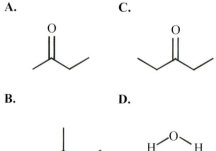

62

GO ON TO THE NEXT PAGE.

54. Aldehydes are readily oxidized to yield carboxylic acids, but ketones are inert to oxidation. Which is the most likely explanation regarding this difference in reactivity?

   A. Aldehydes have a proton attached to the carbonyl that is abstracted during oxidation. Ketones lack this proton and so cannot be oxidized.
   B. Reducing agents like HNO_3 are sterically hindered by ketone's carbonyl carbon.
   C. Aldehydes and ketones are of similar hybridization.
   D. The rate of the forward oxidation reaction is equal to the rate of the reverse reduction reaction in ketones.

55. 1,3-cyclohexane dione is shown below.

[1,3 cyclohexane dione]

Which of the following is not a tautomer of 1,3-cyclohexane dione?

A.

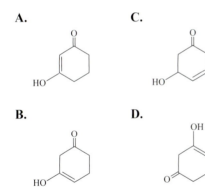

B.

C.

D.

56. Glucose reduces Tollens reagent to give an aldonic acid, ammonia, water, and a silver mirror. Methyl β-glucoside does not reduce Tollens reagent. Based on the structures shown below, which of the following best explains why methyl β-glucoside gives a negative Tollens test?

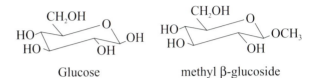

Glucose   methyl β-glucoside

   A. Aldehydes are not oxidized by Tollens reagent.
   B. Ketones are not oxidized by Tollens reagent.
   C. Hemiacetal rings are stable and do not easily open to form straight chain aldehydes.
   D. Acetal rings are stable and do not easily open to form straight chain aldehydes.

STOP.

3-10
Carboxylic Acids

You should be able to recognize and give the common name for the two simplest **carboxylic acids** shown below.

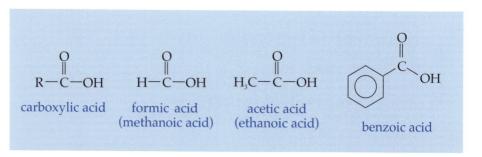

carboxylic acid | formic acid (methanoic acid) | acetic acid (ethanoic acid) | benzoic acid

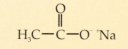

Sodium acetate
(sodium ethanoate)
A salt of acetic acid.

Carboxylic acids where the R group is an alkyl group are called *aliphatic acids*. The salts of carboxylic acids are named with the suffix *-ate*. The *-ate* replaces the *-ic* (or *-oic* in IUPAC names), so that "acetic" becomes "acetate". (Acetate is sometimes abbreviated –OAc.) In IUPAC rules, the carbonyl carbon of a carboxylic acid takes priority over all groups discussed so far.

On the MCAT, look for carboxylic acid to behave as an acid or as the substrate in a **nucleophilic substitution reaction**. Like any carbonyl compound, its stereochemistry makes it susceptible to nucleophiles. When the hydroxyl group is protonated, the good leaving group, water, is formed and substitution results.

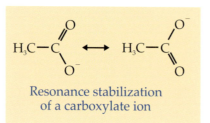

Resonance stabilization of a carboxylate ion

As far as organic acids go, carboxylic acids are very strong. When the proton is removed, the conjugate base is stabilized by resonance.

Electron withdrawing groups on the α-carbon help to further stabilize the conjugate base and thus increase the acidity of the corresponding carboxylic acid.

3-11
Physical Properties

Carboxylic acids are able to make strong double **hydrogen bonds** to form a dimer. The dimer significantly increases the boiling point of carboxylic acids by effectively doubling the molecular weight of the molecules leaving the liquid phase. Saturated carboxylic acids with more than 8 carbons are generally solids. The double bonds in unsaturated carboxylic acids impede the crystal lattice and lower melting point.

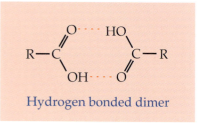

Hydrogen bonded dimer

Carboxylic acids with four carbons or less are miscible with water. Carboxylic acids with five or more carbons become increasingly less soluble in water. Carboxylic acids with more than 10 carbons are insoluble in water. Carboxylic acids are soluble in most nonpolar solvents because the dimer form allows the carboxylic acid to solvate without disrupting the hydrogen bonds of the dimer.

When a carboxylic acid loses CO_2 the reaction is called __decarboxylation__. Although the reaction is usually exothermic, the energy of activation is usually high, making the reaction difficult to carry out. The energy of activation is lowered when the β-carbon is a carbonyl because either the anion intermediate is stabilized by resonance or the acid forms a more stable cyclic intermediate. (A carboxylic acid with a carbonyl β-carbon is called a *β-keto acid*.)

3-12
Decarboxylation

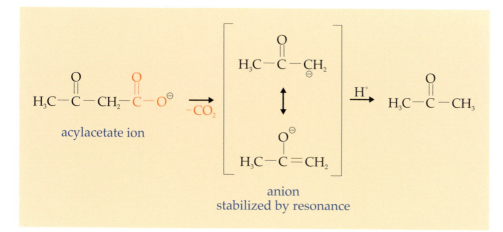

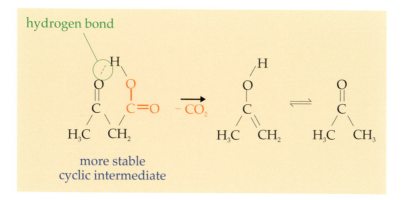

Notice that the first reaction starts with the anion and the second reaction starts with the acid. Notice also that the final products of both reactions are tautomers.

Derivatives of carboxylic acids contain the *acyl* group.

Inorganic acid chlorides like $SOCl_2$, PCl_3, and PCl_5 each react with carboxylic acids by nucleophilic substitution to form *acyl chlorides* (also called acid chlorides).

3-13
Carboxylic Acid Derivatives

$$R-\overset{\overset{\displaystyle O}{\|}}{C}-OH \ + \ SOCl_2 \ \xrightarrow{H^+} \ R-\overset{\overset{\displaystyle O}{\|}}{C}-Cl \ + \ SO_2\uparrow \ + \ HCl\uparrow$$

acyl group

Acyl chlorides are Bronsted-Lowry acids, and, just like aldehydes, they donate an α-hydrogen. The electron withdrawing chlorine stabilizes the conjugate base more than the lone hydrogen of an aldehyde, making acyl chlorides significantly stronger acids than aldehydes.

Acid chlorides are the most reactive of the carboxylic acid derivatives because of the stability of the Cl⁻ leaving group.

Acid chlorides are the most reactive of the carboxylic acid derivatives. Acid chlorides love nucleophiles.

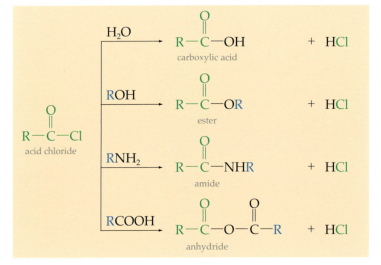

All carboxylic acid derivatives hydrolyze to give the carboxylic acid. Typically, hydrolysis can occur under either acidic or basic conditions.

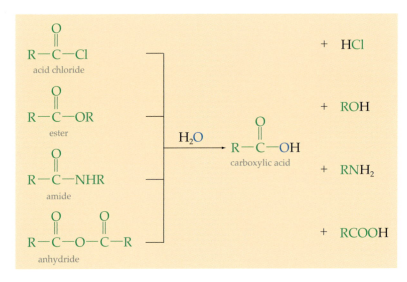

Alcohols react with carboxylic acids through nucleophilic substitution to form **es-ters**. A strong acid catalyzes the reaction by protonating the hydroxyl group on the carboxylic acid.

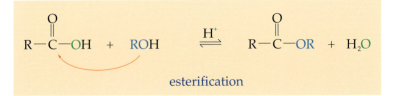

The yield in this reaction can be adjusted in accordance with LeChatlier's principle by adding water or alcohol. A more effective method for preparing esters is to use an anhydride instead of a carboxylic acid in the above reaction.

Alcohols react in a similar way with esters in a reaction called **transesterification**, where one alkoxy group is substituted for another. An equilibrium results in this reaction as well, where the result can be controlled by adding an excess of the alcohol in the product or the reactant.

Transesterification is just trading alkoxy groups on an ester.

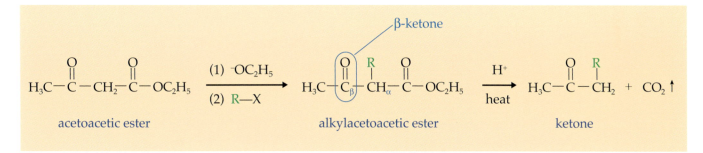

transesterification

Once again, you should watch for the β-dicarbonyl compounds, which increase the acidity of the alpha hydrogens between the carbonyls. Specifically, with esters you have acetoacetic ester. **Acetoacetic ester synthesis** is the production of a ketone from acetoacetic ester due to the strongly acidic properties of the alpha hydrogen. A base is added to remove the alpha hydrogens. The resulting enolate ion is alkylated by an alkyl halide or tosylate leaving the alkylacetoacetic ester. Alkyacetoacetic ester is a β-keto ester that can be decarboxylated by the addition of acid. The acetoacetic ester synthesis is finished with the decarboxylation leaving the ketone.

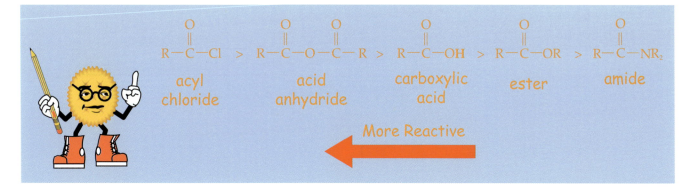

Acetoacetic ester synthesis

Amides are formed when an **amine**, acting as a nucleophile, substitutes at the carbonyl of a carboxylic acid or one of its derivatives. (Amines are discussed in the next section of this lecture.)

In all of the reactions with carboxylic acid derivatives, the carbonyl carbon is acting as the substrate in nucleophilic substitution. Rather than memorize all these reactions, you should remember that carboxylic acids and their derivatives undergo nucleophilic substitution; aldehydes and ketones prefer nucleophilic addition.

Many of these reactions are reversible, but equilibrium will prefer the more stable products. In other words, since a strong base makes a poor leaving group, the equilibrium will favor the formation of the compound whose leaving group is a stronger base. This explains the order of reactivity of carboxylic acid derivatives.

Questions 57 through 64 are **NOT** based on a descriptive passage.

57. All of the following can form hydrogen bonds with water EXCEPT:

  A. aldehydes
  B. carboxylic acids
  C. ethers
  D. alkenes

58. Which of the following are products when an alcohol is added to a carboxylic acid in the presence of a strong acid?

   I. water
  II. ester
 III. aldehyde

  A. I only
  B. II only
  C. I and II only
  D. I and III only

59. Carboxylic acids typically undergo all of the following reactions EXCEPT:

  A. nucleophilic addition
  B. nucleophilic substitution
  C. decarboxylation
  D. esterification

60. Which of the following will most easily react with an amine to form an amide?

  A. acyl chloride
  B. ester
  C. carboxylic acid
  D. acid anhydride

61. Which of the following compounds will result in a positive haloform reaction, which only occurs with methyl ketones?

  A. $CH_3C\equiv N$
  B. $C_6H_5COCH_3$
  C. CH_3CH_2CHO
  D. CH_3CH_2COOH

62. Phthalic anhydride reacts with two equivalents of ammonia to form ammonium phthalamate. One equivalent is washed away in an acid bath to form phthalamic acid.

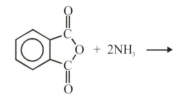

Phthalic anhydride

What two functional groups are created in phthalamic acid?

  A. a carboxylic acid and an amide
  B. a carboxylic acid and a ketone
  C. a carboxylic acid and an aldehyde
  D. an aldehyde and an amide

63. The normal reactivity of methyl benzoate is affected by the presence of certain substituents. Which of the following substituents will decrease methyl benzoate reactivity making it safer for transport?

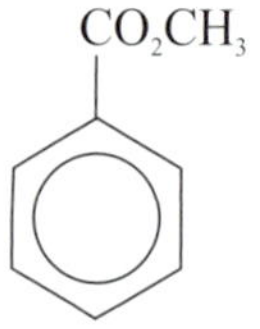

[Methyl benzoate]

  A. NO_2
  B. hydrogen
  C. Br
  D. CH_3

64. When mildly heated with aqueous base or acid, nitriles are hydrolyzed to amides. What may be the product of hydrolysis under stronger conditions?

  A. aldehyde
  B. ketone
  C. ester
  D. carboxylic acid

STOP.

Amines are derivatives of **ammonia**. You should be able to identify ammonia and all types of amines.

3-14

Amines

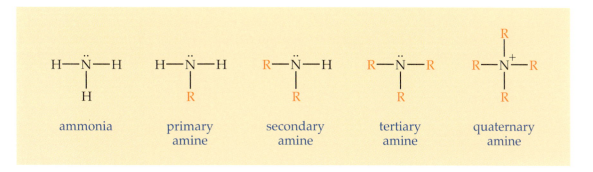

ammonia — primary amine — secondary amine — tertiary amine — quaternary amine

Notice that **nitrogen can take three or four bonds**. When nitrogen takes four bonds it has a positive charge. Also notice the lone pair of electrons on nitrogen. When you see nitrogen on the MCAT and it has only three bonds, you should draw in the lone pair of electrons immediately. On the MCAT, there are three important considerations when dealing with nitrogen containing compounds:

1. they may act as a Lewis base donating their lone pair of electrons;

2. they may act as a nucleophile where the lone pair of electrons attacks a positive charge; and

3. nitrogen can take on a fourth bond (becoming positively charged).

Ammonia and amines act as weak bases by donating their lone pair of electrons. Electron withdrawing substituents decrease the basicity of an amine whereas electron donating substituents increase the basicity of an amine. However, steric hindrance created by bulky functional groups tends to hinder the ability of an amine to donate its lone pair, thus decreasing its basicity. For the MCAT you should know this general trend of amine basicity from highest to lowest when the functional groups are electron donating: 2°, 1°, ammonia.

Aromatic amines (amines attached directly to a benzene ring) are much weaker bases than nonaromatic amines because the electron pair can delocalize around the benzene ring. Substituents that withdraw electrons from the benzene ring will further weaken the aromatic amine.

Since amines like to donate their negative electrons, they tend to stabilize carbocations when they are part of the same molecule.

3-15

Physical Properties

Given the shape of amines we might expect some secondary and tertiary amines to be optically active. However, at room temperature the lone pair of electrons moves very rapidly (as many as 2×10^{11} times per second in ammonia) from one side of the molecule to the other, inverting the configuration. Thus each chiral molecule spends equal time as both its enantiomers. If we imagine that the tertiary amine drawn above is rapidly inverting, it becomes easier to appreciate the manner in which large substituents sterically hinder the electrons.

Ammonia, primary amines, and secondary amines can **hydrogen bond** with each other. All amines can hydrogen bond with water. This makes the lower molecular weight amines very soluble in water. Amines with comparable molecular weights have higher boiling points than alkanes but lower boiling points than alcohols.

Don't become confused by memorizing too much detail about the physical properties of ammonia and amines. For the MCAT, just keep in mind that ammonia and amines hydrogen bond, which raises boiling point and increases solubility.

3-16 Condensation with Ketones

Amines react with aldehydes and ketones losing water to produce **imines** and **enamines**. (Substituted imines are sometimes called *Schiff bases*.) In this reaction the amine acts as a nucleophile, attacking the electron deficient carbonyl carbon of the ketones. As expected, the ketone undergoes nucleophilic addition. An acid catalyst protonates the product to form an unstable intermediate. The intermediate loses water and a proton to produce either an enamine or an imine. If the original amine is secondary (2°), it has no proton to give up, so the ketone must give up its alpha proton. As a result, an enamine is produced. If the original amine is primary (1°), it gives up its proton to form an imine.

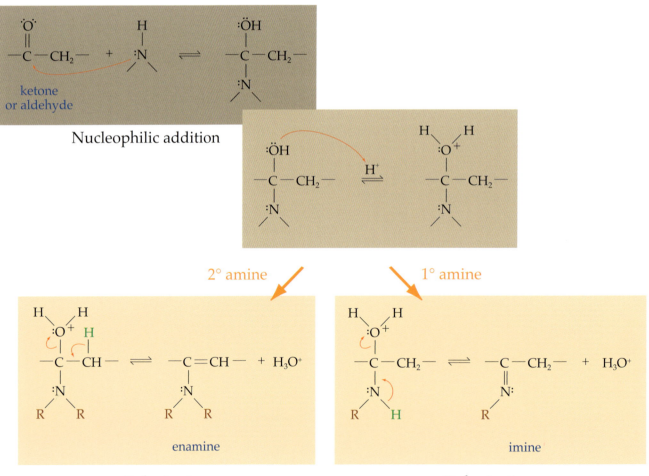

Nucleophilic addition

2° amine   1° amine

enamine   imine

Dehydration   Dehydration

Note that if too much acid is used in this reaction, the amine will become protonated before the first step. The protonated amine will have a positive charge and become a poor nucleophile, preventing the first step of the reaction from going forward.

The imine product shown exists as a tautomer with its corresponding enamine.

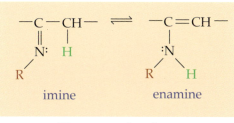

Tautomerization

It is possible to replace the oxygen of a ketone or aldehyde with two hydrogens by adding hot acid in the presence of amalgamated zinc (zinc treated with mercury); however, some ketones and aldehydes may not be able to survive such a treatment. For these ketones and aldehydes, the **Wolff-Kishner Reduction** may be used. The first step of the Wolff-Kishner Reduction follows the same mechanism as imine formation shown on the previous page only a hydrazine is used rather than an amine. The addition of hydrazine to the ketone or aldehyde produces a hydrozone by nucleophilic addition. A hot strong base is added to the hydrazone to deprotanate the nitrogen and produce the desired product with water and nitrogen gas as by-products. A high-boiling solvent is usually used to facilitate the high temperature.

3-17 Wolff-Kishner Reduction

The Wolff-Kishner Reduction does nothing more than reduce a ketone or aldehyde by removing the oxygen and replacing it with two hydrogens. You can do the same thing by adding hot acid to a ketone or aldehyde, but some ketones and aldehydes can't survive the hot acid. That's where the Wolff-Kishner Reduction comes in.

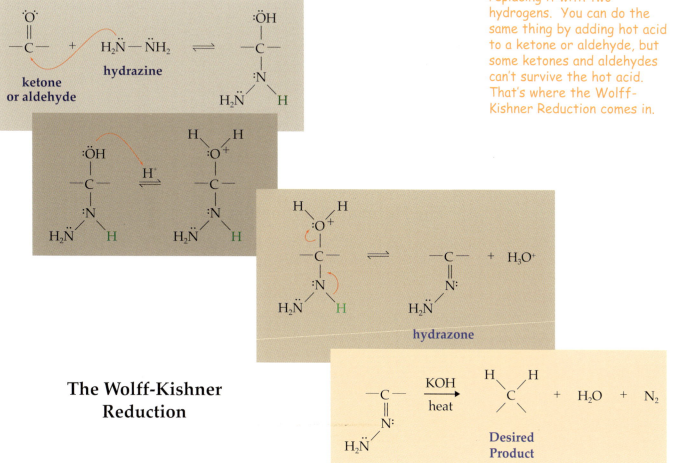

The Wolff-Kishner Reduction

3-18
Alkylation and the Hofmann Elimination

Amines can be alkylated with alkylhalides.

$$NH_3 \quad + \quad R-X \quad \longrightarrow \quad RNH_2 \quad + \quad HX$$

$$NRH_2 \quad + \quad R-X \quad \longrightarrow \quad R_2NH \quad + \quad HX$$

$$NR_2H \quad + \quad R-X \quad \longrightarrow \quad R_3N \quad + \quad HX$$

$$NR_3 \quad + \quad R-X \quad \longrightarrow \quad R_4N^+ \quad + \quad X^-$$

This is a nucleophilic substitution reaction with the amine acting as a nucleophile.

As a leaving group, an amino group would be $^-NH_2$, so amino groups are very poor leaving groups. However, an amino group can be converted to a quaternary ammonium salt by repeated alkylations. The quaternary ammonium salt is an excellent leaving group.

The elimination of a quarternary ammonium salt usually follows an E2 mechanism requiring a strong base. The quarternary alkyl halide, typically an ammonium iodide, is converted to a quarternary ammonium hydroxide using silver oxide.

$$R-\overset{+}{N}(CH_3)_3 \, ^-I \; + \; \tfrac{1}{2}Ag_2O \; + \; H_2O \quad \longrightarrow \quad R-\overset{+}{N}(CH_3)_3 \, ^-OH \; + \; AgI \downarrow$$

Heating the quarternary ammonium hydroxide results in the **Hofmann elimination** to form an alkene.

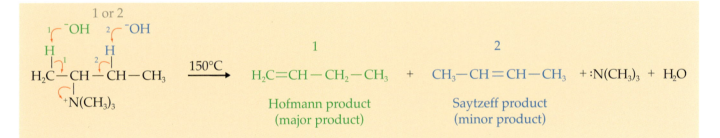

The Hofmann Elimination

Notice that the LEAST stable alkene is the major product in the Hofmann elimination, called the Hofmann product.

3-19
Amines and Nitrous Acid

Nitrous acid is a weak acid. A strong acid can dehydrate nitrous acid to produce nitrosonium ion and water.

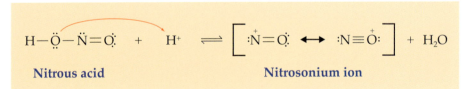

Most reactions with amines and nitrous acid involve the nitrosonium ion.

Primary amines react with nitrous acid to form *diazonium salts*. Aliphatic (nonaromatic) amines form extremely unstable salts that decompose spontaneously to form nitrogen gas. Aromatic amines also form unstable diazonium salts, but at temperatures below 5°C they decompose very slowly.

The reaction, called **diazotization of an amine** goes as follows. Nitrous acid is protonated by a strong acid to form the nitrosonium ion. Nitrosonium ion reacts with the primary amine to form *N*-nitrosoammonium, an unstable compound. *N*-nitrosoammonium deprotonates to form *N*-nitrosoamine. *N*-nitrosoamine tautomerizes to diazenol. In the presence of acid, diazenol dehydrates to diazonium ion.

This reaction is pretty long. When thinking about nitrous acid and primary amines, just think diazonium ion, and remember that only aromatic amines work.

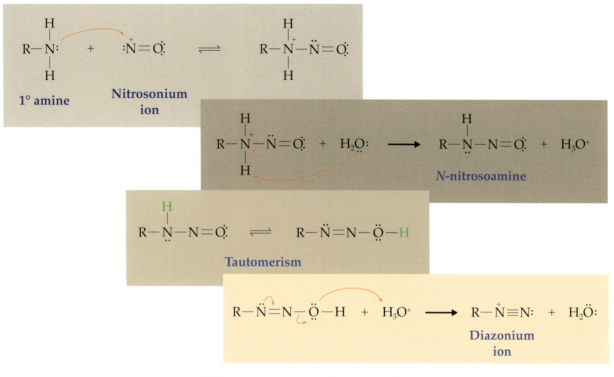

Diazotization of an Amine

The diazonium group can be easily replaced by a variety of other groups, making the diazotization of an amine a useful reaction.

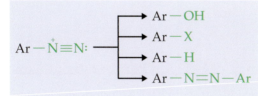

diazonium group

Unlike primary amines, secondary amines have an extra R group instead of the tautomeric proton. No tautomer can form. Notice from the diazotization reaction above that, if the *N*-nitrosoamine can't make a tautomer, the reaction will be stopped at the *N*-nitrosoamine. When nitrous acid is added to a secondary amine, the product is an *N*-nitrosoamine.

3-20
Amides

Amides that have no substituent on the nitrogen are called primary amides. Primary amides are named by replacing the -ic in the corresponding acid with -amide. For instance, acetamide is formed when the –OH group of acetic acid is replaced by $–NH_2$. Substituents on the nitrogen are prefaced by N-. For instance, if one hydrogen on acetamide is replaced by an ethyl group, the result is N-ethylacetamide.

Amides can behave as a weak acid or a weak base. They are less basic than amines due to the electron withdrawing properties of the carbonyl. Amides are hydrolyzed by either strong acids or strong bases.

Amides with a hydrogen attached to the nitrogen are able to hydrogen bond to each other.

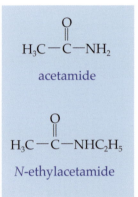

acetamide

N-ethylacetamide

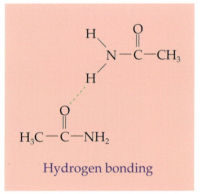

Hydrogen bonding

3-21
β-Lactams

Cyclic amides are called lactams. A Greek letter is assigned to the lactam to denote size. β-lactams are 4-membered rings, γ-lactams have 5 members, δ-lactams have 6 members, and so on. Although amides are the most stable of the carboxylic acid derivatives, β-lactams are highly reactive due to large ring strain. Nucleophiles easily react with β-lactams. β-lactams are found in several types of antibiotics.

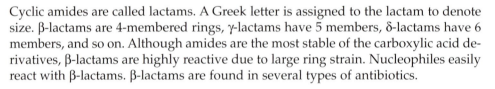

a β-lactam

3-22
The Hofmann Degradation

Primary amides react with strongly basic solutions of chlorine or bromine to form primary amines with carbon dioxide as a by-product. This reaction is called the **Hofmann degradation**. The amide is deprotoned by the strong base. The deprotonated amide picks up a halogen atom leaving a halide ion. The product is an N-haloamide. The N-haloamide is more acidic than the original primary amide and is deprotonated as well. Now a tricky rearrangement occurs. The R group of the amide migrates to the nitrogen to form an isocyanate. Isocyanate reacts with water to form a carbamic acid. The carbamic acid is decarboxylated, giving off carbon dioxide and leaving the amine.

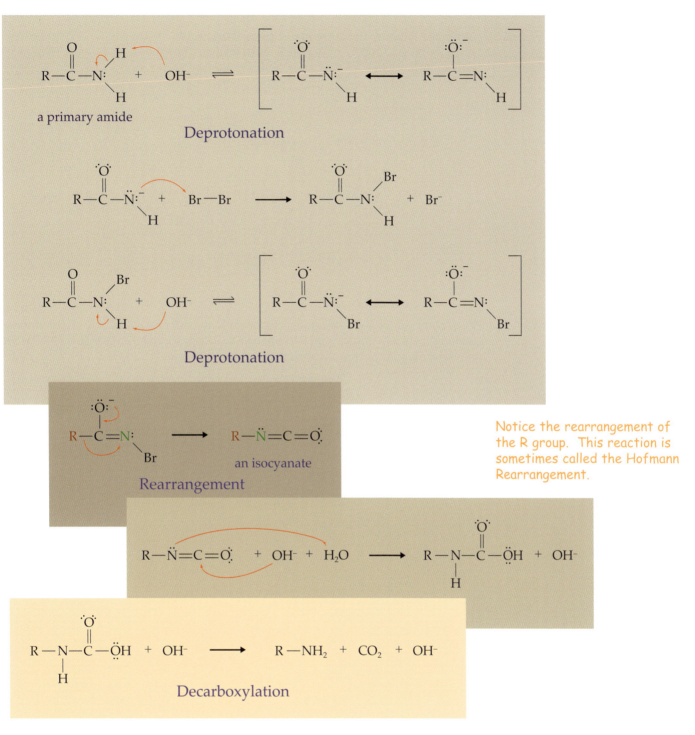

a primary amide

Deprotonation

Deprotonation

Rearrangement

an isocyanate

[in orange]Notice the rearrangement of the R group. This reaction is sometimes called the Hofmann Rearrangement.

Decarboxylation

The Hofmann Degradation

The advantage of the Hofmann degradation over other methods of producing amines is that other methods rely upon an S_N2 mechanism. This prevents the production of amines on a tertiary carbon. The Hofmann degradation can produce amines with a primary, secondary, or tertiary alkyl position.

3-23
Phosphoric Acid

You need to know the structure of **phosphoric acids** for the MCAT. When heated, phosphoric acid forms **phosphoric anhydrides**. Phosphoric acids react with alcohols to form esters.

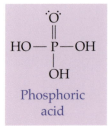

Phosphoric acid

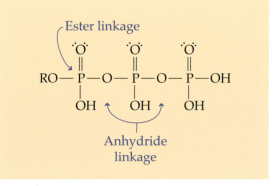

In a living cell at a pH of about 7, triphosphates exist as negatively charged ions, making them less susceptible to nucleophilic attack and relatively stable. ATP is an example of an important triphosphate.

65. If all substituents are alkyl groups, which of the following is the least basic amine?

A. primary
B. secondary
C. tertiary
D. quaternary

66. Ammonia is best described as:

A. a Lewis acid
B. a Lewis base
C. an electrophile
D. an aromatic compound

67. Which of the following would have the lowest solubility in water?

A.

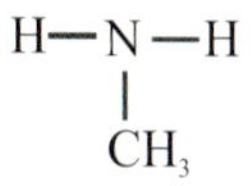

H—N—H
    |
    CH$_3$

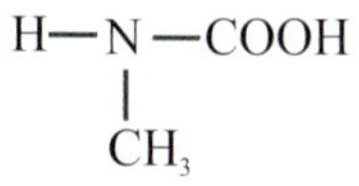

C.

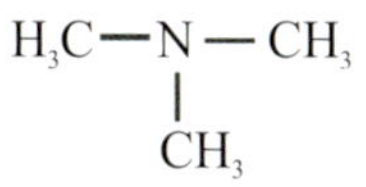

H$_3$C—N—CH$_3$
      |
      CH$_3$

B.

H—N—COOH
    |
    CH$_3$

D.

H$_3$C—N—COOH
      |
      CH$_3$

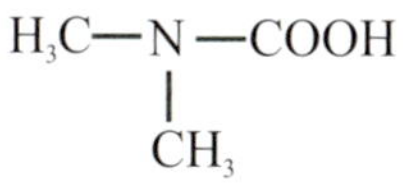

68. Which of the following is a possible product of the reaction shown below?

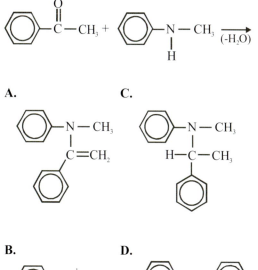

A.

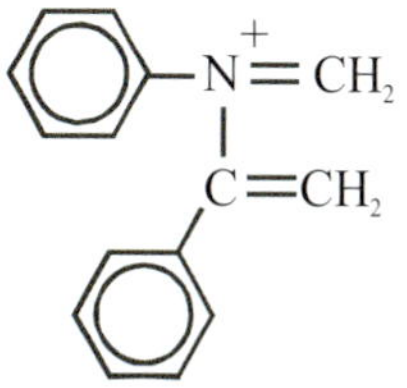

C.

B.

D.

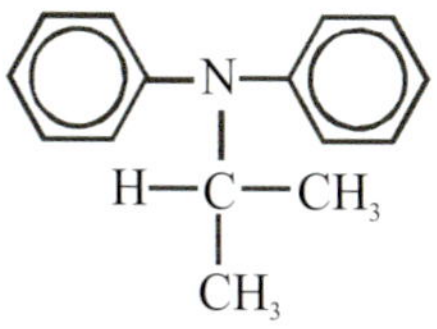

69. Ethylamine can be alkylated with iodomethane in the presence of a strong base. The strong base is needed:

A. to neutralize the strong acid ethyl-methylamine that is formed during the reaction.
B. to neutralize the strong acid HI that is formed during the reaction.
C. to protonate the methyl group.
D. to deprotonate the methyl group.

70. In the prepolymer shown below, which of the following moities contains the most reactive bond?

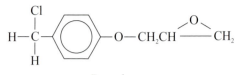

Prepolymer

A.

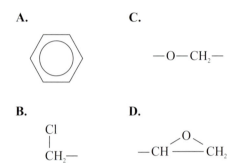

B.

Cl
|
CH_2—

C.

—O—CH_2—

D.

—CH$\overset{O}{\diagdown}$CH$_2$

71. In a coordinate covalent bond, the shared electrons are furnished by only one species. Which of the following molecules is LEAST likely to be involved in a coordinate covalent bond?

A. sodium chloride (NaCl)
B. chlorate ion (ClO_3^-)
C. ammonia (NH_3)
D. water (H_2O)

72. When D_2O is added to cyclohexanone, all acidic hydrogens (atomic weight = 1) are replaced with deuterons (atomic weight = 2). What is the new atomic weight of cyclohexanone following D_2O treatment?

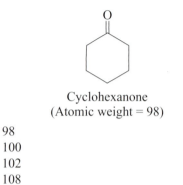

Cyclohexanone
(Atomic weight = 98)

A. 98
B. 100
C. 102
D. 108

STOP.

4-1

Fatty Acids

Fatty acids are long carbon chains with a carboxylic acid end. They serve three basic functions in the human body: 1. they serve as hormones and intracellular messengers (i.e. *eicosanoids* such as *prostaglandins*); 2. they are components of the phospholipids and glycolipids of cell membranes; 3. they act as fuel for the body. The first of these functions will not be tested on the MCAT unless it is explained in a passage. For the second function of fatty acids you should be able to recognize the structure of a phospholipid as shown in Lecture 3 of the biology manual.

As fuel for the body, fatty acids are stored in the form of *triacylglycerols*. Triacylglycerols can be hydrolyzed to form glycerol and the corresponding fatty acids in a process called **lipolysis**. Notice that this process is simply the reverse of esterification. In the lab triacylglycerols can be cleaved by the addition of NaOH, a process called **saponification**. Saponification is the production of soap.

For nomenclature purposes, the carbonyl carbon of a fatty acid is assigned the number 1. The carbon next to the carbonyl is called the α-carbon (alpha carbon) and the carbon at the opposite end of the chain is called the Ω-carbon (omega carbon). The pK_a of most fatty acids is around 4.5, so most fatty acids exist in their anion form in the cellular environment.

The carbon chains on fatty acids may be **saturated or unsaturated**. Fatty acids are **amphipathic**, meaning they contain a hydrophobic and a hydrophilic end. Since the hydrophobic carbon chain predominates, fatty acids are **nonpolar**.

$$H-\underset{\underset{\displaystyle |}{\displaystyle |}}{\overset{\overset{\displaystyle H}{\displaystyle |}}{C}}-O-\overset{\overset{\displaystyle O}{\displaystyle ||}}{C}-(CH_2)_n-CH_3$$

$$H-\underset{\displaystyle |}{\overset{\displaystyle |}{C}}-O-\overset{\overset{\displaystyle O}{\displaystyle ||}}{C}-(CH_2)_n-CH_3 \quad \xrightarrow[+H_2O]{lipases} \quad H-\underset{\displaystyle |}{\overset{\displaystyle |}{C}}-OH \quad + \quad HO-\overset{\overset{\displaystyle O}{\displaystyle ||}}{C}-(CH_2)_n-CH_3$$

$$H-\underset{\underset{\displaystyle H}{\displaystyle |}}{\overset{\displaystyle |}{C}}-O-\overset{\overset{\displaystyle O}{\displaystyle ||}}{C}-(CH_2)_n-CH_3$$

triacylglyceride   **glycerol**   **fatty acids**

Fatty acids are highly reduced, which allows them to store more than twice the energy (about 9 kcal/gram) of carbohydrates or proteins (about 4 kcal/gram). Fatty acids are stored as **triacylglycerols** in **adipose cells**. Lipolysis of triacylglycerols takes place inside the adipose cells when blood levels of epinephrine, norepinephrine, glucagon, or ACTH are elevated. The resulting fatty acid products are then exported to different cells for the utilization of their energy. Once inside a cell, the fatty acid is linked to Coenzyme A and carried into the mitochondrial matrix by the γ-amino acid L-carnitine. The fatty acid is then oxidized two carbons at a time with each oxidation yielding an NADH, FADH$_2$, and an acetyl CoA. Each acetyl CoA enters the Krebs cycle for further oxidation by condensation with oxaloacetate.

4-2
Amino Acids

Amino acids are the building blocks of proteins. A single protein consists of one or more chains of amino acids strung end to end by **peptide bonds.** Hence the name **polypeptide**. You must be able recognize the structure of an amino acid and a polypeptide. A peptide bond creates the functional group known as an **amide** (an amine connected to a carbonyl carbon). It is formed via condensation of two amino acids. The reverse reaction is the hydrolysis of a peptide bond.

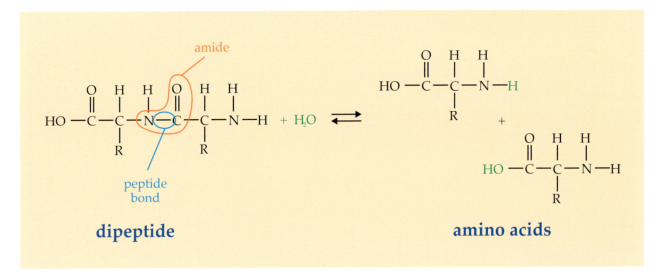

dipeptide

amino acids

Amino acids used by the human body are α-amino acids. They are called alpha-amino acids because the amine group is attached to the carbon which is alpha to the carbonyl carbon, similar to α-hydrogens of ketones and aldehydes.

Since nitrogen is comfortable taking on four bonds and oxygen is comfortable with a partial negative charge, electrons delocalize creating a resonance that gives the peptide bond a partial double bond character. The double bond character prevents the bond from rotating freely and affects the secondary and to some extent the tertiary structure of the polypeptide.

Notice the R group on each amino acid. The R group is called the **side chain** of the amino acid. Nearly all organisms use the same **20 α-amino acids** to synthesize proteins. Many amino acids and amino acid derivatives, such as *hydroxyproline* and *cystine*, can be created by post-translational modifications after the polypeptide is formed. **Ten** amino acids are **essential**. ("Essential" means that they cannot be synthesized by the body, so they must be ingested. Some books list 8 or 9 amino acids as essential. The discrepancy involves whether or not to list as essential those amino acids that are derivatives of other essential amino acids.) Each amino acid differs only in its R group. The R groups have different chemical properties. These properties are divided into four categories: 1. acidic; 2. basic; 3. polar; and 4. nonpolar. All acidic and basic R groups are also polar. Generally, if the side chain contains carboxylic acids, then it is acidic; if it contains amines, then it is basic. Only the three basic amino acids have an **isoelectric point** (discussed below) above a pH of 7; all other amino acids have an isoelectric point below 7.

nonpolar	polar	acidic	basic
valine	serine	aspartic acid	histidine
isoleucine	threonine	glutamic acid	arginine
proline	cysteine		lysine
methionine	tyrosine		
alanine	glutamine		
leucine	asparagine		
tryptophan			
phenylalanine			
glycine			

It is unlikely that the MCAT would require you to know into which chemical category that an amino acid will fall; however, here are the amino acids listed under their specific categories, just in case.

Polar side groups are **hydrophilic** and will turn to face an aqueous solution such as cytosol. Nonpolar side groups are **hydrophobic** and will turn away from an aqueous solution. These characteristics affect a protein's tertiary structure.

Although we often draw an amino acid as:

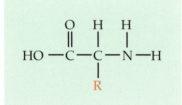

it actually never exists as such. In the cytosol, amino acids exist in one of the three forms drawn below:

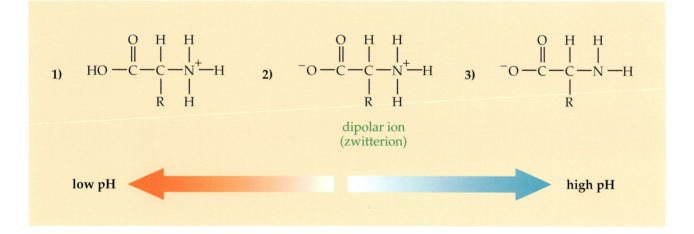

Close examination of species 1 reveals it to be a diprotic acid. If we choose an amino acid with no ionizable substituents on its R group, and we titrate it with a strong base, we observe the following: As the pH increases, the stronger acid, the carboxylic acid, is first to lose its proton, creating species 2, its conjugate base. When species 1 and 2 exist in equal proportions, we have reached the half-equivalence point. As we continue the titration, we remove the proton from all of the carboxylic acids until we have 100% of species 2. The pH at this point is called the **isoelectric point, pI**. (Technically, the pI for any amino acid is the pH where the population has no net charge and the maximum number of species are zwitterions.) Continuing the titration, the base begins to remove a proton from the amine. When we have equal amounts of 2 and 3, we are at the second half-equivalence point of our titration. Once we have removed the acidic proton from each amine group leaving 100% of species 3, we have reached the second equivalence point. The isoelectric point is dictated by the side group of an amino acid. The more acidic the side group, the lower the pI; the more basic the side group, the greater the pI.

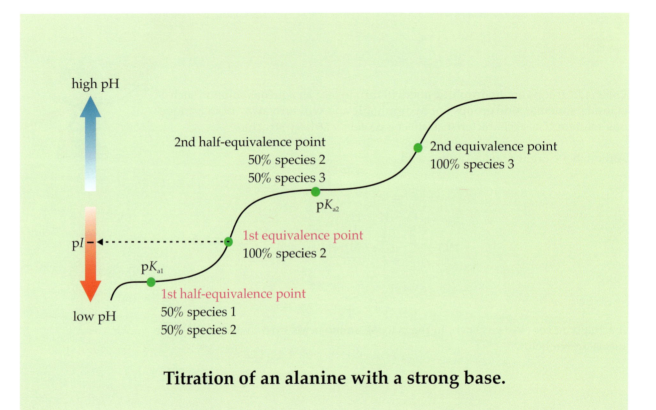

Titration of an alanine with a strong base.

Questions 73 through 80 are **NOT** based on a descriptive passage.

73. Electrophoresis can separate amino acids by subjecting them to an electric field. The electric field applies a force whose strength and direction is dependent upon the net charge of the amino acid. If a solution of amino acids at a pH of 8 underwent electrophoresis, which of the following would most likely move the furthest toward the anode?

    A. lysine
    B. arginine
    C. glutamate
    D. histidine

74. Fatty acids and glycerol react within the body to form tri-acylglycerides. Which of the following functional groups are contained in any triacylglyceride?

    A. aldehyde
    B. carboxylic acid
    C. ester
    D. amine

75. The partial double bond character of a peptide bond has its greatest effect in which structure of an enzyme?

    A. primary
    B. secondary
    C. tertiary
    D. quaternary

76. Which of the following nutrients has the greatest heat of combustion?

    A. carbohydrate
    B. protein
    C. saturated fat
    D. unsaturated fat

77. A student conducted the titration of an amino acid with a strong base. The point in the titration when 50% of the amino acid exists as a zwitterion is called:

    A. the isoelectric point.
    B. the equivalence point.
    C. the half-equivalence point.
    D. the end point.

78. Which of the following amino acids has the lowest solubility in aqueous solution?

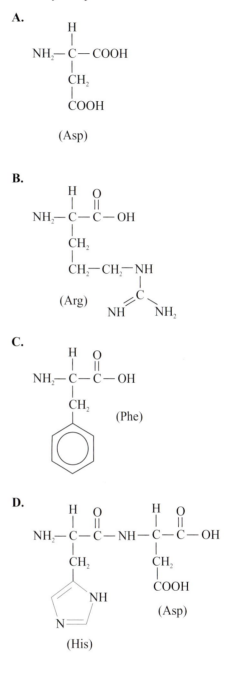

GO ON TO THE NEXT PAGE.

79. How many complete monomers can be extracted from the compound below and utilized for analysis?

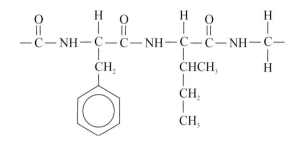

- A. 2
- B. 3
- C. 4
- D. 8

80. Based on structural properties alone, which of the following compounds is most likely to interrupt alpha-helix structures found in myoglobin?

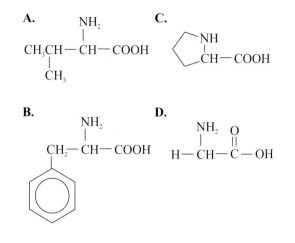

STOP.

Carbohydrates can be thought of as carbon and water. For each carbon atom there exists one oxygen and two hydrogens. The formula for any carbohydrate is:

4-3

Carbohydrates

$$C_n(H_2O)_n$$

The carbohydrate most likely to appear on the MCAT is fructose or glucose. Both are six carbon carbohydrates called **hexoses**. These may appear as Fischer projections or ring structures. The Fischer projections are shown below:

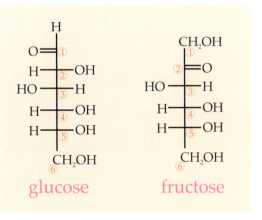

glucose   fructose

Notice that glucose is an aldehyde and fructose is a ketone. Polyhydroxyaldehydes like glucose are called **aldoses**. Polyhydroxyketones like fructose are called **ketoses**. Carbohydrates are also named for the number of carbons they possess: triose, tetrose, pentose, hexose, heptose, and so on. The names are commonly combined making glucose an **aldohexose**.

Notice also that several of the carbons are chiral. Carbohydrates are labeled D or L as follows: When in a Fischer projection as shown, if the hydroxyl group on the highest numbered chiral carbon points to the right, the carbohydrate is labeled D; if to the left, then L.

In a carbohydrate the alcohol group on the chiral carbon farthest from the carbonyl may act as a nucleophile and attack the carbonyl. When this happens, nucleophilic addition to an aldehyde or ketone results and the corresponding hemiacetal is formed, creating a ring structure. Carbon 1 in the diagram below is now called the anomeric carbon. The **anomeric carbon** can be identified as the only carbon attached to two oxygens because its alcohol group may point upwards or downwards on the ring structure resulting in either the α or β anomer. The anomer shown in the diagram below is the α anomer.

The cyclic structures are named according to the number of ring members (including oxygen): a five-membered ring is called a **furanose**; a six-membered ring is called a **pyranose**. So the glucose ring becomes **glucopyranose**.

The human body can assimilate only D-fructose and D-glucose and cannot assimilate L-fructose and L-glucose. D is for delicious.

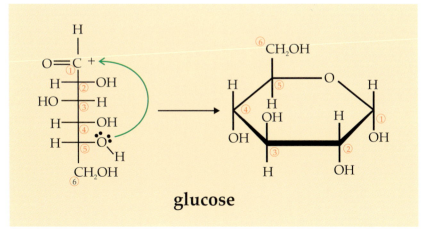

glucose

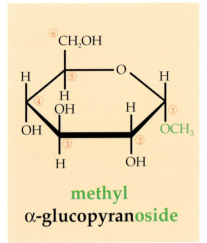

methyl
α-glucopyranoside

Names of reducing sugars end in -ose; names of nonreducing sugars end in -oside. This detailed nomenclature of carbohydrates is unlikely to be tested directly on the MCAT, but it doesn't hurt to know it.

Sugars that are acetals (not hemiacetals) are called glycosides. The names of such sugars end in -oside. For instance, if the hydroxyl group on the anomeric carbon of glucose were replaced with an O-methyl group, it would form methyl glucopyranoside. The group attached to the anomeric carbon of a glycoside is called an *aglycone*.

Tollens reagent is a basic reagent that detects aldehydes. Aldoses have an aldehyde on their open-chain form and reduce Tollens reagent. Tollens reagent promotes enediol rearrangement of ketoses so that ketoses also reduce Tollens reagent. Recall from Lecture 3 that acetals are used as blocking groups because they do not react with basic reducing agents. Since Tollens reagent must react with the open-chain form of a sugar, glycosides (which are closed ring acetals) do NOT reduce Tollens reagent, while nonglycosides do.

Disaccharides and polysaccharides are glycosides where the aglycone is another sugar. The anomeric carbon of a sugar can react with any of the hydroxyl groups of another sugar, but there are only three bonding arrangements that are common: a 1,4′ link; a 1,6′ link; and a 1,1′ link. The numbers refer to the carbon numbers on the sugars. The linkages are called glycosidic linkages. A disaccharide or polysaccharide will only react with Tollens reagent if there is an anomeric carbon that is not involved in a glycosidic bond and is free to react.

There are several disaccharides and polysaccharides for which you should know the common name.

Sucrose: 1,1′ glycosidic linkage: glucose and fructose (This linkage is alpha with respect to glucose and beta with respect to fructose. It is more accurately called a 1,2′ linkage because the anomeric carbon on fructose is numbered 2, not 1 like glucose.)

Maltose: α-1,4′ glucosidic linkage: two glucose molecules

Lactose: β-1,4′ galactosidic linkage: galactose and glucose

Cellulose: β-1,4′ glucosidic linkage: a chain of glucose molecules

Amylose: α-1,4′ glucosidic linkage: a chain of glucose molecules

Amylopectin: α-1,4′ glucosidic linkage: a branched chain of glucose molecules with α-1,6′ glucosidic linkages forming the branches

Glycogen: α-1,4′ glucosidic linkage: a branched chain of glucose molecules with α-1,6′ glucosidic linkages forming the branches

Glycosidic linkages are broken via hydrolysis. Without an enzyme, they are broken down only slowly by water. Animals do not possess the enzyme to break the β-1,4′ glucosidic linkage in cellulose. Some adult humans lack the enzyme to break the β-1,4′ galactosidic linkage in lactose.

81. How many stereoisomers exist of D-altrose, shown below?

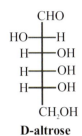

D-altrose

- **A.** 2
- **B.** 8
- **C.** 16
- **D.** 32

82. Which of the following types of reactions describes ring formation in glucose when the alcohol group nucleophilically attacks the carbonyl carbon atom?

- **A.** hemiacetal formation
- **B.** hemiketal formation
- **C.** acetal formation
- **D.** ketal formation

83. Which of the following is the ketose most abundant in fruits?

- **A.** fructose
- **B.** glucose
- **C.** proline
- **D.** glycerol

84. From only the drawing shown below, which of the following statements can be discerned as true?

- **I.** The molecule is a carbohydrate.
- **II.** The stereochemical designation of the molecule is D.
- **III.** The molecule rotates polarized light clockwise.

- **A.** I only
- **B.** II only
- **C.** I and II only
- **D.** I, II, and III

85. Which of the following statements are true concerning carbohydrates?

- **I.** Carbohydrates can exist as meso compounds.
- **II.** The human body is capable of digesting all isomers of glucose.
- **III.** Glucose is an aldehyde.

- **A.** III only
- **B.** I and II only
- **C.** I and III only
- **D.** I, II, and III

86. Aspartame, saccharine and sodium cyclamate are all synthetic sweeteners used to replace glucose.

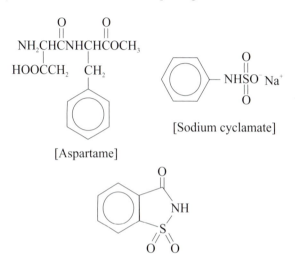

[Sodium cyclamate]

[Aspartame]

[Saccharin]

Which of the following properties are shared by both glucose and the synthetic sweeteners?

- **I.** All activate gustatory receptors at the tip of the human tongue.
- **II.** All can hydrogen bond.
- **III.** All are carbohydrates.

- **A.** I only
- **B.** III only
- **C.** I and II only
- **D.** I, II, and III

87. Fructose can cyclize into a five-membered ring known as a furanose. The hydroxyl group on which carbon of fructose behaves as a nucleophile during the formation of a furan?

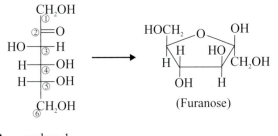

(Furanose)

   A.   carbon 1
   B.   carbon 3
   C.   carbon 5
   D.   carbon 6

88. Sugar A and B are what type of carbohydrates, respectively?

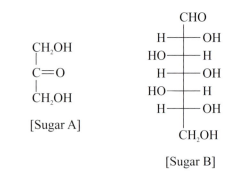

[Sugar A]

[Sugar B]

   A.   ketotriose and ketohexose
   B.   aldotriose and aldohexose
   C.   aldotriose and ketoheptose
   D.   ketotriose and aldoheptose

STOP.

There are three types of lab techniques that you must know for the MCAT: spectroscopy, spectrometry, and separations. Spectroscopy will be either **nuclear magnetic resonance (nmr)**, **infrared spectroscopy (IR)**, or **ultraviolet spectroscopy (UV)**. You will need to understand how **mass spectrometry** works. Separation techniques will include **chromatography, distillation, crystallization**, and **extraction**.

4-4

Lab Techniques

NMR refers to **nuclear magnetic resonance** spectroscopy. The nucleus most commonly studied with nmr is the hydrogen nucleus, but it is possible to study the nucleus of carbon-13 and other atoms as well.

4-5

NMR

Nuclei with an odd atomic number or odd mass number exhibit *nuclear spin* that can be observed by an nmr spectrometer. The spin creates a magnetic field around the nucleus similar to the field created by a small magnet. When placed in an external magnetic field, the nucleus aligns its own field with or against the external field. Nuclei aligned with the magnetic field have a lower energy state than those aligned against the field. The stronger the magnetic field, the greater the difference between these energy states.

When photons (electromagnetic radiation) of just the right frequency (energy state) are shone on the nuclei, those nuclei whose magnetic fields are oriented with the external magnetic field can absorb the energy of the photon and flip to face against the external field. A nucleus that is subjected to this perfect combination of magnetic field strength and electromagnetic radiation frequency is said to be in resonance. An nmr spectrometer can detect the energy absorption of a nucleus in resonance.

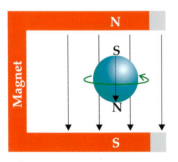 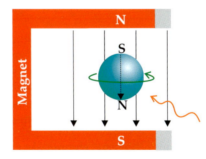 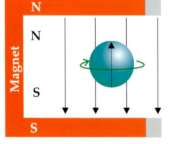

low energy state   high energy state

In nmr, the frequency of the electromagnetic radiation is held constant while the magnetic field strength is varied.

Absent any electrons, all protons absorb electromagnetic energy from a constant-strength magnetic field at the same frequency (about 60 MHz in a magnetic field of 14,092 gauss). However, hydrogen atoms within different compounds experience unique surrounding-electron densities and are also uniquely affected by the magnetic fields of other nearby protons. The electrons *shield* the protons from the magnetic field. As a result, the external field must be strengthened for a shielded proton to achieve resonance. Thus protons within a compound absorb electromagnetic energy of the *same frequency* at *different magnetic field strengths*.

An nmr spectrum (shown on the next page) is a graph of the magnetic field strengths absorbed by the hydrogens of a specific compound at a single frequency. The field strength is measured in *parts per million, ppm*, and, despite the *decreasing* numbers, *increases* from left to right. The leftward direction is called *downfield* and the rightward is called *upfield*. All the way to the right is a peak at 0 ppm. This peak

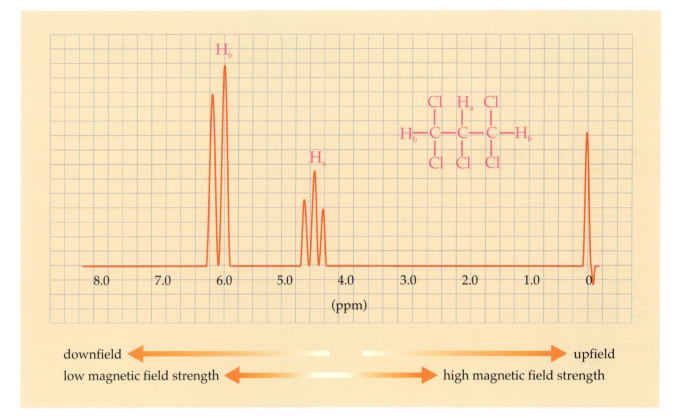

is due to a reference compound (tetramethylsilane, discussed below) used to calibrate the instrument.

Although nmr is based on quantum mechanics and can be a very complex subject, there is actually very little to understand about nmr for the MCAT. First and most importantly, remember that, **unless otherwise indicated, nmr is concerned with hydrogens**. Given an nmr spectrum, you should be able to identify which peaks belong to which hydrogens on a given compound, or which of four compounds might create the given spectrum. To do this you must understand the following:

- **Each peak** represents **chemically equivalent hydrogens**;

- **Splitting** of peaks is created by "neighboring hydrogens".

$$CH_3-Si-CH_3$$

Tetramethylsilane

Each peak indicates one or a group of chemically equivalent hydrogens (in other words, hydrogens indistinguishable from each other by way of their positions on the compound). Such hydrogens are said to be *enantiotropic*. Enantiotropic hydrogens are represented by the same peak in an nmr spectrum. They have the same **chemical shift**. Chemical shift is the difference between the resonance frequency of the chemically shifted hydrogens and the resonance frequency of hydrogens on a reference compound such as tetramethylsilane. Tetramethylsilane (shown above) is the most common nmr reference compound because it contains many hydrogens that are all enantiotropic and are very well shielded. In the graph above, although not all of the H_b are attached to the same carbon, they are stereochemically similar, and thus represented by the same group of peaks. Their chemical shift is approximately 6.0 ppm.

The area under a peak is proportional to the number of hydrogens represented by that peak. The more chemically equivalent hydrogens, the greater the area. The tallest peak does not necessarily correspond to the greatest area. The **integral trace** is a line drawn above the peaks that rises each time it goes over a peak. The rise of the integral trace is in proportion to the number of chemically equivalent hydrogens in the peak beneath it. A newer instrument, called a *digital trace*, records numbers which correspond to the rise in the line. The exact number of hydrogens cannot be determined from the integral trace or the digital trace; only the ratio of hydrogens from one peak to another can be determined.

Lateral position on a spectrum is dictated by *electron shielding*, thus limited predictions can be made based upon electron-withdrawing and electron-donating groups. Electron-withdrawing groups tend to lower shielding and thus decrease the magnetic field strength at which resonance takes place. This means that hydrogens with less shielding tend to have peaks downfield or to the left. Likewise, electron-donating groups tend to increase shielding and increase the required field strength for resonance.

Splitting (called **spin-spin splitting**) results from neighboring hydrogens that are not chemically equivalent. (*Spin-spin coupling* is the same thing except that it also includes hydrogens that are chemically equivalent. The MCAT will not test this distinction.) The number of peaks due to splitting for a group of chemically equivalent hydrogens is given by the simple formula, **_n_ + 1**, where *n* is the number of **neighboring hydrogens** that are not chemically equivalent. A neighboring hydrogen is one that is on an atom adjacent to the atom to which the hydrogen is connected.

For proton nmr spectroscopy, follow these steps:

- Identify chemically equivalent hydrogens.

- Identify and count neighboring hydrogens that are not chemically equivalent. Use n + 1 to figure the number of peaks created by splitting for the chemically equivalent hydrogens.

- If necessary, identify electron withdrawing/donating groups near the chemically equivalent hydrogens. Withdrawing groups will move their signal to the left.

Something else you should know: Aldehyde protons have a very distinctive shift at 9.5 ppm. Watch for it.

In a rare situation, carbon nmr may also appear on the MCAT. Remember, the nucleus must have an odd atomic or mass number to register on nmr, so carbon-13 is the only carbon isotope to register. Treat carbon nmr the same way as proton nmr, except ignore splitting.

Of course, nmr can be more complicated than is described here. However, like everything else on the MCAT, any complications tested will be explained and answerable from this small body of knowledge just presented. We have provided one more spectrum on the next page in order for you to test your understanding. Before reading further, turn the page and see if you can predict which hydrogens belong to which groups of peaks.

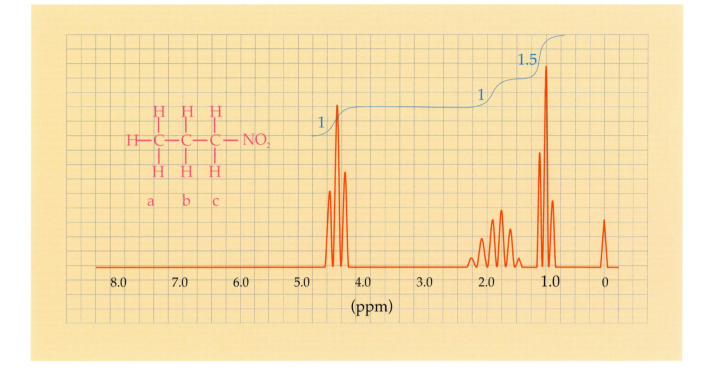

ANSWER: Each letter, *a*, *b*, and *c*, represents a group of chemically equivalent hydrogens. The groups of peaks from left to right correspond to the *c*, *b*, and *a* hydrogens respectively. Since NO_2 is electron-withdrawing, the *c* hydrogens are further downfield. The *b* hydrogens have 5 neighbors, so their peak has 6 peaks. The digital trace shows the peak furthest upfield as having 1.5 times as many hydrogens as the other peaks. The ratio of *a* hydrogens to *b* or *c* hydrogens is 3 to 2, so this must be the peak representing the *a* hydrogens.

4-6
IR Spectroscopy

A dipole exists when the centers of positive and negative charge do not coincide. When exposed to an electric field, these oppositely charged centers will move in opposite directions; either toward each other or away from each other. In infrared radiation, the direction of the electric field oscillates, causing the positive and negative centers within polar bonds to move toward each other and then away from each other. Thus, when exposed to **infrared radiation**, the polar bonds within a compound stretch and contract in a vibrating motion.

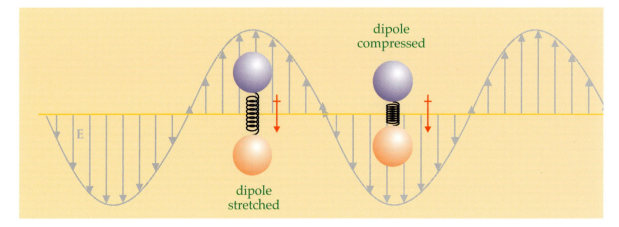

Different bonds vibrate at different frequencies. When the resonance frequency of the oscillating bond is matched by the frequency of infrared radiation, the IR energy is absorbed. In **IR Spectroscopy**, an infrared spectrometer slowly changes the frequency of infrared light shining upon a compound and records the frequencies of absorption in reciprocal centimeters, cm^{-1} (number of cycles per cm).

If a bond has no dipole moment, then the infrared radiation does not cause it to vibrate and no energy is absorbed. However, energy can also be absorbed due to other types of stretching and scissoring motions of the molecules in a compound.

The most predictable section of the IR spectrum is in the 1600 to 3500 cm^{-1} region. Below are some distinguishing characteristics of this range of the IR spectrum for the functional groups MCAT may test. You should be familiar with these shapes and frequencies.

IR questions on the MCAT used to be as easy as reading a chart. Now, the MCAT is sometimes requiring limited memorization of the IR spectra of certain functional groups. The most likely spectra that would be asked by MCAT are the C=O, a sharp dip around 1700 cm^{-1}; and the O-H, a broad dip around 3200-3600.

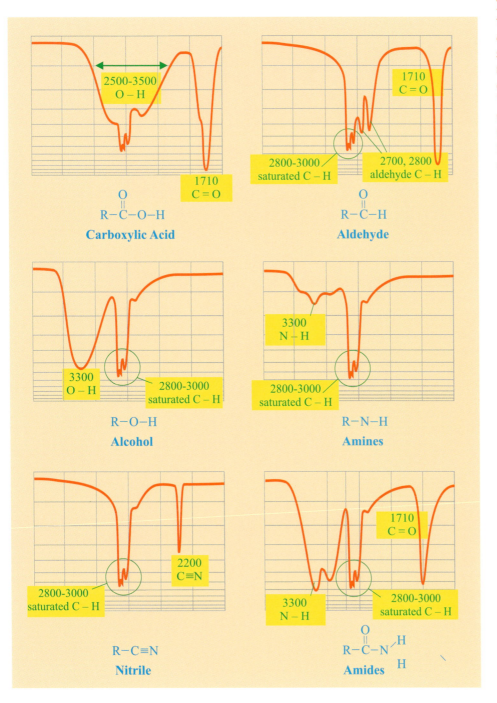

Limited predictions about vibration can be made based upon the *mass of the atoms involved* and the *stiffness of the bond* between them. Atoms with greater mass resonate at lower frequencies; stiffer bonds, such as double and triple bonds, resonate at higher frequencies. Bond strength and bond stiffness follow the same order: $sp > sp^2 > sp^3$.

An IR spectrum can help identify which functional groups are in a compound, but it does not readily reveal the shape or size of the carbon skeleton. However, two compounds are very unlikely to have exactly the same IR spectrum. This makes an IR spectrum like a fingerprint for each compound. Many of the complex vibrations that distinguish one compound from a similar compound are found in the 600 to 1400 cm^{-1} region, called the **<u>fingerprint region</u>**. Below are three sample spectra that include the fingerprint region. Know where the fingerprint region is, and know why it is called the fingerprint region, but use the higher frequency range to identify functional groups.

The fingerprint region of the IR spectrum is unique to nearly all compounds, but it is very difficult to read it. You should know about the fingerprint region, but you should use IR to identify functional groups based upon the region from 1600 to 3500 cm^{-1}.

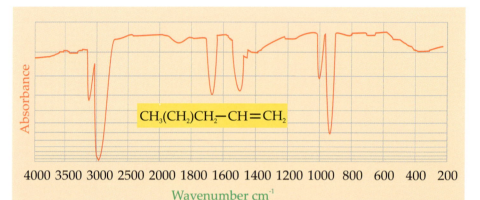

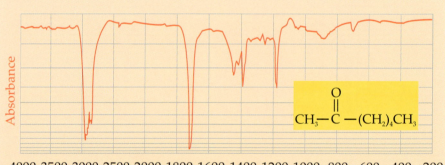

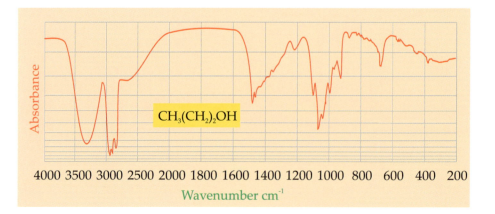

The wavelength of ultraviolet light is between 200 and 400 nm, much shorter than infrared light and at a much higher energy level. Ultraviolet (UV) spectroscopy detects conjugated double bonds (double bonds separated by one single bond) by comparing the intensities of two beams of light from the same monochromatic light source. One beam is shone through a sample cell and the other is shone through a reference cell. The sample cell contains the sample compound to be analyzed dissolved in a solvent. The reference cell contains only the solvent. The sample cell will absorb more energy from the light beam than the reference cell. The difference in the radiant energy is recorded as a UV spectrum of the sample compound.

The UV spectrum provides limited information about the length and structure of the conjugated portion of the molecule. When a photon collides with an electron in a molecule in the sample, the electron may be bumped up to a vacant molecular orbital and the photon absorbed. These are typically π-electron movements from bonding to nonbonding orbitals ($\pi \to \pi^*$). Electrons in σ-bonds usually require more energy to reach the next highest orbital, and thus they are typically unaffected by wavelengths of greater than 200 nm. Conjugated systems with π-bonds, on the other hand, have vacant orbitals at energy levels close to their highest occupied molecular orbital (HOMO) energy levels. The vacant orbitals are called LUMO (lowest unoccupied molecular orbital). UV photons are able to momentarily displace electrons to the LUMO, and the energy is absorbed. If a conjugated system is present in the sample, the sample beam intensity I_s will be lower than the reference beam intensity I_r. The absorbance A is given by $A_\lambda = \log(I_s/I_r)$. The absorbance is plotted on the UV spectra. Absorbance also equals the product of concentration of the sample (c), the length of the path of light through the cell (l), and the *molar absorptivity* (ε)(or *molar extinction coefficient*).

$$A = \varepsilon c l$$

The molar absorptivity is a measure of how strongly the sample absorbs light at a particular wavelength. It is probably easiest to think of it mathematically as $\varepsilon = A/cl$.

Ethylene, though not conjugated, absorbs wavelengths at 171 nm. Absorption at this wavelength is obscured by oxygen in the air. Butadiene has a higher HOMO and lower LUMO than ethylene, allowing for an absorption at 217 nm. Conjugated trienes absorb at even longer wavelengths. The longer the chain of conjugated double bonds, the greater the wavelength of absorption. The rule of thumb is that each additional **conjugated** double bond increases the wavelength by about 30 to 40 nm. An additional alkyl group attached to any one of the atoms involved in the conjugated system increases the spectrum wavelength by about 5 nm. **Isolated** double bonds do not increase the absorption wavelength.

UV spectra lack detail. Samples must be extremely pure or the spectrum is obscured. To the right is a UV spectrum of 2-methyl-1,3-butadiene dissolved in methanol. The methyl group increases the absorption wavelength slightly. The methanol solvent makes no contribution to the spectrum. Spectra are typically not printed, but instead given as lists. The spectrum to the right would be listed as:

$\lambda_{max} = 222$ nm $\varepsilon = 20,000$

4-7
Ultraviolet Spectroscopy

UV starts at around 217 nm with butadiene.

The rule of thumb for UV is 30 to 40 nm increase for each additional conjugated double bond, and a 5 nm increase for each additional alkyl group.

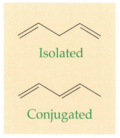

Isolated

Conjugated

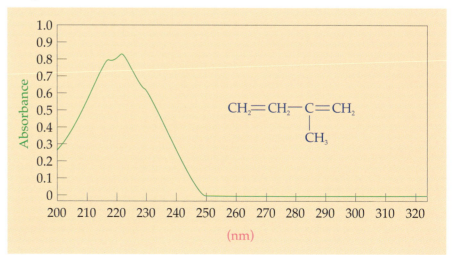

Carbonyls, compounds with carbon-oxygen double bonds, also absorb light in the UV region. For instance, acetone has a broad absorption peak at 280 nm. In this example, the electron can be excited from an unshared pair into a nonbonding π-orbital. ($n \rightarrow \pi^*$)

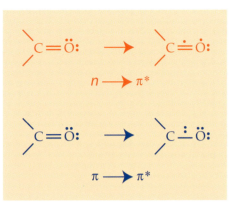

4-8
Visible Spectrum

If a compound has eight or more double bonds, its absorbance moves into the visible spectrum. **β-carotene**, a precursor of vitamin A, has 11 conjugated double bonds. β-carotene has a maximum absorbance at 497 nm. Electromagnetic radiaton of 497 nm has a blue-green color. Carrots, having β-carotene, absorb blue-green light, giving them the **complementary color** of red-orange.

4-9
Mass Spectrometry

Mass spectrometry gives the molecular weight, and, in the case of high resolution mass spectrometry, the molecular formula. In mass spectrometry, the molecules of a sample are bombarded with electrons, causing them to break apart and to ionize. The largest ion is the size of the original molecule but short one electron. This cation is called the *molecular ion*. For instance, if methane were the sample, the molecular ion would be CH_4^+. The ions are accelerated through a magnetic field. The resulting force deflects the ions around a curved path. The radius of curvature of their path depends upon the **mass to charge ratio** of the ion (m/z). Most of the ions have a charge of 1+. The magnetic field strength is altered to allow the passage of different size ions through the flight tube (shown in the diagram). A computer records the amount of ions at different magnetic field strengths as peaks on a chart. The largest peak is called the base peak. The peak made by the molecular ions is called the **parent peak**. Notice that the parent peak is made by molecules that did not fragment.

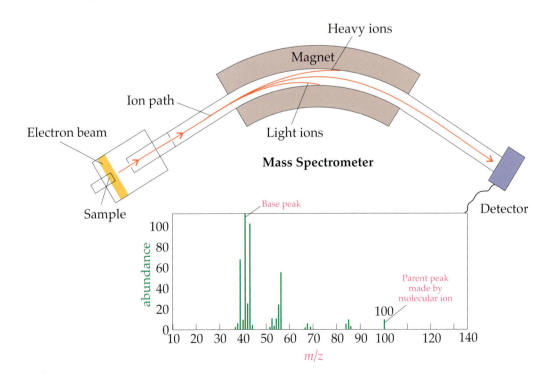

Look for the parent peak all the way to the right of the spectrum. Only heavy isotopes will be further right. All peaks are assigned *abundances* as percentages of the base peak. In the diagram on the previous page, the parent peak has an abundance of 10 because it is 10% as high as the base peak.

Chromatography is the resolution (separation) of a mixture by passing it over or through a matrix that adsorbs different compounds with different affinities, ultimately altering the rate at which they lose contact with the resolving matrix. The mixture is usually dissolved into a solution to serve as the mobile phase, while the resolving matrix is often a solid surface. The surface adsorbs compounds from the mixture, establishing the stationary phase. The compounds in the mixture that have a greater affinity for the surface move more slowly. Typically, the more polar compounds elute more slowly because they have a greater affinity for the stationary phase. The result of chromatography is the establishment of separate and distinct layers, one pertaining to each component of the mixture. Different types of chromatography include:

4-10 Chromatography

Solid to Liquid

Column chromatography is where a solution containing the mixture is dripped down a column containing the solid phase (usually glass beads). The more polar compounds in the mixture travel more slowly down the column, creating separate layers for each compound. Each compound can subsequently be collected as it elutes with the solvent and drips out of the bottom of the column.

In *paper chromatography* (shown on the right) a small portion of the sample to be separated is spotted onto paper. One end of the paper is then placed into a solvent. The solvent moves up the paper via capillary action and dissolves the sample as it passes over it. As the solvent continues to move up the paper, the more polar components of the sample move more slowly because they are attracted to the polar paper. The less polar components are not attracted to the paper and move more quickly.

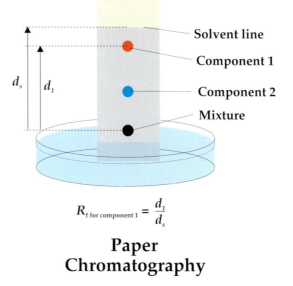

$$R_{f \text{ for component 1}} = \frac{d_1}{d_s}$$

Paper Chromatography

The result is a series of colored dots representing the different components of the sample with the most polar near the bottom and the least polar near the top. An R_f *factor* can be determined for each component of the separation by dividing the distance traveled by the component by the distance traveled by the solvent. Nonpolar components have an R_f factor close to one; polar components have a lower R_f factor. The R_f factor is always between 0 and 1.

Thin layer chromatography is similar to paper chromatography except that a coated glass or plastic plate is used instead of paper, and the results are visualized via an iodine vapor chamber.

Gas to Liquid

In *gas chromatography* the liquid phase is the stationary phase. The mixture is dissolved into a heated carrier gas (usually helium or nitrogen) and passed over a liquid phase bound to a column. Compounds in the mixture equilibrate with the liquid phase at different rates and elute as individual components at an exit port.

4-11
Distillation

<u>Distillation</u> is separation based upon vapor pressure. A solution of two volatile liquids with boiling point differences of approximately 20°C or more may be separated by slow boiling. The **compound with the lower boiling point (higher vapor pressure) will boil off and can be captured** and condensed in a cool tube. Be careful. If a solution of two volatile liquids exhibits a positive deviation to Rault's law, the solution will boil at a lower temperature than either pure compound. The result will be a solution with an exact ratio of the two liquids called an *azeotrope*. An azeotrope cannot be separated by distillation. 5% water and 95% ethanol make an azeotrope that has a lower boiling point than pure water or pure ethanol. An azeotrope can also form when the solution has a higher boiling point than either pure substance. *Fractional distillation* is simply a more precise method of distillation. In fractional distillation, the vapor is run through glass beads allowing the compound with the higher boiling point to condense and fall back into the solution.

4-12
Crystallization

Crystallization is based upon the principle that **pure substances form crystals** more easily than impure substances. The classic example is an iceberg. An iceberg is formed from the ocean but is made of pure water, not salt water. This is because pure water forms crystals more easily. You should know that crystallization is a very inefficient method of separation; it is very difficult to arrive at a pure substance through crystallization. Crystallization of most salts is an exothermic process.

Extraction is based upon <u>solubility due to similar polarities</u>. Like dissolves like. We start with an organic mixture on top of an aqueous layer. They have different polarities and don't mix. There are three steps:

1. add a strong acid and shake. The acid protonates bases like amines in the organic layer, making them polar. The polar amines dissolve in the aqueous layer and are drained off.

2. add a weak base. The base deprotonates only the strong acids like carboxylic acids, making them more polar. The polar carboxylic acids dissolve in the aqueous layer and are drained off.

3. add a strong base. The strong base reacts with the rest of the acids (hopefully all weak acids like phenol). These acids dissolve in the aqueous layer and are drained off.

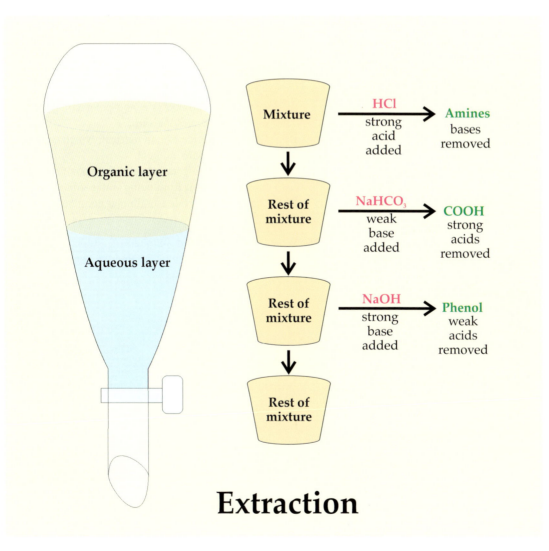

Extraction

89. All of the following are true concerning nmr spectroscopy EXCEPT:

   A. Protons are distinguished when they absorb magnetic energy at different field strengths.
   B. Downfield is to the left on an nmr spectrum.
   C. Functional groups are distinguished when they absorb magnetic energy at different field strengths.
   D. Delocalized electrons generate magnetic fields that can either shield or deshield nearby protons.

90. Extraction is an effective method for separating compounds which can be treated with an acid or base and made to differ in:

   A. boiling point.
   B. molecular weight.
   C. water solubility.
   D. optical activity.

91. A carbonyl will absorb infrared radiation at a frequency of approximately:

   A. 700 – 900 Hz
   B. 1630 – 1700 Hz
   C. 2220 – 2260 Hz
   D. 3300 – 3500 Hz

92. In thin layer chromatography polar compounds will:

   A. rise more slowly through the silica gel than nonpolar compounds.
   B. rise more quickly through the silica gel than nonpolar compounds.
   C. move to the left through the silica gel.
   D. move to the right through the silica gel.

93. Which of the following statements are true concerning separations?

   I. Any two compounds with sufficiently different boiling points can be separated completely by distillation.
   II. Crystallization is an efficient method of compound purification for most compounds.
   III. Distillation is more effective when done slowly.

   A. I only
   B. III only
   C. I and III only
   D. II and III only

94. *Refining* is the separation of crude oil into four primary products:

Petroleum Product	Boiling Point (°C)
Straight-run gasoline	30-180
Kerosene	175-300
Gas oil	295-400
Lubricating wax	425-700

Petroleum product refining can also be described as:

   A. high pressure distillation
   B. nuclear magnetic resonance separation
   C. liquid chromatography extraction
   D. organic phase purification

95. Which statement accounts for the fact that dimethyl sulfoxide is miscible in water, whereas dimethyl sulfide is not?

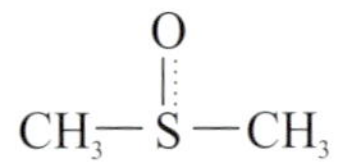

$$CH_3-\overset{\overset{\textstyle O}{\|}}{S}-CH_3 \qquad\qquad CH_3-S-CH_3$$

Dimethyl sulfoxide (bp 187°C) 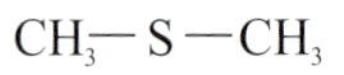   Dimethyl sulfide (bp 37°C)

   A. Dimethyl sulfoxide is a non-polar compound that rapidly penetrates the skin.
   B. Dimethyl sulfide is symmetrical, which causes it to develop a dipole moment.
   C. Dimethyl sulfide has a low boiling point and density issues prevent it from being water soluble.
   D. Dimethyl sulfoxide is a dipolar compound.

96. What is the predicted number of ^{13}C nmr peaks for methylcyclopentane and 1,2-Dimethylbenzene, respectively?

 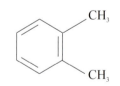

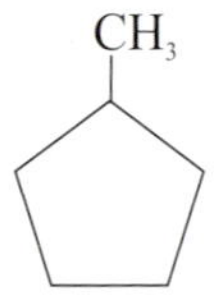

Methylcyclopentane   1,2-Dimethylbenzene

   A. 2,3
   B. 3,4
   C. 4,4
   D. 5,3

STOP.

STOP!

DO NOT LOOK AT THESE EXAMS UNTIL CLASS.

30-MINUTE
IN-CLASS EXAM
FOR LECTURE 1

With few exceptions, enantiomers cannot be separated through physical means. When in racemic mixtures, they have the same physical properties. Enantiomers have similar chemical properties as well. The only chemical difference between a pair of enantiomers occurs in reactions with other chiral compounds. Thus resolution of a racemic mixture typically takes place through a reaction with another optically active reagent. Since living organisms usually produce only one of two possible enantiomers, many optically active reagents can be obtained from natural sources. For instance: (S)-(+)-lactic acid can be obtained from animal muscle tissue; and (S)-(-)-2-methyl-1-butanol, from yeast fermentation.

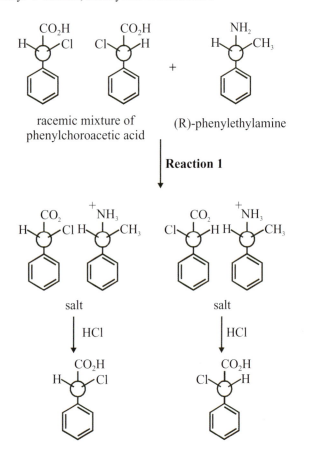

racemic mixture of phenylchoroacetic acid

(R)-phenylethylamine

Figure 1 Separation of enantiomers

In the resolution of a racemic acid, a solution of (R)-phenylethylamine is reacted with a racemic mixture of phenylchloroacetic acid to form the corresponding salts. The salts are then separated by careful fractional crystallization. Hydrochloric acid is added to the separated salts, and the respective acids are precipitated from their solutions.

Resolution of a racemic base can be accomplished in the same manner with tartaric acid.

1. Quinine, a natural anti-malarial, is commonly used as an optically active reagent to resolve acidic enantiomers. How many chiral carbons exist in the quinine molecule drawn below?

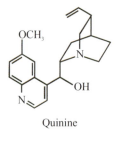

Quinine

A. 1
B. 2
C. 3
D. 4

2. Which of the following alcohols is a natural product of anaerobic respiration?

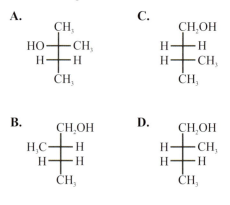

3. The salts created in Reaction 1 are:

A. diastereomers
B. enantiomers
C. structural isomers
D. meso compounds

102

GO ON TO THE NEXT PAGE.

4. The following reaction proceeds with retention of configuration:

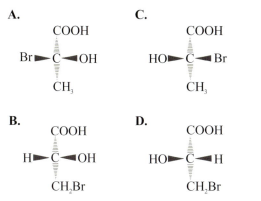

$$CH_2BrCHOHCO_2H \xrightarrow{Zn, H^+} CH_3CHOHCO_2H$$

If the product is the naturally occurring lactic acid, which of the compounds below could be a reactant?

A.

COOH
Br━C━OH
CH₃

C.

COOH
HO━C━Br
CH₃

B.

COOH
H━C━OH
CH₂Br

D.

COOH
HO━C━H
CH₂Br

5. D-(+)-glyceraldehyde undergoes the series of reactions below to yield two isomers of tartaric acid. What type of isomers are they?

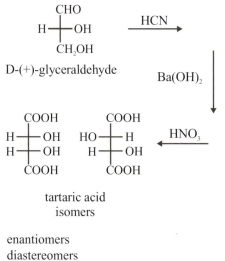

CHO
H━OH
CH₂OH

D-(+)-glyceraldehyde

→ HCN

Ba(OH)₂ ↓

COOH   COOH
H━OH   HO━H   ← HNO₃
H━OH   H━OH
COOH   COOH

tartaric acid
isomers

A.   enantiomers
B.   diastereomers
C.   structural isomers
D.   conformational isomers

6. Which of the following compounds might be used to resolve a racemic mixture of acidic enantiomers?

A.

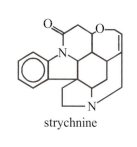

strychnine

B.

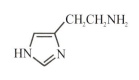

CH₂CH₂NH₂

HN N

histamine

C.

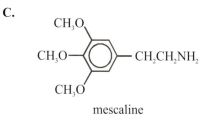

CH₃O
CH₃O━⬡━CH₂CH₂NH₂
CH₃O

mescaline

D.

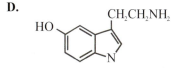

CH₂CH₂NH₂

HO

serotonin

GO ON TO THE NEXT PAGE.

A chemical reaction is *stereoselective* when a certain stereoisomer or set of stereoisomers predominate as products. A reaction is *stereospecific* if different isomers lead to isomerically opposite products.

Bromine adds to 2-butene to form the *vic*-dihalide, 2,3-dibromobutane. A student proposed the following two mechanisms for the addition of bromine to alkenes.

In order to test each mechanism the student designed two experiments.

Mechanism A

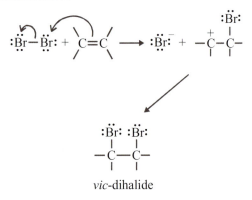

vic-dihalide

Mechanism B

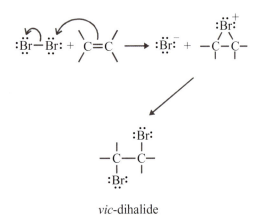

vic-dihalide

Experiment 1

Cyclopentene was dissolved in CCl_4. Bromine was added to the solution at low temperatures and low light. The product tested negative for optical activity. An optically active reagent was then added and, upon fractional distillation, two fractions were obtained. Each fraction was then precipitated and rinsed in an acid bath. The final products were found to have opposite observed rotations.

Experiment 2

The same procedure as in Experiment 1 was followed for both the *cis* and *trans* isomers of 2-butene. The results depended upon which isomer was used.

7. In the second step of *Mechanism B*, the bromine ion acts as:

A. a halophile.
B. a catalyst.
C. an electrophile.
D. a nucleophile.

8. If *Mechanism B* is correct, how many fractions should the student obtain from the distillation in Experiment 2 when the trans isomer is used?

A. 1
B. 2
C. 3
D. 4

9. What is the expected angle between the bonds of the carbocation in *Mechanism A?*

A. 90°
B. 109°
C. 120°
D. 180°

10. The results of the experiments demonstrate that *Mechanism B* is correct. The addition of bromine to alkenes is:

A. stereoselective but not stereospecific.
B. stereospecific but not stereoselective.
C. both stereoselective and stereospecific.
D. neither stereoselective nor stereospecific.

11. If, instead of CCl_4, water is used as the solvent in a halogen addition reaction, a halohydrin is formed. The student proposed that such a reaction would follow *Mechanism A* with water replacing bromine as the nucleophile. If this hypothesis is correct, which of the following is the most likely product for the addition of bromine to propene in water?

    A.   1,2-dibromopropane
    B.   1,3-dibromo-2-propanol
    C.   1-bromo-2-propanol
    D.   2-bromo-1-propanol

12. If *Mechanism B* is correct, the trans isomer in Experiment 2 will produce:

    A.   a meso compound.
    B.   a pair of enantiomers.
    C.   only one optically active compound.
    D.   a pair of structural isomers.

13. In *Experiment 1*, why did the student use low light and low temperature?

    A.   to decrease the rate of the reaction
    B.   to prevent combustion of the alkene
    C.   to avoid contamination of the product via a radical reaction
    D.   to increase the yield of the endothermic reaction

Passage III (Questions 14-19)

It is possible for asymmetrical molecules, such as enzymes, to distinguish between identical substituents on some symmetrical molecules. Such symmetrical molecules are called *prochiral*. A prochiral molecule is an achiral molecule with three different substituents. If one of the two identical substituents on a prochiral molecule is substituted for a different substituent not already present o the molecule, then the molecule would become chiral. The amino acid glycine is a prochiral molecule.

The molecule in Figure 1 is an example of a prochiral molecule. The asymmetrical enzyme binds only to hydrogen 'a' and not to hydrogen 'b' due to the spatial arrangement of its active site with respect to the other substituents on the prochiral carbon. All known dehydrogenases are stereospecific in this manner.

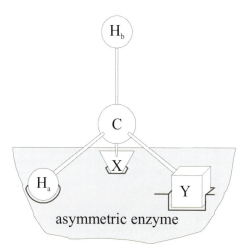

Figure 1 An asymmetrical enzyme distinguishing between identical substituents on a symmetrical molecule.

Experiment 1

An experimenter labeled oxaloacetate with ^{14}C at the carboxyl carbon farthest from the keto group. The oxaloacetate was allowed to undergo the portion of the Kreb's cycle depicted in Figure 2. The acetyl group donated by acetyl CoA is not removed during the Kreb's cycle. The experimenter found that all of the label emerged in the CO_2 of the second decarboxylation.

          GO ON TO THE NEXT PAGE.

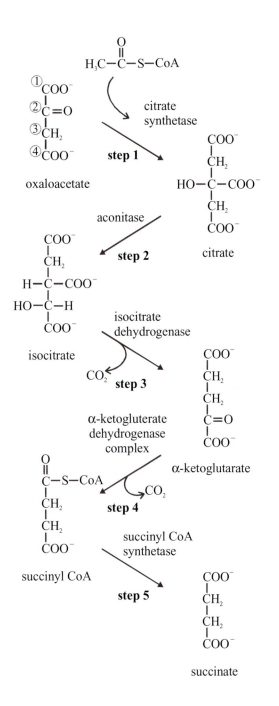

oxaloacetate

citrate

isocitrate

α-ketoglutarate

succinyl CoA

succinate

Figure 2 A portion of the Kreb's cycle

14. Which of the following reactants in step 1 of Figure 2 contains a water soluble vitamin as a component part?

 A. citrate
 B. oxaloacetate
 C. acetyl CoA
 D. citrate synthetase

15. All of the following molecules are prochiral at the third carbon EXCEPT:

 A. succinate
 B. citrate
 C. α-ketoglutarate
 D. isocitrate

16. Which one of the carbons numbered in oxaloacetate is removed from isocitrate by the decarboxylation in step 3 of Figure 2?

 A. 1
 B. 2
 C. 3
 D. 4

17. The hybridization of the labeled carbon in oxaloacetate, citrate, and α-ketogluterate, respectively, is:

 A. sp^2; sp^2; sp^2
 B. sp^2; sp^2; sp^3
 C. sp^2; sp^3; sp^2
 D. sp^3; sp^3; sp^3

18. Which of the following structures is the enol form of α-ketogluteric acid?

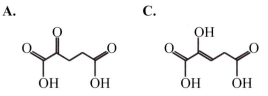
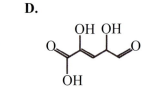

 A.

 C.

 B.

 D.

19. What are the products when deuterium labeled alcohol is reacted with NAD^+ in the presence of alcohol dehydrogenase as shown below?

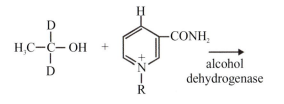

A.

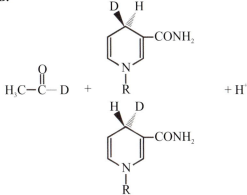

B.

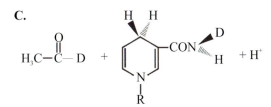

C.

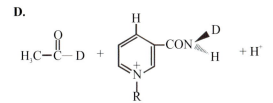

D.

H₃C—C—D +   ... + H⁺

Questions 20 through 23 are **NOT** based on a descriptive passage.

20. Which of the following is true concerning meso compounds?

   I. They are achiral.
   II. They rotate the plane of polarized light.
   III. They contain a chiral carbon.

   A. I only
   B. I and II only
   C. I and III only
   D. II and III only

21. Which of the following is true concerning chirality?

   I. Chiral molecules are never the same as their mirror images.
   II. All chiral molecules have a mirror image which is their enantiomer.
   III. If a molecule is not the same as its mirror image, then it is chiral.

   A. I only
   B. II only
   C. III only
   D. I, II, and III

22. The name of the compound shown below is:

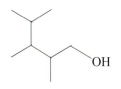

   A. 2-isopropyl-3-methyl-5-pentanol
   B. 3-isopropyl-2-methyl-1-butanol
   C. 2,3,4-trimethyl-1-pentanol
   D. 3,4,5-trimethyl-1-hexanol

23. Which of the following is true concerning conformational isomers?

   A. No conformer can be isolated.
   B. They only exist at high energy levels.
   C. The anti-conformation has the highest energy level.
   D. At low temperatures the anti-conformation is the most common.

STOP. IF YOU FINISH BEFORE TIME IS CALLED, CHECK YOUR WORK. YOU MAY GO BACK TO ANY QUESTION IN THIS TEST BOOKLET.

In-Class Exams

30-MINUTE
IN-CLASS EXAM
FOR LECTURE 2

Passage I (Questions 24-29)

A chemist performs the following experiment.

Step 1

Chlorine is added to (S)-sec-butyl chloride at 300°C. The reaction proceeds with retention of configuration. The products are carefully separated by fractional distillation. The chemist identifies five fractions as isomers of dichlorobutane and labels them: Compounds A, B, C, D, and E. Compounds C and D are formed in a 7 to 3 ratio. The boiling points of all five compounds are listed in Table 1.

Compound	Boiling Point
A	134°C
B	124°C
C	118°C
D	115°C
E	104°C

Table 1 Boiling points of selected fractions from Step 1

Step 2

The labeled compounds are each checked with a polarimeter for the rotation of plane-polarized light. Only Compounds A, B, and C are optically active.

Step 3

Upon nmr spectroscopy, Compounds C and D were revealed to be stereoisomers.

24. After the distillation in Step 1, which of the following properties, if known for each fraction, would identify a fraction as a dichlorobutane?

    A. boiling point
    B. melting point
    C. molecular weight
    D. observed rotation

25. Compounds A and E are:

    A. diastereomers.
    B. enantiomers.
    C. conformational isomers.
    D. constitutional isomers.

26. If (R,R)-2,3-dichlorobutane is found to have a specific rotation of $[\alpha]_D^{20}$ -25.66, then which compound has a specific rotation of $[\alpha]_D^{20}$ +25.66?

    A. Compound A
    B. Compound B
    C. Compound C
    D. Compound D

27. Which of the following is NOT true concerning the compounds listed in Table 1?

    A. Although the relative configuration about the original chiral center is retained, the absolute configuration may have changed.
    B. Both configurations about any new chiral center appeared in equal proportions.
    C. One of the compounds is a meso compound.
    D. Although the relative configuration about the original chiral center is retained, the direction of observed rotation may change.

28. Compound E is most likely which of the following?

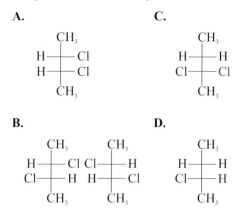

29. If NaOH is added to (S)-sec-butyl chloride, what is the most likely product?

    A. (R)-sec-butyl alcohol
    B. (S)-sec-butyl alcohol
    C. (S)-2-chloro-2-butanol
    D. (R)- 2-chloro-2-butanol

GO ON TO THE NEXT PAGE.

Passage II (Questions 30-36)

The *neighboring mechanism* occurs when a neighboring atom or functional group otherwise not involved in a reaction, affects the reaction by carrying electrons close to the reacting group. If the neighboring group helps to expel the leaving group, it is said to give *anchimeric assistance.*

The halohydrin 3-bromo-2-butanol undergoes the following reactions with hydrobromic acid.

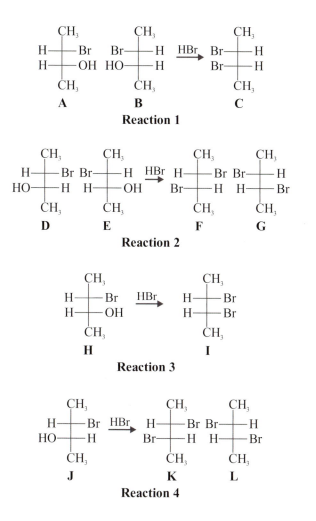

Reaction 1

Reaction 2

Reaction 3

Reaction 4

A chemist proposed the following *neighboring mechanism* to explain the results of the above reactions:

Mechanism I

When the alcohol is protonated by the hydrobromic acid, the attached bromine attacks the adjacent carbon, ejecting the leaving group to form a bromonium ion. The bromine ion is then equally likely to attach via pathway a or b in Figure 1. Both the formation of the bromonium ion and attachment of the bromine ion are similar to an S_N2 mechanism where attachment of the nucleophile and detachment of the leaving group occur in a single step.

The process of bromonium ion formation is related to rearrangement of the carbon skeleton of carbocations. A nearby atom or group may relieve the electron deficiency of another atom through induction, resonance, or, as in bromonium ion formation, by actually carrying the electrons to where they are needed.

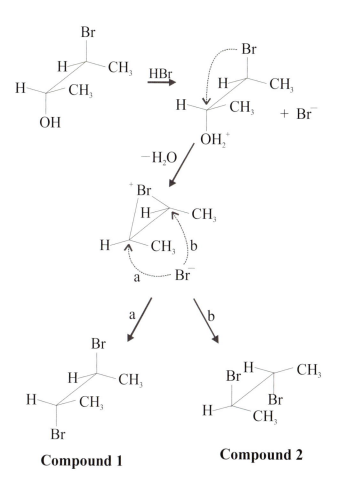

Figure 1 Diagram of Mechanism 1

30. How many stereoisomers exist of 2,3-dibromobutane?

- **A.** 1
- **B.** 2
- **C.** 3
- **D.** 4

GO ON TO THE NEXT PAGE.

31. Which of the following statements is true concerning Reaction 4?

 A. Product K shows retention of configuration at both chiral centers and product L shows inversion of configuration at both chiral centers.
 B. Both products K and L show inversion of configuration at one chiral center and retention of configuration at the other chiral center.
 C. Only product K shows retention of configuration at one chiral center and inversion of configuration at the other chiral center.
 D. Only product L shows retention of configuration at one chiral center and inversion of configuration at the other chiral center.

32. An even mixture of which of the following compounds from the reactions in the passage will rotate plane-polarized light?

 I. A and B
 II. C and I
 III. H and J

 A. I only
 B. II only
 C. III only
 D. I and II only

33. Which of the following techniques could be used to distinguish the products of Reaction 1 from the mixture of products of Reaction 2?

 A. mass spectroscopy
 B. distillation
 C. rotation of polarized light
 D. infrared spectroscopy

34. If no neighboring mechanism occurred in Reaction 4, the expected products would be:

 A. compounds K and L only.
 B. compound K only.
 C. compound L only.
 D. compound C only.

35. Assuming HCl reacts similarly to HBr. which of the following would be the expected product of pathway 'b' of Mechanism 1 for the reaction given below?

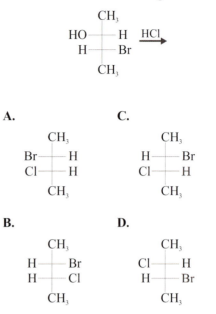

36. According to Mechanism 1, which of the following most likely affects the initial rate of Reaction 3?

 I. the concentration of reactant H
 II. the concentration of HBr
 III. the concentration of product I

 A. I only
 B. II only
 C. I and II only
 D. I, II, and III

Passage III (Questions 37-42)

Complicated alcohols that cannot be obtained on the market are often synthesized in the lab with a Grignard reagent. The Grignard reagent is made by reacting metallic magnesium with an organic halide. Many types of organic halides may be used, including primary, secondary. and tertiary alkylhalides and aromatic halides. However, the reagent is a very powerful base and it is impossible to prepare it from a compound having a hydrogen more acidic than an alkene. The halide may be a chloride, bromide, or iodide but chlorine based reagents require a special solvent.

The basic formula of a Grignard reagent is RMgX. The magnesium-carbon bond is covalent but extremely polar making the Grignard reagent a strong nucleophile. It is this characteristic of the reagent that is used in the synthesis of alcohols.

$$RMgX + O=C\overset{R'}{\underset{H}{<}} \rightarrow R-\overset{R'}{\underset{H}{C}}-OMgX \overset{H^+}{\rightarrow} R-\overset{R'}{\underset{H}{C}}-OH + MgX$$

Reaction 1 Alcohol synthesis from a Grignard reagent

In alcohol synthesis, the reagent reacts with a carbonyl compound to make the magnesium salt of the corresponding alcohol. The product is then bathed in dilute mineral acid forming an alcohol and a water soluble magnesiumhalide salt.

37. Which of the following compounds would make the best solvent in a Grignard synthesis with an alkylbromide?

    A. H_2O
    B. $(C_2H_5)_2O$
    C. $C_2H_3O_2Na$
    D. C_2H_5OH

38. What type of reaction takes place between the Grignard reagent and the carbonyl compound?

    A. S_N1
    B. S_N2
    C. nucleophilic addition
    D. bimolecular elimination

39. Which of the following alcohols would react the most strongly with a Grignard reagent?

    A. CH_3OH
    B. $(CH_3)_3OH$
    C. $CH_3CHOHCH_3$
    D. $CH_3(CH_2)_{11}CH_2OH$

40. Which of the following compounds could be reacted with the Grignard reagent shown below to create a tertiary alcohol?

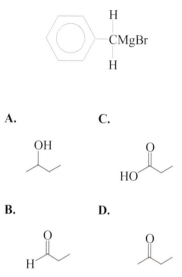

    A.   C.

    B.   D.

41. Which of the following most accurately represents the charge distribution in the magnesium-carbon bond of the Grignard reagent?

    A. $^{\delta+}CMg^{\delta-}$
    B. $^{\delta-}CMg^{\delta+}$
    C. $^{\delta+}CMg^{\delta+}$
    D. $^{\delta-}CMg^{\delta-}$

42. If the alcoholic product of Reaction 1 were oxidized by H_2CrO_4 and acid, what would be the major product?

    A. an aldehyde
    B. a carboxylic acid
    C. a ketone
    D. an alkene

43. The dehydration of 2-pentanol in the presence of a strong acid and heat results in a(n):

    A. alkane
    B. alkene
    C. aldehyde
    D. carboxylic acid

44. Which of the following has the greatest boiling point?

    A. methane
    B. methanol
    C. chloromethane
    D. ammonia

45. NaCl will not react with ethanol via an S_N2 reaction because:

    A. an hydroxide ion is less stable than the chlorine ion.
    B. an hydroxide ion is more stable than the chlorine ion.
    C. steric hindrance prevents the reaction.
    D. the chloride ion is a better nucleophile than the hydroxyl group.

46. Which of the following is the most soluble in water?

    A. 1-butanol
    B. butane
    C. 1-butene
    D. propane

STOP. IF YOU FINISH BEFORE TIME IS CALLED, CHECK YOUR WORK. YOU MAY GO BACK TO ANY QUESTION IN THIS TEST BOOKLET.

STOP.

30-MINUTE
IN-CLASS EXAM
FOR LECTURE 3

In 1877 two chemists working together developed a new method for the preparation of alkylbenzenes and acylbenzenes. In the Friedel-Crafts acylation, named after these two chemists, an acyl group is added to benzene in the presence of a Lewis acid. The Lewis acid usually reacts with the acyl group to form an acylium ion. The acylium ion is stabilized by resonance. Next, the acylium ion acts as an electrophile attacking the benzene ring to form an arenium ion. The arenium ion then loses a proton to generate the final product. Powerful electron-withdrawing groups on the benzene ring such as another acyl group will block this reaction.

Naphthalene is the simplest and most important of the fused ring hydrocarbons. Five percent of all constituents of coal tar are naphthalene. Naphthalene can be manufactured using the Friedel-Crafts reaction via the reaction pathway shown in Scheme 1.

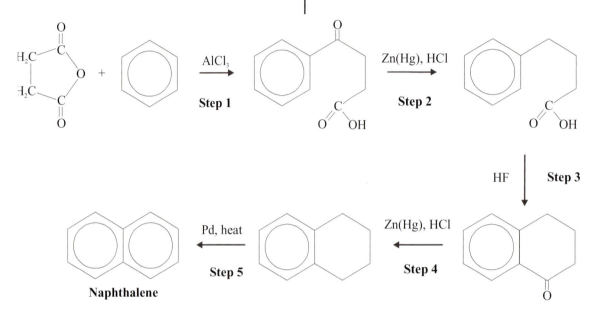

Naphthalene

Scheme 1

47. The Friedel-Crafts reaction occurs twice in Scheme 1. Which two steps represent Friedel-Crafts reactions?

A. steps 1 and 3
B. steps 1 and 5
C. steps 2 and 4
D. steps 3 and 5

48. Step 2 is which of the following types of reactions?

A. an oxidation reaction
B. a reduction reaction
C. an elimination reaction
D. a Friedel-Crafts reaction

49. Why is step 2 necessary in order for ring closure to take place in step 3?

A. Step 2 activates the ring by changing the electron releasing alkyl group to an electron withdrawing acyl group.
B. Step 2 deactivates the ring by changing the electron releasing acyl group to an electron withdrawing alkyl group.
C. Step 2 activates the ring by changing the electron withdrawing acyl group to an electron releasing alkyl group.
D. Step 2 deactivates the ring by changing the electron withdrawing alkyl group to an electron releasing acyl group.

50. What are the most likely products of the following reaction?

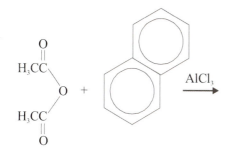

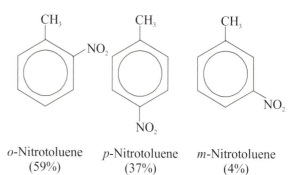

A.

C_2H_8 +

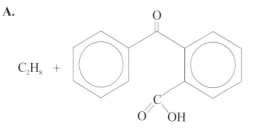

B.

CH_3COH +

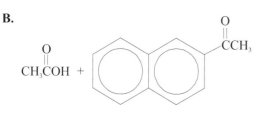

C.

CH_3CH +

D.

CH_3CH +

51. Toluene reacts with nitric acid to form the following products:

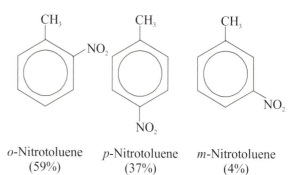

o-Nitrotoluene (59%)   *p*-Nitrotoluene (37%)   *m*-Nitrotoluene (4%)

If the position of substitution were chosen at random, what would be the expected percentage of *m*-nitrotoluene from the reaction?

A. 0%
B. 4%
C. 33%
D. 40%

52. Which of the following is an acylium ion?

A.

$AlCl_4$

C.

CH_3CO^-

B.

D.

CH_3C^+

GO ON TO THE NEXT PAGE.

When unknown compounds are identified without the aid of spectroscopy, classification tests are used. Reacting the carbonyl in a ketone or aldehyde with an amine (2,4 dinitro-phenylhydrazine) to form an imine is the easiest way to detect a ketone or aldehyde (Reaction 1). The imine that forms is a highly colored solid. The color of the solid also helps to indicate structural characteristics. Ketones and aldehydes with no conjugation tend to form imines with yellow to orange colors, while highly conjugated ketones or aldehydes form imines with red color.

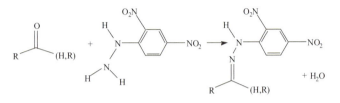

2, 4-nitrophenylhydrazine   dinitrophenylhydrazone

Reaction 1

The presence of a colored solid confirms the presence of a ketone or aldehyde, but the imine formation does not indicate whether the unknown is a ketone or aldehyde. A second classification test is used to distinguish the two functionalities. This test is called the Tollens' test, and the significant reaction is shown in Reaction 2.

Reaction 2

Aldehydes will form a silver mirror or a black precipitate if the test tube is dirty, while ketones will not.

Once the unknown is determined to be a ketone or an aldehyde, the melting point of the imine derivative is determined. The melting point and other physical characteristics (i.e., solubility of unknown and boiling point or melting point of the unknown) are used to determine the unknown's identity. The information is compared to tables in books which contain the melting points of derivatives and other physical data for organic compounds.

53. Why does the Tollens' test produce solid silver with aldehydes and not with ketones?

   A. Ketones are more sterically hindered than aldehydes.
   B. Aldehydes can be oxidized to the carboxylic acid, while ketone cannot.
   C. Ketones do not have an acidic proton while aldehydes do have one.
   D. Aldehydes are more sterically hindered than ketones.

54. A red 2,4 dinitrophenylhydrazone is obtained from the reaction of an unknown with an amine. Of the following four structures, which ketone or aldehyde could have formed this imine?

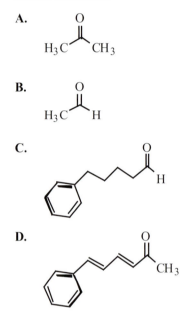

55. What type of reaction is Reaction 1?

   A. bimolecular elimination
   B. dehydration
   C. hydrolysis
   D. saponification

56. In Reaction 1, the nitrogen of the amine is

   A. a nucleophile
   B. an electrophile
   C. an acid
   D. an oxidant

57. The structures shown below are:

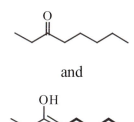

and

A. enantiomers
B. diastereomers
C. epimers
D. tautomers

58. The hemiketal of acetone can be formed by adding:

A. HCl
B. CH₃OH
C. NaOH
D. formaldehyde

59. Instead of using the Tollens' test, a student uses nmr spectroscopy to distinguish an aldehyde from a ketone. What should the student expect to find?

A. More splitting in the nmr peaks of ketones than of aldehydes.
B. Less splitting in the nmr peaks of ketones than of aldehydes.
C. One peak downfield in the aldehyde but not in the ketone.
D. Two peaks upfield in the aldehyde but not the ketone.

Passage III (Questions 60-66)

During high-frequency stimulation of muscles, an anaerobic condition is created. As a result, the pyruvate produced from glycolysis (the breakdown of glucose to produce ATP) is converted to lactate by single enzyme mediation (Figure 1) rather than the pyruvate entering the Krebs cycle. The lactate formation maintains NAD⁺ for glycolsis, but produces less ATP than the completion of the Krebs cycle.

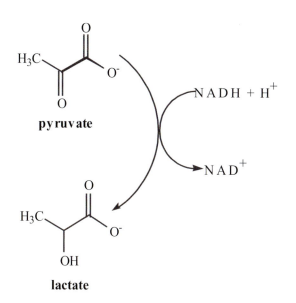

pyruvate

lactate

Figure 1 Conversion of pyruvate to lactate

The lactate produced by this cycle is passed into the blood and is transported to the liver. In the liver, the lactate is converted back to glucose. This cycle is called the Cori cycle.

The increase in the lactic acid produced from glycolysis causes metabolic acidosis and muscle fatigue.

60. Which of the following is true concerning the acidity of pyruvic acid and lactic acid?

A. Pyruvic acid is more acidic.
B. Lactic acid is more acidic.
C. Both acids have the same acidity.
D. Relative acidity cannot be determined based on structures alone.

61. The transformation of pyruvate to lactate is:

A. a decarboxylation
B. an oxidation
C. a reduction
D. hydration

GO ON TO THE NEXT PAGE..

62. The product of the reaction below is:

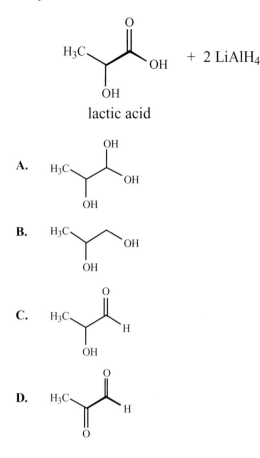

lactic acid

A. <!-- structure: H3C-CH(OH)-CH(OH)-CH2OH with OH groups -->

B. <!-- structure: H3C-CH(OH)-CH2OH -->

C. <!-- structure: H3C-CH(OH)-CHO -->

D. <!-- structure: H3C-CO-CHO -->

63. Why does weightlifting produce lactic acid buildup in muscle tissue?

   A.   Some highly active muscle tissue uses ATP faster than can be supplied by aerobic respiration.

   B.   Some highly active muscle tissue uses ATP faster than can be supplied by anaerobic respiration.

   C.   Lactic acid is always a byproduct of ATP production.

   D.   The Krebs cycle produces lactic acid.

64. Under aerobic conditions additional ATP is produced, following glycolysis, when:

   A.   pyruvate enters the Krebs cycle.

   B.   pyruvate is converted to lactate.

   C.   lactate is converted back to glucose in the liver completing the Cori cycle.

   D.   muscles become fatigued.

65. What is the product of the following reaction:

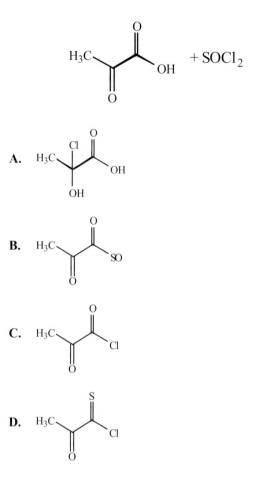

A. <!-- structure -->

B. <!-- structure -->

C. <!-- structure -->

D. <!-- structure -->

66. How do the water solubility and boiling point of pyruvic acid and lactic acid compare?

   A.   Pyruvic acid has a higher boiling point and is more water soluble.

   B.   Lactic acid has a higher boiling point and is more water soluble.

   C.   Pyruvic acid has a higher boiling point but lactate is more water soluble.

   D.   Lactic acid has a higher boiling point but pyruvate is more water soluble.

Questions 67 through 69 are **NOT** based on a descriptive passage.

67. When nucleophilic substitution occurs at a carbonyl, the weakest base is usually the best leaving group. What is the order of reactivity in a nucleophilic substitution reaction from most reactive to least reactive for the following compounds?

I. acid chloride
II. ester
III. amide

A. I, II, III
B. I, III, II
C. III, I, II
D. III, II, I

68. All of the following reactions may result in a ketone EXCEPT:

A. ozonolysis of an alkene.
B. aldol condensation.
C. oxidation of a primary alcohol
D. Friedel-Crafts acylation

69. All of the following qualities of a carbonyl carbon make it a good electrophile EXCEPT:

A. its stereochemistry
B. its partial positive charge
C. its planar shape
D. its lone pair of electrons

STOP. IF YOU FINISH BEFORE TIME IS CALLED, CHECK YOUR WORK. YOU MAY GO BACK TO ANY QUESTION IN THIS TEST BOOKLET.

30-MINUTE
IN-CLASS EXAM
FOR LECTURE 4

In 1888 Emil Fishcer set out to discover the structure of (+)-glucose. Methods for determining absolute configuration had not yet been developed so Fischer arbitrarily limited his attention to the eight D configurations shown in Figure 1. Starting with a sample of glucose and these eight possible structures, Fischer deduced the correct structure of glucose by following a process of elimination similar to the four steps described below.

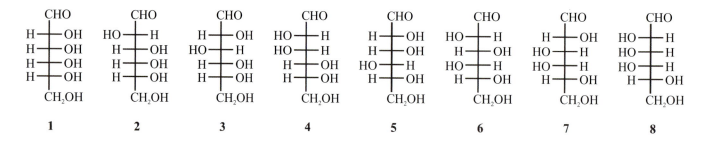

Figure 1

Steps used by Fischer to determine the structure of glucose:

1. Aldoses react with dilute nitric acid at both the CHO group and the terminal CH_2OH group to produce a CO_2H group at either end. Glucose produces an optically active compound in this reaction.

2. Aldoses can be degraded by the following two reactions. First the aldehyde is oxidized with bromine water to form a carboxylic acid. Next the carboxylic acid is decarboxylated with hydrogen peroxide and ferric sulfate leaving an aldehyde. The new aldose is one carbon shorter. When glucose is degraded in this manner, and the product is oxidized by dilute nitric acid, an optically active compound is formed.

3. The Kiliani-Fischer synthesis lengthens the carbon chain of an aldose by one carbon at the aldehyde end and forms a new aldose with its corresponding epimers. When glucose and its epimer are produced from the corresponding pentose via the Kiliani-Fischer synthesis, and then both epimers are reacted with dilute nitric acid, both form optically active compounds.

4. The two remaining possible structures for glucose were now examined. The end groups (CHO and CH_2OH) were exchanged on each. When the end groups were exchanged on one of the sugars it remained as the same compound. However, when the end groups of glucose were exchanged, a new sugar was created.

70. How many stereoisomers are possible for glucose?

   A. 2
   B. 8
   C. 16
   D. 32

71. The reactions between an aldose and dilute nitric acid as described in step 1 are which of the following types of reactions?

   A. reduction
   B. oxidation
   C. hydrolysis
   D. elimination

72. If only step 2 is performed, which of the structures in Figure 1 are eliminated as possible structures of glucose?

   A. 1 and 2 only
   B. 1, 4, and 7 only
   C. 1, 2, 5, and 6 only
   D. 3, 4, 7, and 8 only

GO ON TO THE NEXT PAGE.

73. Which of the following pentoses, when undergoing the Kiliani-Fischer synthesis, will yield D-glucose and D-mannose?

A.
```
        CHO
  HO ——+—— H
   H ——+—— OH
   H ——+—— OH
       CH₂OH
```

C.
```
        CHO
   H ——+—— OH
  HO ——+—— H
  HO ——+—— H
       CH₂OH
```

B.
```
        CHO
   H ——+—— OH
   H ——+—— OH
   H ——+—— OH
       CH₂OH
```

D.
```
        CHO
   H ——+—— OH
   H ——+—— OH
  HO ——+—— H
       CH₂OH
```

74. D-(+)-glyceraldehyde was allowed to undergo the Kiliani-Fischer synthesis, and the reaction ran to completion. After separation of any isomers, how many optically active products were formed?

```
        CHO
   H ——+—— OH
       CH₂OH
```

D-(+)-glyceraldehyde

A. 0
B. 1
C. 2
D. 4

75. Which structures can be eliminated by step 1?

A. 1 and 7 only
B. 4 and 6 only
C. 1, 4, 6, and 7 only
D. 2, 3, 5, and 8 only

76. Before carrying out step 4, Fischer had eliminated all but two possible structures for glucose. Which of the following was the structure that step 4 proved NOT to be glucose?

A. 2
B. 4
C. 5
D. 8

Passage II (Questions 77-82)

In 1951 a chemist made $C_{10}H_{10}Fe$ by reacting two moles of cyclopentadienylmagnesium bromide (a Grignard reagent) with anhydrous ferrous chloride. The structure of the resulting stable solid was uncertain and became an area of great interest in the following years. The structure proposed by the original chemist is shown in Figure 1.

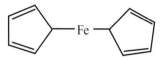

Figure 1. Proposed structure 1

Chemists later proposed a new structure called a "sandwich" complex which is shown in Figure 2.

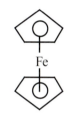

Figure 2. Proposed structure 2

The spectroscopy for $C_{10}H_{10}Fe$ is shown in Tables 1 and 2.

Chemical Shift	Coupling Pattern	Integral Value
4.12 ppm	singlet	10

Table 1 Proton NMR data

Frequency	Description of Peak
2900 cm⁻¹	very strong

Table 2 IR peaks
at frequencies greater than 1500 cm⁻¹

When $C_{10}H_{10}Fe$ is reacted with acetic anhydride in the presence of an acid as shown in Reaction 1, a dark orange solid is formed with the molecular formula $C_{12}H_{12}OFe$. The reaction of $C_{10}H_{10}Fe$ with the anhydride helped scientists to confirm which structure was valid.

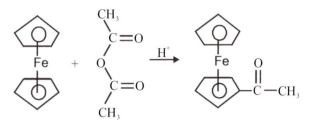

Reaction 1

A summary of the spectroscopy for the product shown in Reaction 1 is given in Tables 3 and 4.

Chemical Shift	Coupling Pattern	Integral Value
2.30 ppm	singlet	3
4.20 ppm	singlet	5
4.50 ppm	doublet	2
4.80 ppm	doublet	2

Table 3 Proton NMR data

Frequency	Description of Peak
2900 cm^{-1}	very strong
1700 cm^{-1}	very strong

Table 4 IR peaks at frequencies greater than 1500 cm^{-1}

77. What is the other product that is produced in Reaction 1 but not shown?

    A. a carboxylic acid
    B. a ketone
    C. an aldehyde
    D. an ester

78. The source of the new peak in the IR data after the reaction with acetic anhydride comes from:

    A. a carbonyl stretch.
    B. a C-H stretch.
    C. the coupling of two protons.
    D. a C-C-H bend.

79. The NMR peak at 2.30 ppm in Table 3 is from protons:

    A. on the carbon of the double bonds in the cyclopentadiene ring.
    B. on the carbon of the methyl group attached to the cyclopentadiene ring.
    C. on the carbon of the methyl group attached to a carbonyl carbon.
    D. on the carbon of the cyclopentadiene ring, not in a double bond.

80. Why is it important that the ferrous chloride be anhydrous in the reaction to form $C_{10}H_{10}Fe$?

    A. The cyclopentadienylmagnesium bromide will react with water.
    B. The ferrous chloride will turn to ferric chloride.
    C. Ferrous chloride will not dissolve in water.
    D. The water would catalyze the reaction and it would erupt.

81. In Figure 2, the five-membered rings are:

    A. aromatic
    B. antiaromatic
    C. nonaromatic
    D. aromaticity can not be determined for any structures that do not contain benzene

82. How does the spectroscopy done before the reaction indicate that structure 1 is not the true structure?

    A. If structure 1 were the true structure, there would be 3 chemical shifts in Table 1.
    B. If structure 1 were the true structure, there would be 4 chemical shifts in Table 1.
    C. If structure 1 were the true structure, there would be a frequency of 1700 cm^{-1} and not a frequency at 2900 cm^{-1} in Table 2.
    D. If structure 1 were the true structure, there would be a frequency of 1700 cm^{-1} as well as the frequency at 2900 cm^{-1} in Table 2.

Passage III (Questions 83-87)

In a student experiment designed to demonstrate microscale extraction techniques, the three compounds shown in Figure 1 are dissolved in diethyl ether and separated. Their physical properties are shown in Table 1.

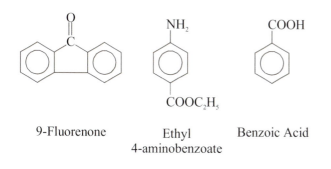

9-Fluorenone

Ethyl 4-aminobenzoate

Benzoic Acid

Figure 1 Compounds to be separated by extraction

The mixture is created by dissolving 50 mg of each compound in 4 mL of diethyl ether. 2 mL of 3 *M* HCl is added creating a two phase system. The system is mixed thoroughly and then allowed to separate. The aqueous layer is removed and the step is repeated with the remainder of the mixture.

6 *M* NaOH is added to the extracted aqueous solution. The solution is cooled in an ice bath and precipitate is collected and washed with distilled water. The precipitate is then weighed and the melting point is determined.

The remaining mixture is now separated by extraction with two 2 mL portions of 3 *M* NaOH. 6 *M* HCl is added to the alkaline solution, which is then cooled to form a precipitate. The precipitate is then weighed and the melting point is determined.

The remaining component is washed with distilled water. Next, 250 mg of Na_2SO_4 are added. The Na_2SO_4 is then filtered off using a filter pipet and the remaining solution is transferred to an Erlenmeyer flask. The Erlenmeyer flask is placed in a warm sand bath. A precipitate forms and is weighed and the melting point determined.

Compound	mp(°C)	bp(°C)	specific gravity
9-Fluorenone	122		
Ethyl 4-aminobenzoate	89		
Benzoic acid	154		
Diethyl ether		40	1.33

Table 1 Physical properties

83. What is the function of the Na_2SO_4 when added to the ether solution?

    A. Na_2SO_4 catalyzes the separation of the 9-fluorenone and ether.
    B. Na_2SO_4 catalyzes the separation of the benzoic acid and ether.
    C. Na_2SO_4 removes the remaining impurities of the solution.
    D. Na_2SO_4 acts as a drying agent.

84. Which of the following comes out in the aqueous layer of the first extraction with 3 *M* HCl?

    A. 9-fluorenone
    B. ethyl 4-aminobenzoate
    C. Benzoic acid
    D. diethyl ether

85. What is the expected molecular weight of the compound extracted by NaOH?

    A. 46
    B. 122
    C. 165
    D. 180

86. In the first extraction, the aqueous layer will be:

    A. below the organic layer because it has a lower density than the organic layer.
    B. below the organic layer because it has a greater density than the organic layer.
    C. above the organic layer because it has a lower density than the organic layer.
    D. above the organic layer because it has a greater density than the organic layer.

87. What is the purpose of the warm sand bath?

    A. Heat evaporates the ether concentrating the 9-fluorenone.
    B. Heat evaporates the ether concentrating benzoic acid.
    C. Heat accelerates the endothermic precipitation reaction.
    D. Heat accelerates the exothermic precipitation reaction.

GO ON TO THE NEXT PAGE.

Questions 88 through 92 are **NOT** based on a descriptive passage.

88. IR spectroscopy is normally used to distinguish between:

A. neighboring protons on different compounds.
B. neighboring protons on the same compound.
C. different functional groups on the same compound.
D. acids and bases.

89. Which of the following is true concerning amino acids?

A. Amino acids are monoprotic.
B. Amino acids have peptide bonds.
C. The side chain on an α-amino acid determines its acidity relative to other α-amino acids.
D. All amino acids have water soluble side groups.

90. Peptide bond formation is an example of:

A. saponification.
B. electrophilic addition.
C. bimolecular elimination.
D. dehydration.

91. Trigylcerides are composed from which of the following?

A. esters, alcohols, and phospholipids
B. fatty acids, alcohol, and esters
C. fatty acids and glycerol
D. glycerol and fatty esters

92. Which of the following is water soluble?

A. a saturated fatty acid
B. an unsaturated fatty acid
C. the side chain on valine
D. glucose

STOP. IF YOU FINISH BEFORE TIME IS CALLED, CHECK YOUR WORK. YOU MAY GO BACK TO ANY QUESTION IN THIS TEST BOOKLET.

ANSWERS &
EXPLANATIONS
FOR
30-MINUTE IN-CLASS
EXAMS

ANSWERS FOR THE 30-MINUTE IN-CLASS EXAMS

Lecture 1	Lecture 2	Lecture 3	Lecture 4
1. D	24. C	47. A	70. C
2. B	25. D	48. B	71. B
3. A	26. C	49. C	72. C
4. D	27. B	50. B	73. A
5. B	28. C	51. D	74. C
6. A	29. A	52. D	75. A
7. D	30. C	53. B	76. B
8. A	31. A	54. D	77. A
9. C	32. C	55. B	78. A
10. C	33. B	56. A	79. C
11. C	34. D	57. D	80. A
12. A	35. C	58. B	81. A
13. C	36. C	59. C	82. A
14. C	37. B	60. A	83. D
15. D	38. C	61. C	84. B
16. A	39. A	62. B	85. B
17. A	40. D	63. A	86. C
18. C	41. B	64. A	87. A
19. A	42. C	65. C	88. C
20. C	43. B	66. B	89. C
21. D	44. B	67. A	90. D
22. C	45. A	68. C	91. C
23. D	46. A	69. D	92. D

MCAT ORGANIC CHEMISTRY

Raw Score	Estimated Scaled Score
23	15
22	14
21	13
19–20	12
18	11
17	10
15-16	9
14	8
12-13	7
11	6
10	5
8-9	4

EXPLANATIONS TO IN-CLASS EXAM FOR LECTURE 1

Passage I

1. **D is correct.**

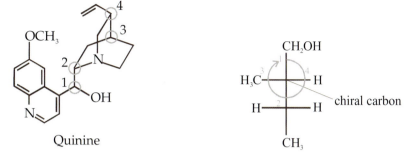

Quinine   chiral carbon

2. **B is correct.** Fermentation is anaerobic respiration. The passage states that (S)-2-methyl-1-butanol is the product of the fermentation of yeast. Looking at this molecule (above right), we prioritize the groups around the chiral carbon. Since the lowest priority group (the proton) is projected sideways, we must reverse the direction of our prioritization circle. This gives us the S configuration.

3. **A is correct.** The salts are stereoisomers because they have the same bond-to-bond connectivity, and they must be diastereomers because they can be separated by physical means (crystallization). Notice from the diagram that they are NOT mirror images of each other, and therefore cannot be enantiomers.

4. **D is correct.** Both A and C are wrong because they have the bromine attached to the wrong carbon to be the reactant. Since we know that configuration is retained, we simply substitute a hydrogen atom for the bromine and look for the molecule with the S configuration. (Remember, we are looking for the configuration of the product, not the reactant, so we must substitute the hydrogen for the bromine.) Retention of configuration does not mean that absolute configuration is retained; it means that there is no inversion. Because the lowest priority group is to the side in a Fischer projection, we reverse the direction of the circle shown below.

5. **B is correct.** The isomer on the left is a meso compound and has no enantiomer. Both isomers have the same bond-to-bond connectivity and are therefore diastereomers.

6. **A is correct.** Strychnine is the only chiral molecule and thus the only possibility. The passage states that the only chemical difference between enantiomers is their reactions with chiral compounds. Strychnine is often employed as a resolving agent for racemic acids.

Passage II

7. **D is correct.** The bromine ion is a negatively charged intermediate looking for a positive charge. Question: What's a halophile? Answer: Who cares? No one taking the MCAT. Answer choice A is a trap.

8. **A is correct.** The trans isomer will produce only a meso compound. If you're confused by this question, see the explanation to question 12 below.

9. **C is correct.** Carbocations are sp^2 hybridized and should be planar with bond angles of 120°.

10. **C is correct.** The reaction produces only certain stereoisomeric products so it is stereoselective. Experiment 2 says that the products depend upon the isomeric formation of the reactants, so it is stereospecific. Any reaction that is stereospecific is also stereoselective, but the converse is not true.

11. **C is correct.** The key is that the secondary carbocation is more stable than the primary (and most likely to form). You don't need to know what a halohydrin is to answer this question. Just look at Mechanism A, and substitute water for bromine as the nucleophile (the negatively charged species).

12. **A is correct.** Since the addition is always anti (attachment on opposite sides), only the meso compound will be formed. This is a very difficult question to visualize. Draw it out.

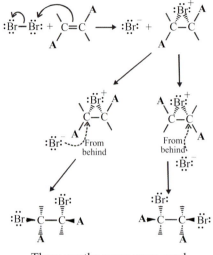

These are the same compound.
It is a meso compound

13. **C is correct.** Bromine will add to the alkane section of the ring when exposed to light via a radical reaction.

Passage III

14. **C is correct.** Acetyl CoA is a coenzyme. Vitamins are components of coenzymes.

15. **D is correct.** Isocitrate's third carbon is chiral. All of the other compounds' third carbons are attached to two distinct substituents and two identical substituents.

16. **A is correct.** The removal of either carbon 2 or 3 would break the chain, so the answer must be either carbon 1 or 4. The radio labeled carbon is carbon 4. Since this is removed in step 4 (as per the passage), the answer must be carbon 1.

17. **A is correct.** The labeled carbon is carbon 4, a carbonyl carbon throughout.

18. **C is correct.** An enol is both an alkene and an alcohol at the same carbon. The question refers to the tautomeric pairing of an alkene and enol. In that pairing, a proton shifts to the carbonyl oxygen and the oxygens' electrons form a carbon-carbon double bond. D is wrong because it does not have a carboxyl at both ends. A is wrong because it is a ketone – not an enol (A is α-ketogluterate). The carbon attached to the alcohol in B does not have a double bond, so it is wrong.

19. **A is correct.** The passage states that all known dehydrogenases are stereospecific in reactions with prochiral molecules. NADH is prochiral at the deuterium labeled carbon in answer choice A. B does not show a stereospecific reaction. In answer choice C a substitution reaction occurred at the amine, and an addition reaction occurred on the ring. This can't be correct. More importantly, in answer choice C the deuterium is not distinguishable from the hydrogen. This is not stereospecific. Answer choice D has too few hydrogens.

Stand Alones

20. **C is correct.** Meso compounds are (by definition) achiral although they do contain chiral carbons. They are not optically active (do not rotate plane-polarized light).

21. **D is correct.** All are true.

22. **C is correct.** If you missed this, try drawing the dash formula representation of this molecule and/or go back and study nomenclature.

23. **D is correct.** Conformational isomers, or conformers, are not true isomers. Conformers are different spatial orientations of the same molecule. Answer choices D and C are opposites, so one is likely to be true. At low temperatures, some conformers can be isolated.

EXPLANATIONS TO IN-CLASS EXAM FOR LECTURE 2

Passage I

Step one produces five dichlorobutanes among other products. These are separated by distillation to give:

(S)-sec-butylchloride

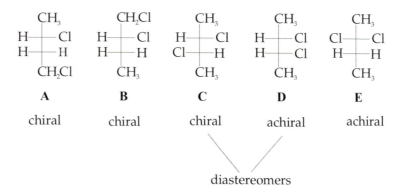

24. **C is correct.** The molecular weight of all the dichloro products would be 127 and differ from all other possible products in this regard.

25. **D is correct.** As per the passage, only compounds C and D are stereoisomers (thus answers A and B are wrong). But all the compounds are dichlorobutane, so any two must be structural isomers. Structural isomerism is the same as constitutional isomerism.

26. **C is correct.** This question simply asks, "Which compound is the enantiomer to (R,R)-2,3-dichlorobutane?" Since we have retention of configuration, only one enantiomer of 2,3-dichlorobutane is made. The one that is made will be a stereoisomer to the meso compound and will rotate plane-polarized light in the opposite direction of (R,R) enantiomer. Enantiomers rotate polarized light, so compound A, B, or C must be this enantiomer. And since C and D are stereoisomers, one must be the meso compound of 2,3-dichlorobutane and one must be the (SS) enantiomer of (R,R)-2,3-dichlorobutane.

27. **B is correct.** From the passage, the configurations of C and D appeared in a 7:3 ratio. As per question 26, C and D are the SS and SR configurations of 2,3-dichlorobutane.

28. **C is correct.** Compound E is achiral, and is not the meso compound because D is (see question 26). Answer A is meso. Answer choice B could not have been formed because there is a change in relative configuration about the original chiral compound. Answer D is chiral. Only answer choice C is left.

29. **A is correct.** A reaction will most likely occur via an S_N2 mechanism with Cl⁻ as the leaving group. The reaction would then proceed with inversion of configuration (and stereochemistry). Since the priority of OH and Cl are both first, the configuration of the product is R.

134 MCAT Organic Chemistry

Passage II

30. **C is correct.** 2,3-dibromobutane has two enantiomers and a meso compound. Four stereoisomers are possible according to the 2^n formula, but since there is a meso, only 3 exist.

31. **A is correct.** In product K the relative configurations are the same as the reactant. In product L, the relative configurations are reversed.

32. **C is correct.** A & B is a racemic mixture. C & I are the same meso compound. H & J are diastereomers, which rotate plane-polarized light to different degrees.

33. **B is correct.** The compounds are diastereomers, so they have different physical properties (like boiling points) and could thus be separated by distillation. A and D are wrong because both compounds have the same mass and the same functional groups. Neither group rotates polarized light, since Reaction 1 produces a meso compound and Reaction 2 produces a racemic mixture.

34. **D is correct.** The reaction would be a simple S_N2 reaction at the hydroxyl carbon proceeding with inversion of configuration to produce the meso compound.

35. **C is correct.** In pathway b, both configurations are inverted, and the halogen already attached to the molecule replaces the OH group.

36. **C is correct.** Although there are two steps, both reactants are required for the first step. The acid is needed to protonate the hydroxyl group. Products do not affect the initial rate.

Passage III

37. **B is correct.** Ether is the best choice for any solvent question on the MCAT. The passage states that the reagent will react with any hydrogen more acidic than an alkene hydrogen. A and D are more acidic than an alkene. C is a salt, not a solvent. In most cases, but not all, a solvent should not react with the reactants.

38. **C is correct.** The partially negative charged carbon on the Grignard reagent acts as a nucleophile and adds to the carbonyl carbon.

39. **A is correct.** Methyl alcohol is the strongest acid and will thus react the most vigorously with a Grignard reagent. The strongest acid is the primary alcohol with the shortest carbon chain.

40. **D is correct.** From the passage we know that the carbon attached to the Mg will act as a nucleophile on the carbonyl carbon. Only D will result in a tertiary alcohol.

41. **B is correct.** The passage states that the bond is covalent and polar and that the carbon is a good nucleophile. Thus the carbon would have a partial negative charge.

42. **C is correct.** Oxidation of a secondary alcohol always produces a ketone.

Stand Alones

43. **B is correct.** The dehydration of an alcohol forms a double bond.

44. **B is correct.** In this case, the differences in molecular weights (methane: 16; methanol: 32; chloromethane: 50.5; ammonia: 17) is outweighed by the extreme bond strength differences. Stronger intermolecular bonds increase boiling point. Hydrogen bonds are the strongest intermolecular bonds. Oxygen is more electronegative than nitrogen and so makes stronger hydrogen bonds. The boiling points are methane: -164; methanol: 65; chloromethane: -24.2; ammonia: -33. Notice that, although ammonia is one-third the weight of chloromethane, its hydrogen bonding gives it a boiling point nearly as high. By comparing the boiling points of ammonia and methanol (or even water), you should notice also how much stronger the hydrogen bonds of oxygen are than those of nitrogen.

45. **A is correct.** The hydroxyl group must be protonated in order for the alcohol to react with the chloride ion in an S_N2 reaction; there is no acid present to protonate the alcohol.

46. **A is correct.** The alcohol can form hydrogen bonds with water.

Copyright © 2005 Examkrackers, Inc.

EXPLANATIONS TO IN-CLASS EXAM FOR LECTURE 3

Passage I

47. **A is correct.** According to the passage, a Friedel-Crafts reaction substitutes *something* (an acyl group) onto a benzene ring in the presence of an acid. Steps 1 and 3 are the only steps that involve substituting onto a benzene ring.

48. **B is correct.** Step 2 must be a reduction reaction because we lose oxygen and gain two hydrogens.

49. **C is correct.** Benzene rings are activated by electron releasing groups and deactivated by electron withdrawing groups, so A and D must be wrong. The passage states that acyl groups are electron withdrawing, so B must be wrong. The passage also states that acyl groups block the Friedel-Crafts reaction. Step 2 removes the ketone, which is an acyl group.

50. **B is correct.** Scheme 1, step 1 shows an anhydride reacting with an aromatic ring in the presence of $AlCl_3$ to form a carboxylic acid and a ketone. This reaction has the same form. This is a Friedel-Crafts reaction.

51. **D is correct.** There are two meta positions out of five possible positions. $2/5 = 0.4$ or 40%.

52. **D is correct.** According to the passage, the acylium ion must be positively charged because it acts as an electrophile, so A and C are out. B is no good because the acylium ion attacks the benzene ring so it must be producible from the anhydride in step 1. That leaves only D.

Passage II

53. **B is correct.** Reaction 2 shows an aldehyde being oxidized to a carboxylate ion to form the precipitate. Answer A is true, but does not answer the question. C and D are false.

54. **D is correct.** According to the passage, red coloring indicates a highly conjugated product. Only choice D has alternating double and single bonds.

55. **B is correct.** Water is lost.

56. **A is correct.** Nitrogen often acts as a nucleophile.

57. **D is correct.** Tautomerization involves a proton shift where the double bond of the carbonyl shifts to the carbonyl/α-carbon bond when the carbonyl oxygen is protonated. You should memorize tautomer formatio and structure.

58. **B is correct.** Alcohols add to aldehydes and ketones to form hemiacetals and hemiketals, respectively. You should be able to recognize this reaction for the MCAT.

59. **C is correct.** You should know that an aldehyde will demonstrate a peak (downfield) when compared to a ketone.

Passage III

60. **A is correct.** The carbonyl group withdraws negative charge, stabilizing the conjugate base of pyruvate.

61. **C is correct.** Ketones can be reduced to yield secondary alcohols.

62. **B is correct.** The first equivalent of lithium aluminum hydride reduces the carboxylic acid to the primary alcohol, which is then completely reduced by the second equivalent of the hydride. The secondary alcohol does not reduce easily with lithium aluminum hydride.

63. **A is correct.** Lactic acid is a by-product of anaerobic respiration. Under active use conditions, some muscle tissues switch completely to anaerobic respiration.

64. **A is correct.** Aerobic means O_2 is present.

65. **C is correct.** Inorganic acid chlorides react with carboxylic acids by nucleophilic substitution to form acyl clorides; you should memorize this reaction.

66. **B is correct.** Lactate can form hydrogen bonds, which increase its water solubility and boiling point.

Stand Alones

67. **A is correct.** The chlorine ion is the weakest base, then the alkoxide ion, then the NH_2^-. Note that you don't need to know what an acid chloride is to answer the question.

68. **C is correct.** Oxidation of a primary alcohol produces an aldehyde, not a ketone; note that you don't need to know the Friedel-Crafts reaction to answer this question.

69. **D is correct.** Carbonyl carbons don't have a lone pair of electrons.

EXPLANATIONS TO IN-CLASS EXAM FOR LECTURE 4

Passage I

See page 132 for a complete diagram of Passage I. Structure 1 is eliminated by steps 1, 2, and 3; structure 2 is eliminated by steps 2 and 3; structure 4 is not eliminated except by step 4; structures 5 and 6 are eliminated by step 2; structure 7 is eliminated by steps 1 and 3; and structure 8 is eliminated by step 3.

70. **C is correct.** Glucose has four chiral carbons so there are 2^4 possible stereoisomers for glucose. The passage shows half of them.

71. **B is correct.** Converting an aldehyde or a primary alcohol into a carboxylic acid is done via oxidation. If you didn't remember this, you are reminded in step 2 of the passage.

72. **C is correct.** Step 2 removes the top carbon from each structure and places a CH_2OH group group at both ends of the new, 5-carbon structures. When looking at the original 8 aldohexose structures, you should notice that molecules 1 & 2 are epimers with respect to carbon #2; 3 & 4 are epimers with respect to carbon # 2; 5 & 6 are epimers with respect to carbon # 2, and 7 & 8 are epimers with respect to carbon #2. Since the treatment of step 2 is removing carbon # 1 from all 8 aldohexoses and replacing carbon #2 with a non-chiral center, then performing step 2 will convert compounds 1 & 2 to the same compound after treatment; the same is true for structures 3 & 4, 5 & 6, and 7 & 8. Thus, If you can eliminate compound 1, then you can eliminate compound 2, and vice versa; the same can be applied to 3 & 4, 5 & 6, and 7 & 8. It should be obvious that structures 1 & 2 give optically inactive molecules with a plane of symmetry; thus answer choices B and D can be eliminated because they do not contain both compounds 1 & 2. Molecules 3 and 4 and 7 & 8 give optically active compounds. Molecules 5 and 6 generate a plane of symmetry through the new carbon # 3 (previously carbon # 4); eliminating answer choice A.

73. **A is correct.** C and D are wrong because for a D-isomer, the hydroxyl group on the second carbon from the bottom must be on the right. Furthermore, if the hexoses that are created by the Kiliani-Fischer synthesis from B, C, and D were degraded and oxidized by nitric acid, all would result in meso compounds (optically inactive). To see this, add one chiral carbon just below the aldehyde (making both epimers). Now replace the end groups with carboxylic acids. All now form (at least one) meso compound. You don't need to know the structure of mannose for the MCAT and it is not given in the passage, so you know that this is extra information. Ignore it. As for answer A, the passage explains that the Kiliani-Fischer synthesis adds one more chiral carbon above the other chiral carbons of an aldose as viewed in a Fischer projection. Answer A must be correct because structure 3 in Figure 1 is glucose. If you recognized the structure of glucose, you could have made this question easier, but the passage also states (in step 2) that, when degraded and oxidized by nitric acid, glucose leaves an optically active compound.

74. **C is correct.** A pair of enantiomers would be formed by the addition of one chiral carbon. Only one configuration of glyceraldehyde is used, so that chiral carbon does not increase the number of enantiomers.

75. **A is correct.** 1 and 7 produce meso compounds, which are optically inactive.

76. **B is correct.** This question is answerable from the information in step 4 alone. If you do step 4 on all the answer choices, only structure 4 produces the same sugar.

Passage II

77.   **A is correct.** Anhydrides can participate in an acylation reaction in which half of the anhydride adds to another molecule and the other half yields a carboxylic acid. Simply counting the total atoms in the reactants and subtracting the total atoms of the products shown for reaction 1 can give you a clue to answer this question.

78.   **A is correct.** You should probably memorize that a carbonyl stretch is 1700. Remember that IR measures the existence of functional groups.

79.   **C is correct.** The integral value is three. This is the only place where there are three protons.

80.   **A is correct.** A Grignard is a strong base and will react with water.

81.   **A is correct.** This should be an easy question. Each ring in isolation (cyclopentadienyl anion; not bonding to the metal atom) has a negative charge giving it 6 pi electrons, which equals $4n + 2$ where $n = 1$.

82.   **A is correct.** The protons close to the iron would have a different chemical shift than the protons farther from the iron. There are three different carbons with hydrogens attached: the ones attached to the iron, the ones attached to those, and the ones attached to those.

Passage III

83.   **D is correct.** Water has some slight solubility in organic extracts. Inorganic anhydrous salts such as magnesium, sodium, and calcium sulfate readily form insoluble hydrates, removing the water from wet organic phases. Answers A and B must be wrong because the ether is distilled from the last fraction in the sand bath. There is no basis for thinking sodium sulfate could remove impurities.

84.   **B is correct.** The acid protonates the basic amino group on ethyl 4-aminobenzoate, making it soluble in the aqueous solution. The other compounds are not basic and would not be made soluble by the acid.

85.   **B is correct.** The benzoic acid will be deprotonated by NaOH, making it soluble in the aqueous layer. The MW of benzoic = 122.

86.   **C is correct.** From the table, we see that diethyl ether has a greater density than water, which will make it sink. However, this is NOT always true for extractions; sometimes the aqueous layer is heavier.

87.   **A is correct.** From Table 1 we see that ether has a low boiling point. As the ether evaporates, the neutral compound, 9-fluorenone, is concentrated.

Stand Alones

88.   **C is correct.** IR distinguishes functional groups.

89.   **C is correct.** All amino acids are at least diprotic compounds; under appropriate conditions, both the carboxyl and amino groups can act as acids (some side chains can also act as acids, making some amino acids triprotic), so A is wrong. Proteins have peptide bonds, not amino acids, so B is wrong. D is wrong because some amino acids (like leucine) have nonpolar side groups.

90.   **D is correct.** Water is removed to form peptide bonds.

91.   **C is correct.** Fatty acids and the three-carbon backbone of glycerol form triglycerides.

92.   **D is correct.** Valine's side chain is hydrophobic. Fats are hydrophobic, and glucose is soluble in water.

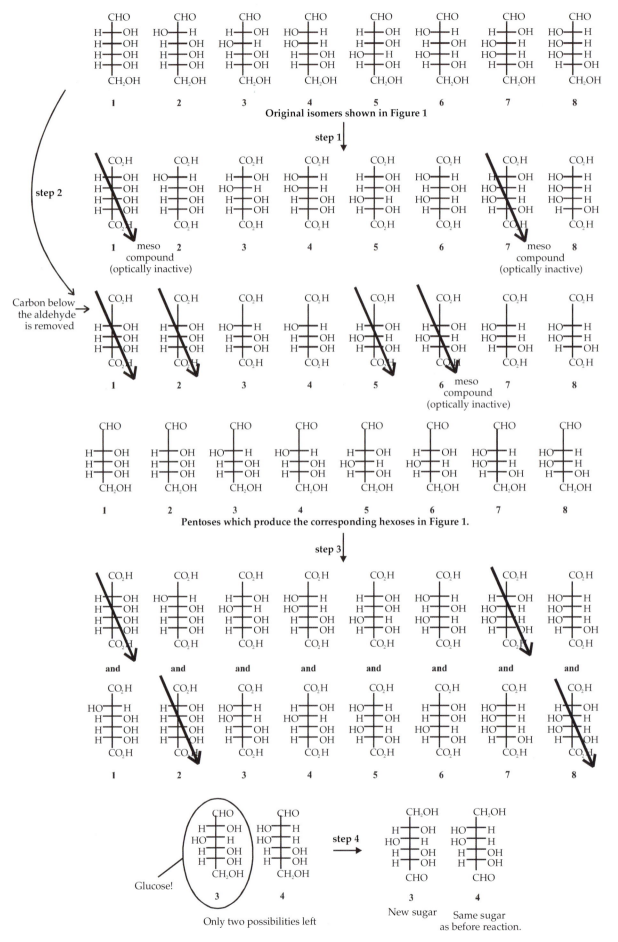

Steps used by Fischer to determine glucose

Original isomers shown in Figure 1

Pentoses which produce the corresponding hexoses in Figure 1.

ANSWERS &
EXPLANATIONS
FOR
LECTURE QUESTIONS

ANSWERS TO THE LECTURE QUESTIONS

Lecture 1	Lecture 2	Lecture 3	Lecture 4
1. A	25. A	49. D	73. C
2. B	26. C	50. A	74. C
3. D	27. D	51. D	75. B
4. C	28. D	52. A	76. C
5. B	29. D	53. D	77. C
6. B	30. C	54. A	78. C
7. B	31. B	55. C	79. A
8. B	32. C	56. D	80. C
9. A	33. C	57. D	81. C
10. C	34. D	58. C	82. A
11. B	35. A	59. A	83. A
12. D	36. D	60. A	84. C
13. D	37. B	61. B	85. A
14. C	38. D	62. A	86. C
15. C	39. B	63. A	87. C
16. B	40. B	64. D	88. D
17. A	41. C	65. D	89. C
18. C	42. B	66. B	90. C
19. B	43. A	67. C	91. B
20. D	44. D	68. A	92. A
21. B	45. C	69. B	93. B
22. D	46. C	70. D	94. A
23. B	47. B	71. A	95. D
24. C	48. B	72. C	96. C

EXPLANATIONS TO THE QUESTIONS IN LECTURE 1

1. **A is correct.** Of course no MCAT test-taker would be expected to know this reaction. The entire first half of this question is misdirection. The clue is that there must be six carbons because there is a substituent on the sixth carbon. Next, the carbons must be numbered starting from one end of the chain. Carbon one is the anomeric carbon (the one attached to the oxygen in the ring and an O-methyl group). The O-methyl group on this carbon is represented by the first methyl in the name *methyl* β-2,3,4,6-tetra-O-methyl-D-glucoside. There are four more O-methyl groups attached to their respective numbered carbons. Answer **B** doesn't have a sixth carbon if we account for five methyl groups. Answers C and D don't have enough methyl groups.

2. **B is correct.** Of course you don't need to know the structure of benzamide. But you should know that it's an amide derivative of benzene. B is the only amine with benzene. Also, you will see in Organic Chemistry Lecture 2 that benzene undergoes substitution, so answers C and D imply that a nitrogen has replaced a carbon atom in the benzene ring; these structures cannot be correct. Answer choice A is the amine derivative of benzene, aniline, not the amide derivative. And finally, D requires a positive charge on the nitrogen atom.

3. **D is correct.** The most stable bond is the bond with the highest bond energy. Remember, bond energy is the average energy needed to break a bond (closely related to bond dissociation energy). Bond energy is actually negative potential energy, so the higher the magnitude, the lower the energy level, the more energy necessary to break the bond, and the more stable the bond. The highest bond energy is between the methyl group bonded to a ring structure. All ring structures are unsaturated.

4. **C is correct.** You must be able to recognize the basic functional groups.

5. **B is correct.**

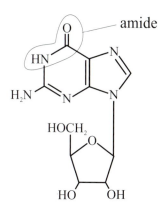

guanosine

6. **B is correct.** Amines (—NH_2) behave as weak Lewis bases and are most similar to ammonia (NH_3). A Lewis base is any species that can donate a pair of electrons and form a coordinate covalent bond. Amides contain a carbonyl carbon and therefore are not similar to ammonia. Ether and ethanol are not nitrogen-containing compounds.

7. **B is correct.**

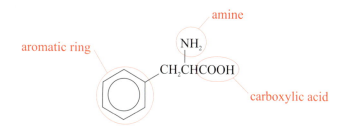

8. **B is correct.** The following IUPAC rules of nomenclature must be used to name an alkane:

    • Find the longest continuous carbon chain to serve as parent name – in this case, nonane.

    • Number the carbons of the parent chain, beginning at the end nearest to the most branch points.

    • Identify and number the parent chain substituents – in this case, two methyl (on carbons 4,7) and one ethyl (on carbon 3) groups.

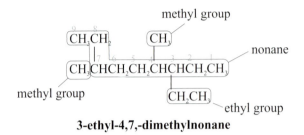

3-ethyl-4,7,-dimethylnonane

9. **A is correct.** B is missing a hydrogen. C has the charges reversed. In D, nitrogen has five bonds.

10. **C is correct.** The number of σ-bonds on the three species respectively is 3, 4, 3.

11. **B is correct.** The bonds are stabilized by resonance and are shorter and stronger than carbon-carbon alkane bonds but longer and weaker than carbon-carbon alkene bonds.

12. **D is correct.** A π-bond has 100% *p* character and is at a higher energy level than a σ-bond.

13. **D is correct.** Moving atoms is a violation of the rules of resonance. The actual molecule is always at a lower energy level than any of its resonance structures. Although A and B are true, they don't answer the question. Notice that A and B say the same thing. This is a good indicator that they are both wrong.

14. **C is correct.** *sp* hybridization allows the formation of a triple bond, which consists of one σ-bond and two π-bonds. Triple bonds display 180° bond angle linear geometry and are stronger than double or single bonds. Double bonds are sp² hybridized with 120° trigonal planar geometry. *sp³* hybridization, such as seen in the single bonds of tetrahedral compounds (i.e., methane), have 109.5° angles.

15. **C is correct.** NaCl and CCl$_4$ are provided as reference compounds.

Compound	Dipole moment (D)
NaCl	8.75
CH$_3$Cl	1.95
H$_2$O	1.85
H$_2$C=N=N	1.50
Benzene	0
CCl$_4$	0

16. **B is correct.** The rule of thumb is that any carbon chain with four or fewer carbons is usually a gas. 2-methylbutane is a five-carbon compound and is therefore a liquid. A skeletal backbone of 16 carbons or more is usually seen in lipids and waxes.

17. **A is correct.** At least one of the double-bonded carbons in every other answer choice has two substituents exactly the same.

18. **C is correct.** C is the only carbon attached to four different substituents so is therefore the only chiral carbon.

19. **B is correct.** B is a meso compound with a plane of symmetry through the middle of the oxygen atom and the third carbon. All three other molecules are chiral.

20. **D is correct.** A has no chiral carbon. B is named improperly. It is a trichloro compound. C is a meso compound. In D, the number 4 carbon is chiral. Any chiral molecule has an enantiomer.

21. **B is correct.** Both carbons are chiral in each compound, but B is a meso compound.

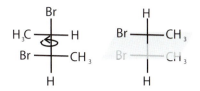

22. **D is correct.** All isomers are made up of the same set of elements and have identical molecular weights. Structural isomers are further subdivided by carbon chain differences, functional group position, and type variations. For instance, ethyl alcohol and dimethyl ether are structural isomers.

$$CH_3CH_2OH \qquad CH_3OCH_3$$

    Ethyl alcohol   Dimethyl ether

23. **B is correct.** Absolute configuration describes the R or S configuration around a chiral atom. Observed rotation describes the direction of rotation of plane-polarized light. The direction of rotation cannot be predicted by the absolute configuration alone.

24. **C is correct.** Diastereomers – epimers, anomers, and geometric isomers – are stereoisomers that are not mirror images of each other. A meso compound is an achiral molecule, which is identical to its mirror image.

EXPLANATIONS TO THE QUESTIONS IN LECTURE 2

25. **A is correct.** A contains no tertiary carbons.

26. **C is correct.** Bromine is the most selective.

27. **D is correct.** Cycloheptane has the most ring strain and is at the greatest energy level. It will produce more heat per mole than methane or ethane because it is a larger molecule.

28. **D is correct.** *Cis* groups on cyclohexane will never be both equatorial or both axial while in the chair configuration.

29. **D is correct.** Only termination does not produce a radical. Conjugation is not a step in halogenation.

30. **C is correct.** Alkanes (i.e., *n*-butane) are a class of saturated hydrocarbons containing only carbon-carbon single bonds. They are unreactive and are either straight-chained or branched. Cycloalkanes (i.e., cyclobutane), on the other hand, contain rings of carbon atoms. Although free rotation is possible around carbon-carbon single bonds in alkanes, geometric hindrance greatly reduces the possibility of rotation in cycloalkanes. For this reason, cycloalkanes are "stuck" as cis or trans isomers. The cis isomer has both substituents on the same side of the ring, while the trans form has substituents on opposite sides of the cycloalkane ring.

31. **B is correct.** Primary hydrogen atoms are attached to primary carbons. Primary carbons are bound to only one other carbon. This parent compound houses five primary carbons with three hydrogens on each one.

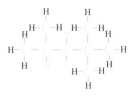

32. **C is correct.** There are four main reaction types seen in organic chemistry: addition, elimination, substitution and rearrangement. In an *addition reaction* (A + B → C), two reactants add together to form a single product. One reactant splitting into two products is known as an *elimination reaction* (A → B + C). *Substitutions*

(A—B + C—D → A—C + B—D) occur when two reactants exchange parts to yield two new products. *Rearrangement reaction* (A → B) is defined by a reactant undergoing bond reorganization to give an entirely new product.

---

33. **C is correct.** The most stable alkene is the most substituted. *Trans* is more stable than *cis*.

34. **D is correct.** The most reactive will be the one with the lowest energy of activation. Since D makes the most stable carbocation (a tertiary carbocation), it is the most reactive in an electrophilic addition reaction.

35. **A is correct.** Don't let the ring structure intimidate you. Look for the functional groups and ask yourself "How do they react?" The only functional group that we know here is alkene. It's not electrophilic addition; it must be ozonolysis of an alkene. Ozone is highly reactive. It rips right through the double bond of an alkene. The result is a cleavage of the alkene at the double bond to form two aldehydes.

36. **D is correct.** This reaction is dehydration of an alcohol and proceeds with rearrangement of the carbocation intermediate from secondary to tertiary. (See page 35.)

37. **B is correct.** This is hydration of an alkene and follows Markovnikov's rule.

38. **D is correct.** Anthracene is a larger version of benzene, a prototypic aromatic compound. It satisfies Huckel's rule, which states that if a compound has *planar, monocyclic rings with 4n + 2 š electrons* (n being any integer, including zero), it is by definition an aromatic compound. Benzene houses six š electrons, a pair for each double bond (while anthracene has 14 π electrons).

39. **B is correct.** The question stem presents a mechanism for an elimination reaction (the product gains a double bond) that relies on a rapid C—H bond dissociation as the rate-limiting step. When the heavier deuterium (D) is used instead of a pure hydrogen atom, the reaction rate decreases because of a stronger carbon—deuterium bond.

40. **B is correct.** Isoprene is a diene (alkene), which occupies an irregular shape as a result of all those double bonds. When stretched, disorganized chains straighten out but can always revert back to their original random state. Isoprene *vulcanization* (cross-link induction) serves to prevent stretching.

---

41. **C is correct.** The hydroxide ion is more basic than the chloride ion and substitution will not result unless the hydroxide is protonated to make water, which is less basic than the chloride ion. The answer choices requiring knowledge of solvents should be immediately dismissed as being too difficult for the MCAT.

42. **B is correct.** This is an S_N1 reaction and increasing the concentration of the nucleophile will not affect the rate of the reaction because the slow step is the formation of a carbocation. Adding heat always increases the rate of the reaction.

43. **A is correct.** Reduction of a ketone produces a secondary alcohol. In this case two ketones were reduced. You might recognize $LiAlH_4$ as a reducing agent but you don't need to.

44. **D is correct.** D is not a hydrogen bond. For a hydrogen bond to occur, a N, O, or F must be intermolecularly bonded (the hydrogen bond itself) to a H that is covalently bonded to another N, O, or F.

45. **C is correct.** Regardless of whether or not the mechanism is S_N1 or S_N2, the hydroxyl group will not leave until it has been protonated. For S_N1, the formation of the cation, although rate determining, is very fast after protonation. For S_N2, the chloride ion must collide with the opposite side of a protonated molecule, so many collisions do not result in a reaction. Thus, S_N1 is faster. Tertiaries are the fastest to react in S_N1, then secondaries. Primaries react only through S_N2. Tertiaries react in less than a minute; secondaries in 1 to 5 minutes; while primaries may take days. This is a very tough MCAT question. You may have two of these per MCAT at the most. The important thing on a question like this is not to spend too much time. Narrow it down to A or C and take your best guess.

46. **C is correct.** Anti-Markovnikov alkene free radical addition is demonstrated by reaction mechanisms 1 and 2, both of which rely on peroxides as reagents. Based on the experimental results provided by the question stem, anti-Markovnikov addition only succeeds using HBr.

47. **B is correct.** S_N1 *substitution reaction:*

- two-step reaction
- follows first order reaction kinetics (rate = $k[S]$)
- proceeds through a carbocation intermediate
- prefers tertiary carbons to increase carbocation stability
- prefers protic solvent
- produces a racemic mixture of products

S_N2 *substitution reaction:*

- one-step reaction
- follows second-order reaction kinetics (rate = $k[S][Nucleophile]$)
- proceeds through a transition state
- prefers primary carbons
- prefers aprotic solvent
- produces optically active product
- causes an inversion of stereochemistry

48. **B is correct.** S_N1 mechanism depends on the rate-limiting step, which is the carbocation formation and is nucleophile independent; all subsequent steps occur at a much faster rate and do not affect the rate of the reaction.

EXPLANATIONS TO THE QUESTIONS IN LECTURE 3

49. **D is correct.** Even if you don't recognize the reaction, the name aldol means that the product must be an alcohol. This eliminates C. You should recognize that the alpha hydrogen is the most reactive hydrogen on an aldehyde or ketone. For A or B to be correct, the carbonyl hydrogen must be removed while the alpha hydrogen remains intact. Not likely. Notice also that since in an aldol reaction between two aldehydes the product must be an aldehyde, A, B, and C are eliminated; they are ketones.

50. **A is correct.** Only H_x is an alpha hydrogen. Aldehydes and ketones typically undergo nucleophilic addition, not substitution.

51. **D is correct.** The reduction of an aldehyde results in a primary alcohol. A and B are the same molecule; both secondary alcohols.

52. **A is correct.** Ketones reduce more easily than esters. The first step is ketal formation to form blocking groups so that the ketone is not reduced. If the first step were omitted, the ketone would be reduced to a secondary alcohol.

53. **D is correct.** Water is a stronger acid than alcohol, which is stronger than aldehyde, which is stronger than ketone.

54. **A is correct.** When aldehydes are oxidized, they lose the hydrogen attached to the carbonyl carbon. Ketones have no such hydrogen to lose.

55. **C is correct.** Tautomerization is an equilibrium represented by a proton shift. Ketones tautomerize to form enols where the carbonyl carbon from the ketone becoms part of an alkene by forming a double bond with a neighboring carbon. In choice C, the carbonyl carbon does not form part of the alkene.

56. **D is correct.** The Tollens test gives a silver mirror for reducing sugars. Reducing sugars are hemiacetals in their ring form and either aldehydes or ketones in their straight-chain form. Acetals do not open easily because they contain the blocking groups discussed under "Formation of Acetals". However, to answer this question you just need to see that methyl β-glucoside is an acetal. Choice A is incorrect because glucose is an aldehyde and reduces Tollens reagent. Choice B is irrelevant because neither sugar is a ketone. Additionally, Tollens reagent promotes enediol rearrangement of ketones to aldehydes. Choice C is incorrect because glucose is a hemiacetal that opens to an aldehyde and reacts with Tollens reagent.

57. **D is correct.** Alkenes have no N, O, or F with which to hydrogen bond.

58. **C is correct.** This is an esterification reaction. (See page 66.)

59. **A is correct.** Carboxylic acids typically undergo nucleophilic substitution, not addition.

60. **A is correct.** This question may require a little too much knowledge for the MCAT. It is more likely that a question like this will be associated with a passage that explains reactivity of carboxylic acid derivatives. To find the answer, we look at the strengths of the leaving groups:

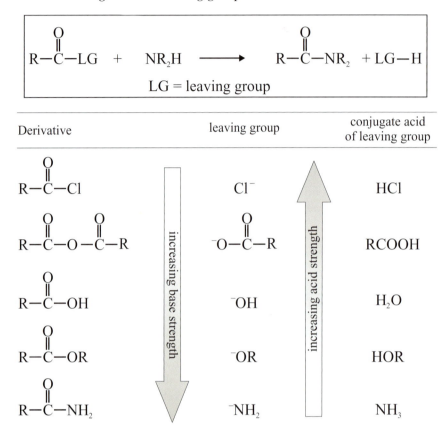

The weakest leaving group is the most stable and the most likely to be formed.

61. **B is correct.** This is the only methyl ketone listed.

62. **A is correct.** The anhydride reacts with ammonia to form an amide and a carboxylate ion. The addition of acid to the carboxylate creates carboxylic acid.

63. **A is correct.** NO_2 is an electron withdrawing substituent (deactivating) that stabilizes the methyl benzoate, decreasing reactivity. This will make the compound safer for transport and storage.

64. **D is correct.** Stronger conditions take the reaction further. Under acidic and basic conditions, an amide hydrolyzes to a carboxylic acid.

---

65. **D is correct.** The quaternary amine with all alkyl groups is not basic at all since its electrons have already been donated.

66. **B is correct.** Ammonia can donate a pair of electrons to act as a Lewis base.

67. **C is correct.** This molecule cannot hydrogen bond as easily as the others.

68. **A is correct.** The amine acts as a nucleophile and adds to the ketone. You should be able to predict this based upon your knowledge of amines and/or ketones.

69. **B is correct.** This is a simple alkylation of an amine. You should have this reaction memorized. Even if you don't, only B and D are possibilities for a base. Ethyl-methylamine is not an acid.

70. **D is correct.** Epoxides, oxygen-containing cyclic compounds, have much higher reactivity levels than other

ethers. This is due to a highly strained three-member ring that can be opened by nucleophilic attack. Benzene is stabilized by electron delocalization, which is possible in aromatic compounds.

71.   **A is correct.** Sodium chloride is a prototypic example of an ionic bond. In a coordinate covalent bond, both shared electrons come from the same atom; for instance, a Lewis base (i.e., ammonia) or oxygen-containing compound (i.e., water). Although both shared electrons come from the same atom, a coordinate covalent bond is a single bond similar in chemical properties to a covalent bond.

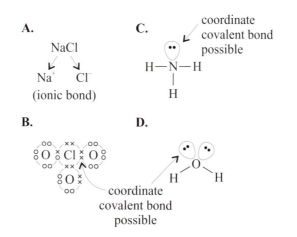

72.   **C is correct.** Cyclohexanone ketone is flanked by four acidic alpha hydrogens, which will be replaced by deuterium. Since each deuterium is twice as heavy as hydrogen, the atomic weight is expected to increase by four (from 98 to 102).

EXPLANATIONS TO THE QUESTIONS IN LECTURE 4

73.   **C is correct.** By definition, in electrophoresis negatively charged amino acids will move toward the anode. Only amino acids with an acidic isoelectric point will be negatively charged at a pH of 8. All amino acids except histidine, arginine, and lysine have acidic isoelectric points. Most likely on the MCAT, a question like this one would be accompanied with isoelectric points given in a passage. However, it is possible that a rare question would require you to memorize the three basic amino acids: histidine, arginine, and lysine.

74.   **C is correct.** This reaction is between a carboxylic acid and an alcohol to form an ester. See page 66.

75.   **B is correct.** The amino acid bias and shapes of the secondary structures (α-helix and β-pleated sheets) is partially explained by the rigid structure of the peptide bond, whose double bond character prevents rotation. This rigidity provides steric constraints on hydrogen bond formation for some amino acids that precludes them from participating, or even breaking secondary structure.

76.   **C is correct.** Saturated fats have the greatest energy storage potential, about twice that of carbohydrates and proteins.

77.   **C is correct.** The isoelectric point is where 100% of the amino acid exists as a zwitterion. The isoelectric point occurs at the first equivalence point.

78.   **C is correct.** The solubilities of amino acids differ based upon the R group. Phenylalanine has a benzene R group and is the least polar amino acid listed. The carboxylic acids and amines on the other R groups increase solubility. You may have also memorized the four groups of amino acid side chains as either nonpolar, polar, acidic, or basic. Acidic, basic, and polar amino acids have greater water solubility than nonpolar amino acids.

79. **A is correct.** You may read this question and be uncertain of what it means by "monomer". Such an experience is not uncommon on the MCAT. The minimum that you need to understand for this question is that a monomer is some type of "equivalent unit". Since it is an MCAT question, you should assume that monomer refers to something that you already know. You make this assumption because MCAT doesn't test science that is not covered in these books. Next you need to recognize the chemical shown as a polypeptide. You need to know that polypeptides are divided into amino acid residues, and you must be able to recognize where these residues begin and end.

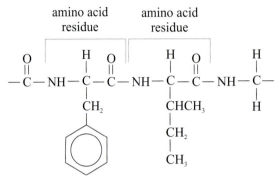

80. **C is correct.** A proline residue interrupts alpha-helix formation (and beta-pleated sheets) because the amide nitrogen has no hydrogen to contribute to the hydrogen bonding that drives and stabilizes the alpha-helix structure. Also, proline induces a kink, or turn in the polypeptide chain that further disrupts hydrogen bonding between neighboring amino acids in secondary structure.

---

81. **C is correct.** The formula for the number of isomers of a carbohydrate is 2^n, where n is the number of chiral carbons.

82. **A is correct.** In this question you must know that glucose is an aldehyde and that an aldehyde and alcohol react to form, first, a hemiacetal. If a second equivalent of alcohol is added, an acetal will form.

83. **A is correct.** Of the choices, only fructose is a ketose. Notice that you did not have to know anything about fruit in this question. This question could have been rephrased as, "Which of the following is a ketose?"

84. **C is correct.** The general formula for a carbohydrate is $C_n(H_2O)_n$. Since this carbohydrate is in the Fischer projection with the aldehyde or ketone at the top, and the bottom chiral carbon is positioned to the right, it is of the D configuration. The only way to know about polarized light is to use a polarimeter.

85. **A is correct.** Carbohydrates have different functional groups on either end and cannot exist as a meso compound. Humans cannot digest all isomers of carbohydrates. Humans cannot digest L-glucose for example. You must know that glucose is an aldehyde.

86. **C is correct.** You may not remember that the gustatory receptors at the tip of the tongue stimulate a sweet taste. You don't need to because you should recognize that glucose and the artificial sweeteners can all hydrogen bond. You should also know that glucose ($C_{12}O_6H_{12}$) is a carbohydrate (is made from carbon and water alone), but the synthetic sweeteners are not. They contain nitrogen and other elements not contained in carbohydrates.

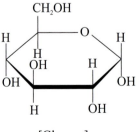

[Glucose]

87. **C is correct.** Carbon 5 hydroxyl group acts as a nucleophile by attacking the number 2 carbonyl carbon, leading to α or β furanose ring formation.

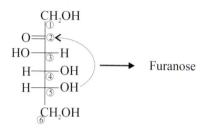

88. **D is correct.** Sugar A is a ketotriose and Sugar B is an aldoheptose.

___

89. **C is correct.** nmr deals with protons, not functional groups. D is true but is far more information about nmr than you are required to know.

90. **C is correct.** Extraction is separation based upon solubilitiy differences between molecules in a mixture.

91. **B is correct.** It is possible that one question on the MCAT may require specific knowledge of the IR table of frequencies for groups as basic as the carbonyl.

92. **A is correct.** The silica gel in TLC is polar and adsobs polar compounds stronger than nonpolar compounds; this results in polar compounds rising (migrating) more slowly.

93. **B is correct.** Distillation will not completely separate two compounds which form an azeotrope. Crystallization is a very inefficient method of purification. Distillation is more effective when done slowly.

94. **A is correct.** The *distillation process*, a workhorse of the chemical industry, relies on extreme varying of boiling points to separate complex chemical mixtures like petroleum. The tall towers seen at oil refineries are in fact distillation columns. *Liquid chromatography* is column chromatography, which separates compounds based on polarity, size, charge, and/or liquid or gas phase differences. *Nuclear magnetic resonance* (nmr) spectroscopy induces energy absorption to determine different types of carbon and/or hydrogen present in a compound.

95. **D is correct.** Dimethyl sulfoxide is a dipolar compound with a high boiling point as a result. It is miscible in water because it can hydrogen bond.

96. **C is correct.**

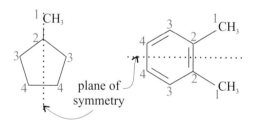

4 peaks on C^{13} nmr

INDEX

E

eclipsed 19

eicosanoids 75

electromagnetic waves 22

Electron donating groups 40-41

electron shielding 86

electron withdrawing group 40, 47

electronegativity 2, 15, 45

Electrophilic addition 36-37, 41, 60, 122, 138

elimination 33-35, 44-46, 107, 110, 112, 118, 122, 138

enamines 71

enantiomeric purity 24

enantiomers 23-24, 44, 70, 96-97, 99, 104, 113, 125, 127-128, 130, 137

enantiotropic 85

Enantiotropic hydrogens 85

enolate ion 56, 58

entgegen 25

epimers 25, 113, 118, 130, 137

Epoxides 51-52, 141

equatorial hydrogens 28

esters 48-49, 55, 65-66, 122, 139

ether 9, 38, 48, 51-52, 121, 128, 131, 135, 137

Extraction 84, 93-94, 121, 143

F

Fischer projection 3, 81, 125, 130, 142

formal charge 2

G

gas chromatography 92

geminal diol 58

geometric isomers 23-25, 137

Grignard 47-48, 107, 119, 128, 130

H

halogens 2, 4, 30, 32-33, 37-40

halohydrin 39, 99, 105, 125

Heat of Combustion 30, 79

hemiacetals 57

hemiketals 57

heterogeneous catalyst 36

HOMO 89-90

Huckel's rule 14, 42, 138

hybrid orbitals 12-13

hybridization 2, 12, 17-18, 62, 100, 136, 139

Hydration of an alkene 37, 41, 47

Hydroboration 38, 47

hydrogen bond 16, 43, 45, 51, 56, 71, 138, 140-141, 143

hydrogens 2-4, 28, 39, 47, 56, 59, 73, 76, 81, 84-87, 126, 129-130, 137, 141-142

hydrophilic 75, 77

hydrophobic 75, 77, 131

hydroxyproline 76

I

imines 71, 112

index of hydrogen deficiency 4

induced dipoles 15-16

infrared spectroscopy (IR) 84

instantaneous dipole moment 16

integral trace 86

Intermolecular attractions 16

inversion 45, 54, 106, 125, 127-128, 139

inverted 22, 128

isoelectric point 77-79, 141-142

K

ketal 57-58, 82, 139

ketones 48-50, 55-58, 60, 62, 67, 69, 71, 76, 112-113, 129, 138-139, 141

L

leaving group 35, 44-46, 50, 53, 58, 63, 66-67, 105, 115, 127, 140

levorotary 23

Lewis dot structure 1

lipolysis 75-76

localized 11

London Dispersion Forces 16

LUMO 89-90

M

Markovnikov's rule 36-37, 39, 138

Mass spectrometry 84, 90

mercurinium ion 37

meso compounds 25, 29, 82, 96, 101, 126, 130

meta 39-40, 129

methyl 9-10, 25, 27, 30-31, 35, 45-47, 62, 68-69, 72, 90, 96, 101, 120, 125, 128, 135-136, 139, 141

molecular ion 90

molecular shape 13

N

neighboring hydrogens 85-86

Newman projection 3

nitriles 71

U

Ultraviolet (UV) spectroscopy 89

unsaturated 9, 14, 60, 64, 75, 79, 122, 135

V

valence 2, 12

vic-dihalides 38

W

Ω-carbon 75

water 13, 16, 27, 33-35, 37-39, 46-47, 50-51, 53, 56, 58, 63-66, 68, 71-73, 81, 92, 94, 99-100, 107-108, 114, 118, 120-122, 125, 128-131, 138-139, 141-143

Z

zusammen 25

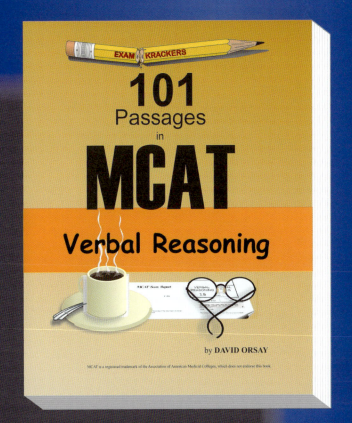

An Unedited Student Review of This Book

The following review of this book was written by Teri R—. from New York. Teri scored a 43 out of 45 possible points on the MCAT. She is currently attending UCSF medical school, one of the most selective medical schools in the country.

"The Examkrackers MCAT books are the best MCAT prep materials I've seen-and I looked at many before deciding. The worst part about studying for the MCAT is figuring out what you need to cover and getting the material organized. These books do all that for you so that you can spend your time learning. The books are well and carefully written, with great diagrams and really useful mnemonic tricks, so you don't waste time trying to figure out what the book is saying. They are concise enough that you can get through all of the subjects without cramming unnecessary details, and they really give you a strategy for the exam. The study questions in each section cover all the important concepts, and let you check your learning after each section. Alternating between reading and answering questions in MCAT format really helps make the material stick, and means there are no surprises on the day of the exam-the exam format seems really familiar and this helps enormously with the anxiety. Basically, these books make it clear what you need to do to be completely prepared for the MCAT and deliver it to you in a straightforward and easy-to-follow form. The mass of material you could study is overwhelming, so I decided to trust these books—I used nothing but the Examkrackers books in all subjects and got a 13-15 on Verbal, a 14 on Physical Sciences, and a 14 on Biological Sciences. Thanks to Jonathan Orsay and Examkrackers, I was admitted to all of my top-choice schools (Columbia, Cornell, Stanford, and UCSF). I will always be grateful. I could not recommend the Examkrackers books more strongly. Please contact me if you have any questions."

Sincerely,
Teri R—

About the Author

Jonathan Orsay is uniquely qualified to write an MCAT preparation book. He graduated on the Dean's list with a B.A. in History from Columbia University. While considering medical school, he sat for the real MCAT three times from 1989 to 1996. He scored in the 90 percentiles on all sections before becoming an MCAT instructor. He has lectured in MCAT test preparation for thousands of hours and across the country for every MCAT administration since August 1994. He has taught premeds from such prestigious Universities as Harvard and Columbia. He was the editor of one of the best selling MCAT prep books in 1996 and again in 1997. Orsay is currently the Director of MCAT for Examkrackers. He has written and published the following books and audio products in MCAT preparation: "Examkrackers MCAT Physics"; "Examkrackers MCAT Chemistry"; "Examkrackers MCAT Organic Chemistry"; "Examkrackers MCAT Biology"; "Examkrackers MCAT Verbal Reasoning & Math"; "Examkrackers 1001 questions in MCAT Physics", "Examkrackers MCAT Audio Osmosis with Jordan and Jon".

About the Editor

Dr. Jerry Johnson earned his B.S. in biology in 1999 and his Ph.D. in Biochemistry in 2003 from the University of Houston. As a student he conducted biochemistry workshops for the University and conducted research on mechanisms of mitochondrial reactive oxygen species production and oxidative phosphorylation. As a post-doctoral and NEI fellow at the University of Houston, College of Optometry Dr. Johnson continued his biochemistry workshops, conducted research on retinal toxicology and development and accepted an adjunct professorship with the University of Houston-Downtown campus to teach Cell Biology. Beginning in the fall of 2005, Dr. Johnson joined the faculty of the University of Houston-Downtown as a full-time Assistant Professor of Biology and Biochemistry. In addition to his teaching of biochemistry and cell biology, Dr. Johnson continues to conduct research focusing on mitochondrial physiology and enzymology, reactive oxygen species production and mechanisms of retinal development, toxicology and aging.

www.examkrackers.com
www.examkrackers.com

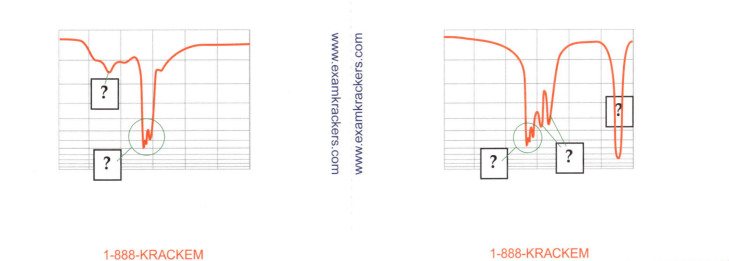

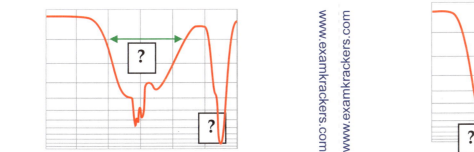

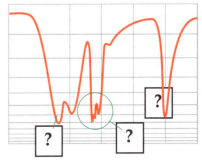

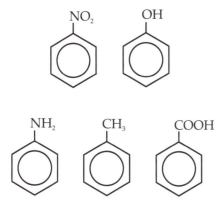

Name the Derivatives

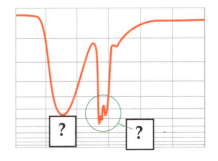

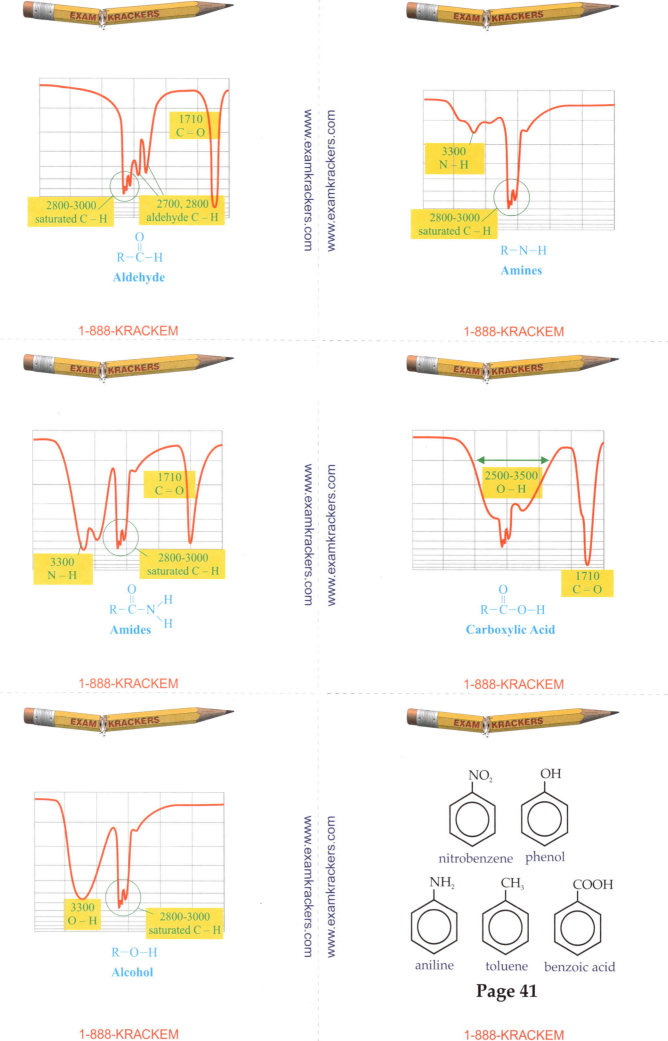

1710
C = O

2800-3000
saturated C – H

2700, 2800
aldehyde C – H

$$\overset{\displaystyle O}{\underset{\displaystyle R-C-H}{\|}}$$

Aldehyde

3300
N – H

2800-3000
saturated C – H

R – N – H

Amines

1710
C = O

3300
N – H

2800-3000
saturated C – H

$$\overset{\displaystyle O}{\underset{\displaystyle R-C-N}{\|}}\overset{H}{\underset{H}{<}}$$

Amides

2500-3500
O – H

1710
C = O

$$\overset{\displaystyle O}{\underset{\displaystyle R-C-O-H}{\|}}$$

Carboxylic Acid

3300
O – H

2800-3000
saturated C – H

R – O – H

Alcohol

NO_2

nitrobenzene

OH

phenol

NH_2

aniline

CH_3

toluene

COOH

benzoic acid

Page 41

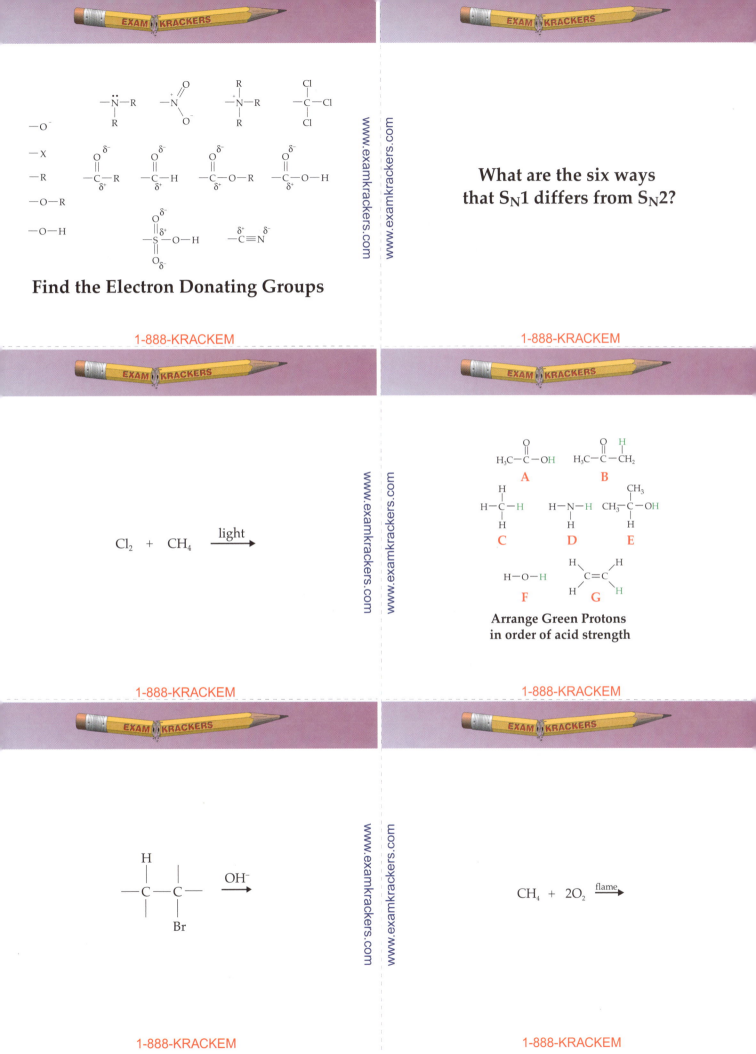

Find the Electron Donating Groups

What are the six ways that S_N1 differs from S_N2?

$$Cl_2 \ + \ CH_4 \xrightarrow{\text{light}}$$

Arrange Green Protons in order of acid strength

$$\overset{\displaystyle H}{\underset{\displaystyle Br}{-C-C-}} \xrightarrow{\text{OH}^-}$$

$$CH_4 \ + \ 2O_2 \xrightarrow{\text{flame}}$$

The nucleophile: S_N2 requires a strong nucleophile, while nucleophilic strength doesn't affect S_N1.

1st S: S_N2 reactions don't occur with a sterically hindered **Substrate**. S_N2 requires a methyl, primary, or secondary substrate, while S_N1 requires a secondary or tertiary substrate.

2nd S: A highly polar **Solvent** slows down S_N2 reactions by stabilizing the nucleophile.

3rd S: The **Speed** of an S_N2 reaction depends upon the concentration of the substrate and the nucleophile, while the speed of an S_N1 depends only on the substrate.

4th S: S_N2 inverts **Stereochemistry** about the chiral center, while S_N1 creates a racemic mixture.

5th S: S_N1 may be accompanied by carbon **Skeleton** rearrangement, but S_N2 never rearranges the carbon skeleton.

www.examkrackers.com

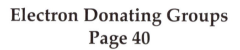

Electron Donating Groups
Page 40

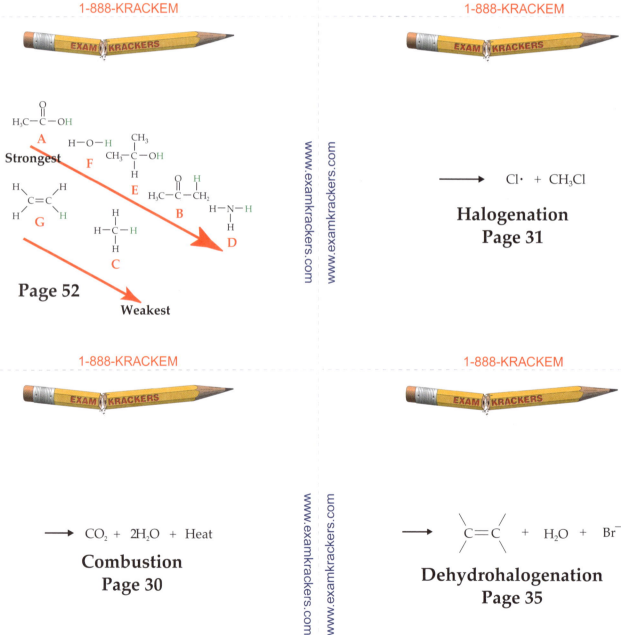

Page 52

Strongest

Weakest

www.examkrackers.com

$$\longrightarrow \quad Cl\cdot \ + \ CH_3Cl$$

Halogenation
Page 31

$$\longrightarrow \quad CO_2 \ + \ 2H_2O \ + \ Heat$$

Combustion
Page 30

www.examkrackers.com

$$\longrightarrow \quad C=C \ + \ H_2O \ + \ Br^-$$

Dehydrohalogenation
Page 35

$$CH_2{=}CH_2 \ + \ H_2 \xrightarrow{\text{Ni, Pd, or Pt}}$$

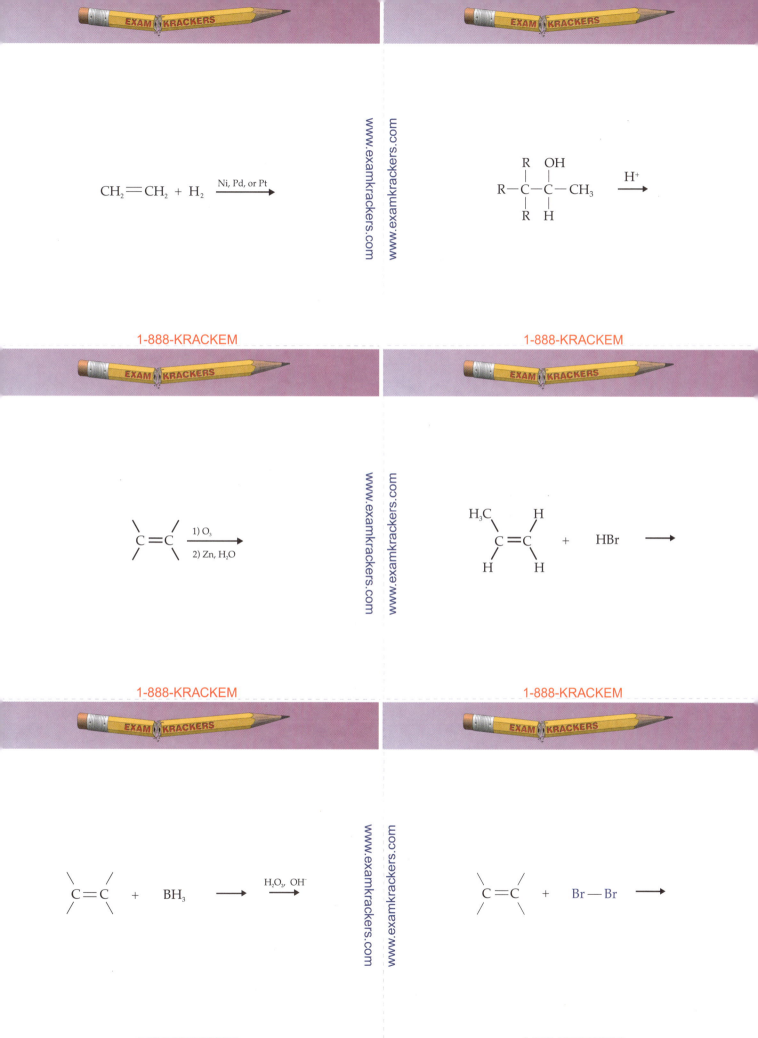

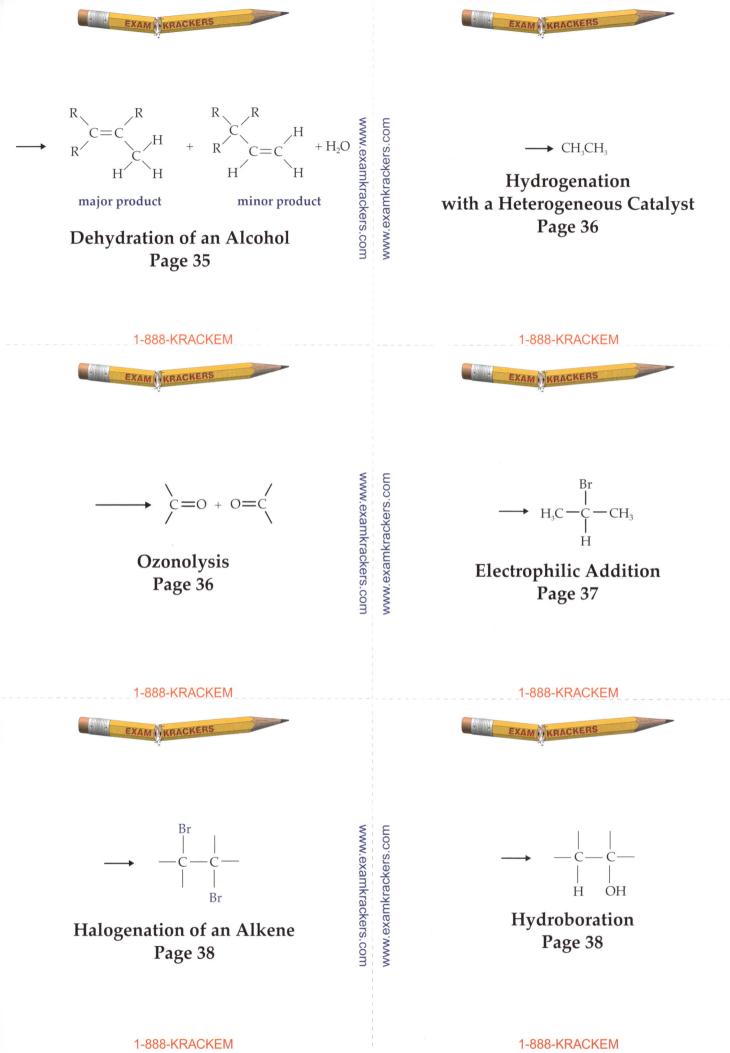

→

major product   +   minor product   + H₂O

Dehydration of an Alcohol
Page 35

→ CH₃CH₃

**Hydrogenation
with a Heterogeneous Catalyst
Page 36**

→ C=O + O=C

**Ozonolysis
Page 36**

→ H₃C—C—CH₃ (Br above, H below)

**Electrophilic Addition
Page 37**

→ —C—C— (Br above, Br below)

**Halogenation of an Alkene
Page 38**

→ —C—C— (H and OH below)

**Hydroboration
Page 38**

www.examkrackers.com

www.examkrackers.com

www.examkrackers.com

$$\text{C}=\text{C} \quad + \quad \text{Hg(OAc)}_2 \xrightarrow{\text{H}_2\text{O}} \xrightarrow{\text{NaBH}_4}$$

$$\text{RMgX} \quad + \quad \overset{R}{\underset{R}{\text{C}}}=\text{O} \xrightarrow{\quad} \xrightarrow{\text{H}_3\text{O}^+}$$

aldehyde

ketone

$\xrightarrow{\text{NaBH}_4}$

ester

$\xrightarrow{\text{LiAlH}_4}$

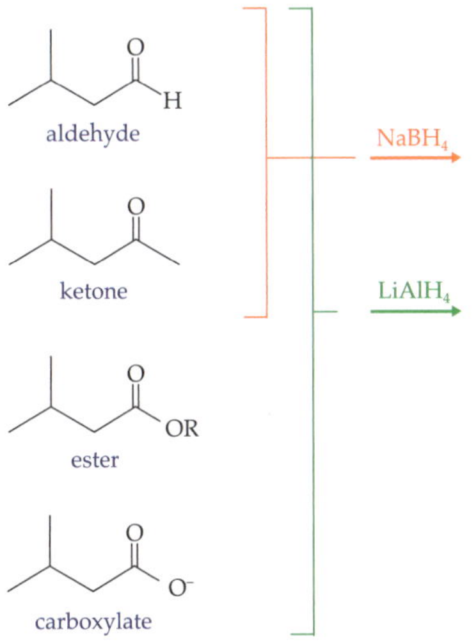

carboxylate

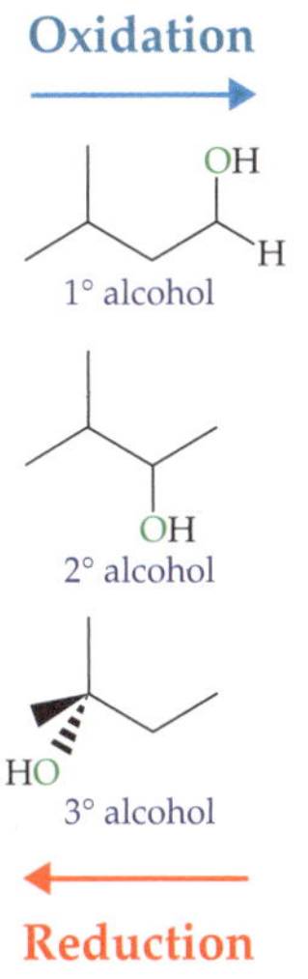

Oxidation

1° alcohol

2° alcohol

3° alcohol

Reduction

$$\text{CH}_3\text{CH}_2\text{OH} \quad + \quad \text{HCl} \xrightarrow{\quad}$$

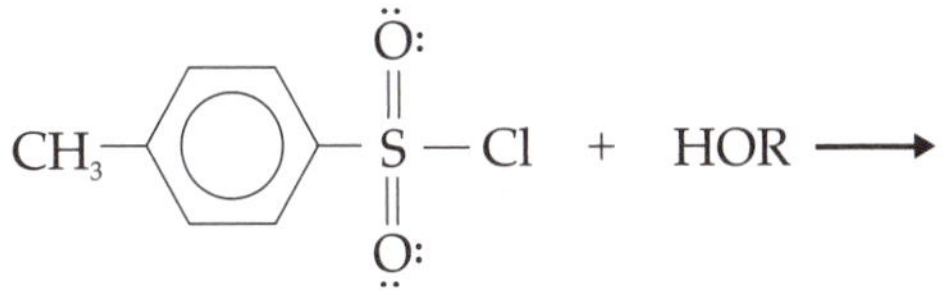

$$\text{CH}_3-\overset{\overset{\ddot{\text{O}}:}{\|}}{\underset{\underset{\ddot{\text{O}}:}{\|}}{\text{S}}}-\text{Cl} \quad + \quad \text{HOR} \xrightarrow{\quad}$$

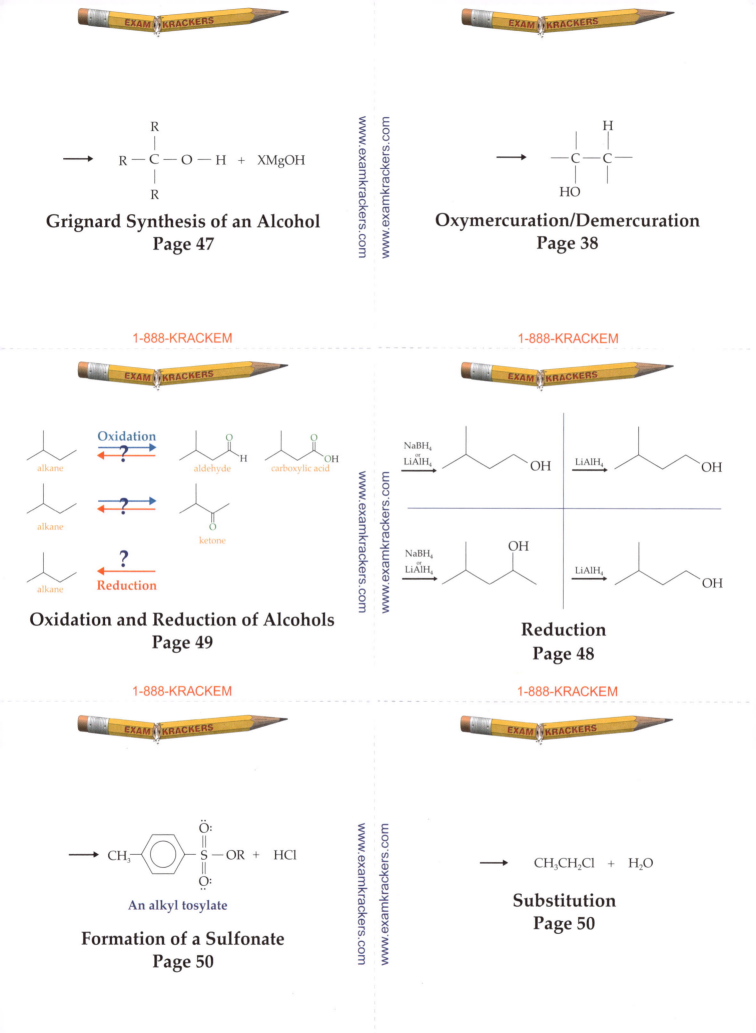

→ R—C—O—H + XMgOH

(with R groups on the central carbon)

Grignard Synthesis of an Alcohol
Page 47

→ —C—C—
HO

Oxymercuration/Demercuration
Page 38

Oxidation
?
?
Reduction

alkane → aldehyde → carboxylic acid
alkane → ketone
alkane

Oxidation and Reduction of Alcohols
Page 49

NaBH₄ or LiAlH₄ → OH   LiAlH₄ → OH

NaBH₄ or LiAlH₄ → OH   LiAlH₄ → OH

Reduction
Page 48

→ CH₃—⟨benzene ring⟩—S—OR + HCl
(with O: above and O: below S)

An alkyl tosylate

Formation of a Sulfonate
Page 50

→ CH₃CH₂Cl + H₂O

Substitution
Page 50

ROR + HBr ⟶

$$\underset{\text{vic diol}}{\underset{\overset{\displaystyle H_3C\quad CH_3}{|}}{\overset{\overset{\displaystyle HO\quad OH}{|}}{CH_3-C-C-CH_3}}} \xrightarrow[\text{heat}]{H^+}$$

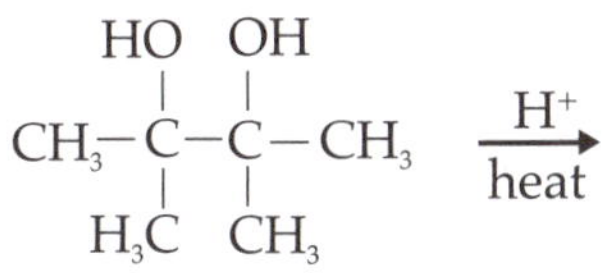

vic diol

$$R-\overset{\overset{\displaystyle H}{|}}{\underset{\underset{\displaystyle H}{|}}{C}}-\overset{\overset{\displaystyle O}{\|}}{C}-H \;+\; \text{ROH} \;\longrightarrow$$

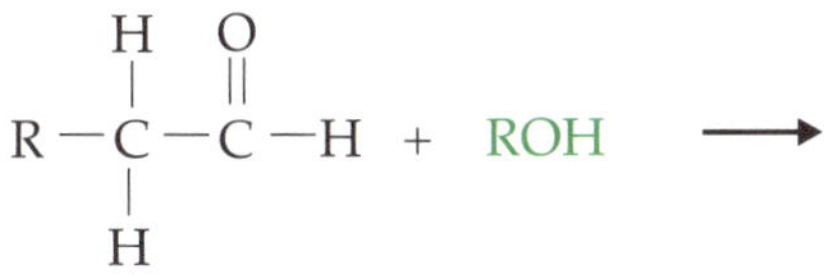

$$\underset{\text{epoxide}}{\overset{\overset{\displaystyle O}{\diagup\;\diagdown}}{-C-C-}}$$

epoxide

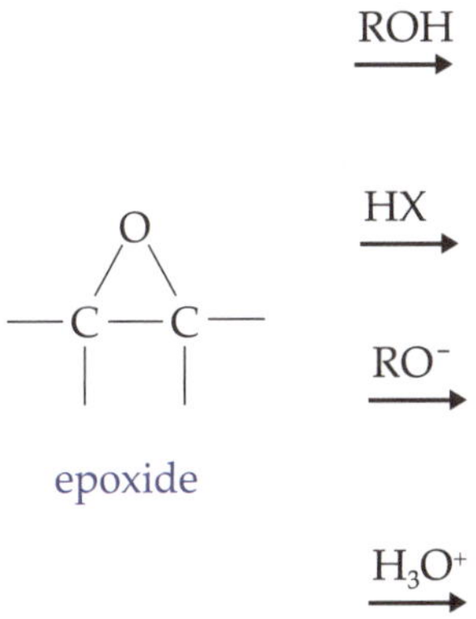

$\xrightarrow{\text{ROH}}$

$\xrightarrow{\text{HX}}$

$\xrightarrow{\text{RO}^-}$

$\xrightarrow{H_3O^+}$

$$R-\overset{\overset{\displaystyle O}{\|}}{C}-H \xrightarrow[H^+]{\text{HOCH}_2\text{CH}_2\text{OH}}$$

$$\underset{\text{aldehyde}}{R-\overset{\overset{\displaystyle O}{\|}}{C}-H} \;+\; H_2O \xrightarrow{\text{OH}^-}$$

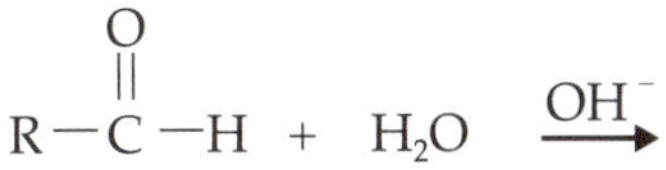

aldehyde

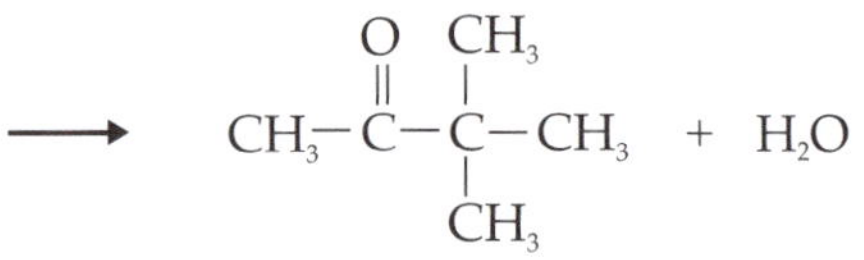

⟶ CH₃–C–C–CH₃ + H₂O
       ‖ |
       O CH₃
          |
          CH₃

Pinacol Rearrangement
Page 51

⟶ ROH + RBr

Acid Cleavage
Page 52

ROH⟶
        OH
        |
      –C–C–
        | |
           OR

RO⁻⟶
        O⁻
        |
      –C–C–
        | |
           OR

HX⟶
        OH
        |
      –C–C–
        | |
           X

H₃O⁺⟶
        OH
        |
      –C–C–
        | |
           OH

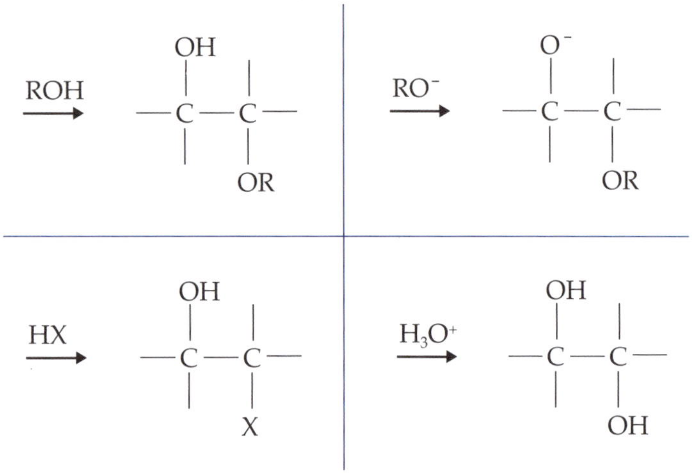

From the Same Reactant
Page 52

⟶ R–C–C–H
      | |
      H OR

      H OH

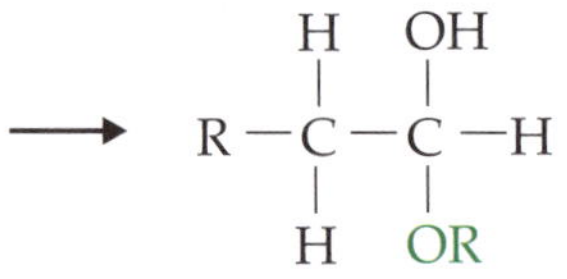

Hemiacetal Formation
Page 57

⟶ R–C–OH
      |
      OH
      |
      H

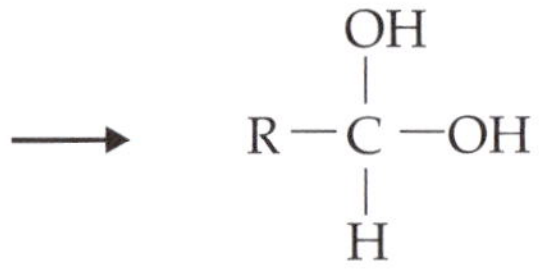

hydrate

Gem Diol Formation
Page 58

⟶ R–C–H
      O   O
       \ /

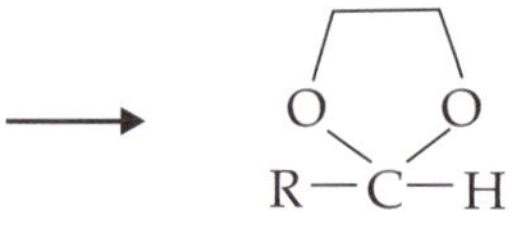

Acetal formation
Blocking Groups
Page 58

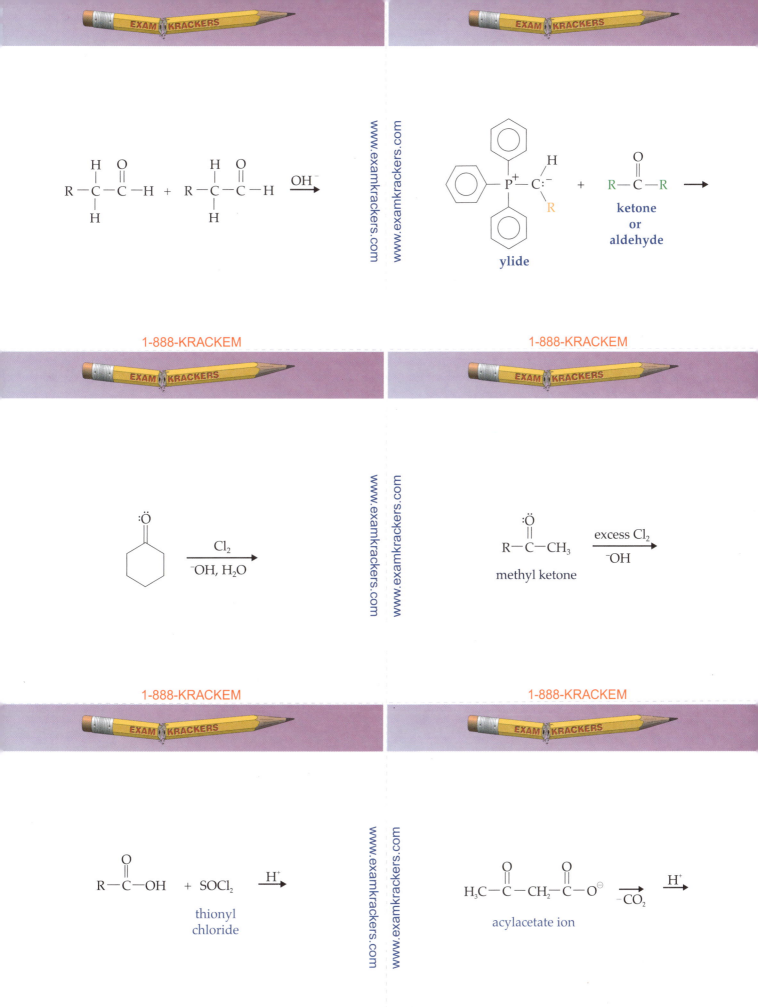

1-888-KRACKEM

1-888-KRACKEM

1-888-KRACKEM

1-888-KRACKEM

1-888-KRACKEM

1-888-KRACKEM

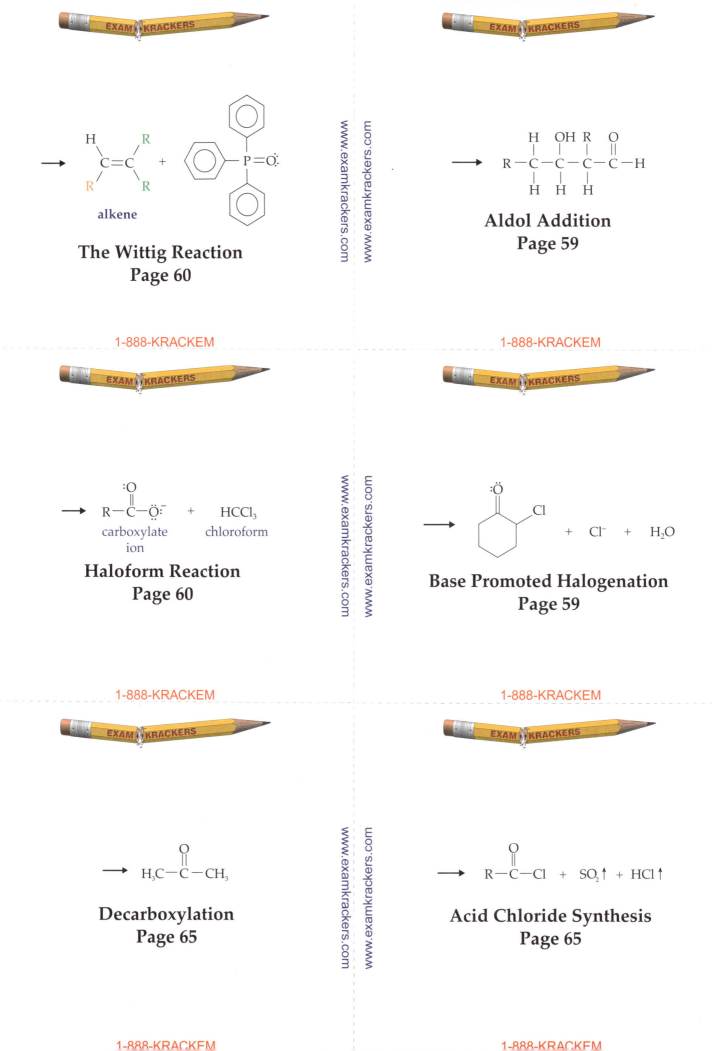

The Wittig Reaction
Page 60

alkene

Aldol Addition
Page 59

carboxylate
ion

chloroform

Haloform Reaction
Page 60

Base Promoted Halogenation
Page 59

Cl^- + H_2O

$H_3C-C-CH_3$

Decarboxylation
Page 65

$R-C-Cl$ + $SO_2\uparrow$ + $HCl\uparrow$

Acid Chloride Synthesis
Page 65

www.examkrackers.com
www.examkrackers.com
www.examkrackers.com

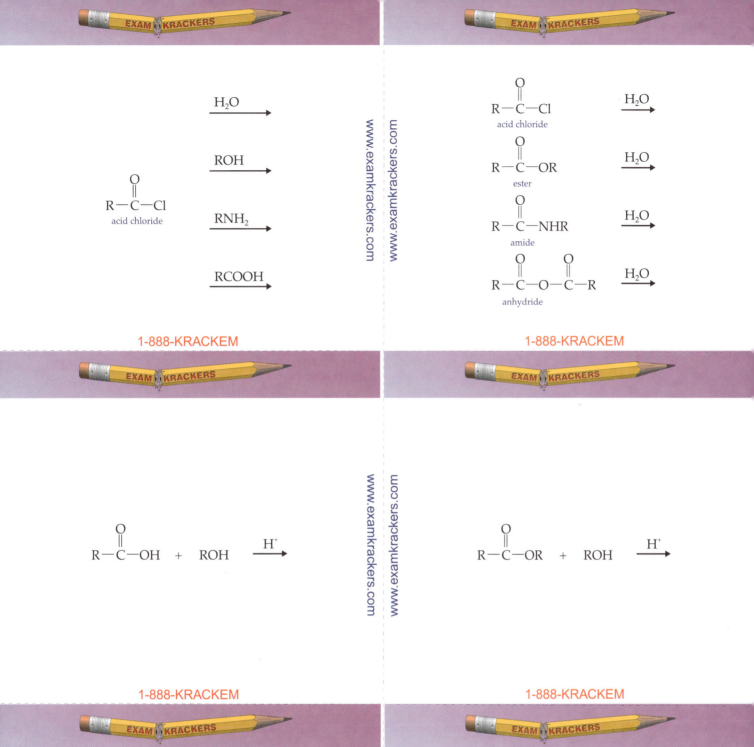

$$\underset{\text{acid chloride}}{R-\overset{\overset{\displaystyle O}{\|}}{C}-Cl} \quad \xrightarrow{\text{H}_2\text{O}}$$

$$\xrightarrow{\text{ROH}}$$

$$\xrightarrow{\text{RNH}_2}$$

$$\xrightarrow{\text{RCOOH}}$$

$$\underset{\text{acid chloride}}{R-\overset{\overset{\displaystyle O}{\|}}{C}-Cl} \quad \xrightarrow{\text{H}_2\text{O}}$$

$$\underset{\text{ester}}{R-\overset{\overset{\displaystyle O}{\|}}{C}-OR} \quad \xrightarrow{\text{H}_2\text{O}}$$

$$\underset{\text{amide}}{R-\overset{\overset{\displaystyle O}{\|}}{C}-NHR} \quad \xrightarrow{\text{H}_2\text{O}}$$

$$\underset{\text{anhydride}}{R-\overset{\overset{\displaystyle O}{\|}}{C}-O-\overset{\overset{\displaystyle O}{\|}}{C}-R} \quad \xrightarrow{\text{H}_2\text{O}}$$

1-888-KRACKEM

1-888-KRACKEM

$$R-\overset{\overset{\displaystyle O}{\|}}{C}-OH \quad + \quad ROH \quad \xrightarrow{\text{H}^+}$$

$$R-\overset{\overset{\displaystyle O}{\|}}{C}-OR \quad + \quad ROH \quad \xrightarrow{\text{H}^+}$$

1-888-KRACKEM

1-888-KRACKEM

$$\underset{\text{acetoacetic ester}}{H_3C-\overset{\overset{\displaystyle O}{\|}}{C}-CH_2-\overset{\overset{\displaystyle O}{\|}}{C}-OC_2H_5} \quad \overset{\text{(1) }^-OC_2H_5}{\underset{\text{(2) R—X}}{\longrightarrow}} \quad \xrightarrow[\text{heat}]{\text{H}^+}$$

$$\underset{\substack{\text{ketone} \\ \text{or aldehyde}}}{-\overset{\overset{\displaystyle \ddot{O}}{\|}}{C}-CH_2-} \quad + \quad \overset{\displaystyle H}{\underset{\displaystyle R \quad R}{:N}} \quad \xrightarrow{\text{H}_3\text{O}^+}$$

1-888-KRACKEM

1-888-KRACKEM

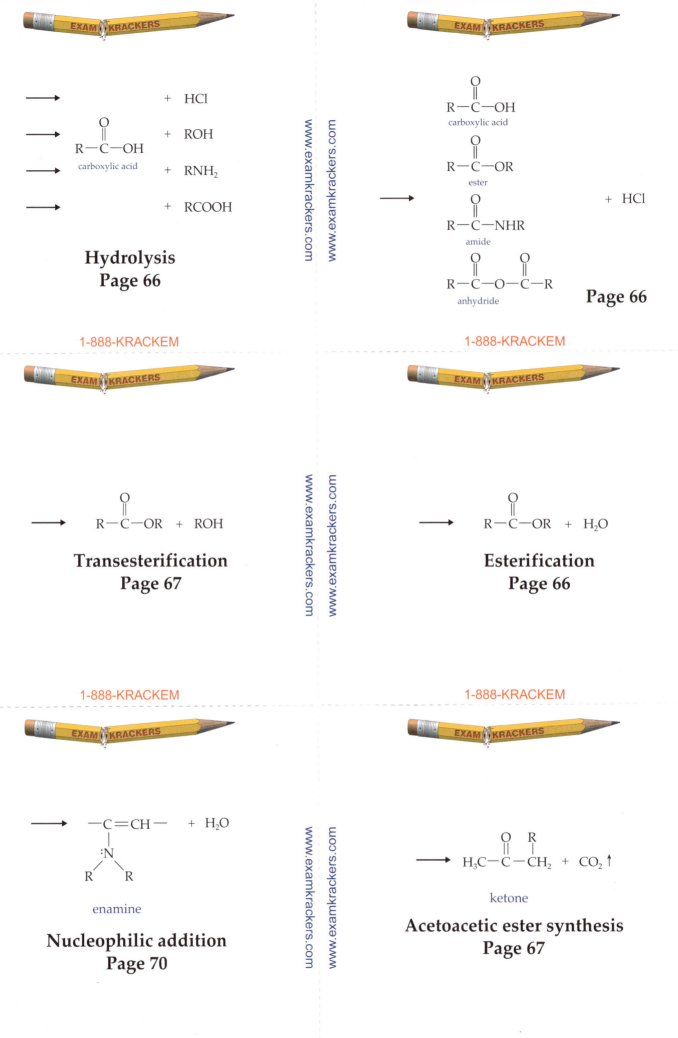

$$\longrightarrow \qquad + \quad HCl$$

$$\longrightarrow \quad \underset{\substack{| \\ \text{carboxylic acid}}}{R-\overset{\displaystyle O}{\overset{\|}{C}}-OH} \quad + \quad ROH$$

$$\longrightarrow \qquad + \quad RNH_2$$

$$\longrightarrow \qquad + \quad RCOOH$$

Hydrolysis
Page 66

$$\underset{\text{carboxylic acid}}{R-\overset{\displaystyle O}{\overset{\|}{C}}-OH}$$

$$\underset{\text{ester}}{R-\overset{\displaystyle O}{\overset{\|}{C}}-OR}$$

$$\underset{\text{amide}}{R-\overset{\displaystyle O}{\overset{\|}{C}}-NHR}$$

$$\underset{\text{anhydride}}{R-\overset{\displaystyle O}{\overset{\|}{C}}-O-\overset{\displaystyle O}{\overset{\|}{C}}-R}$$

$$\longrightarrow \qquad + \quad HCl$$

Page 66

$$\longrightarrow \quad R-\overset{\displaystyle O}{\overset{\|}{C}}-OR \quad + \quad ROH$$

Transesterification
Page 67

$$\longrightarrow \quad R-\overset{\displaystyle O}{\overset{\|}{C}}-OR \quad + \quad H_2O$$

Esterification
Page 66

$$\longrightarrow \quad \underset{\substack{| \\ :N \\ \diagup \quad \diagdown \\ R \qquad R \\ \\ \text{enamine}}}{-C=CH-} \quad + \quad H_2O$$

Nucleophilic addition
Page 70

$$\longrightarrow \quad \underset{\text{ketone}}{H_3C-\overset{\displaystyle O}{\overset{\|}{C}}-\overset{\displaystyle R}{\overset{|}{C}}H_2} \quad + \quad CO_2 \uparrow$$

Acetoacetic ester synthesis
Page 67

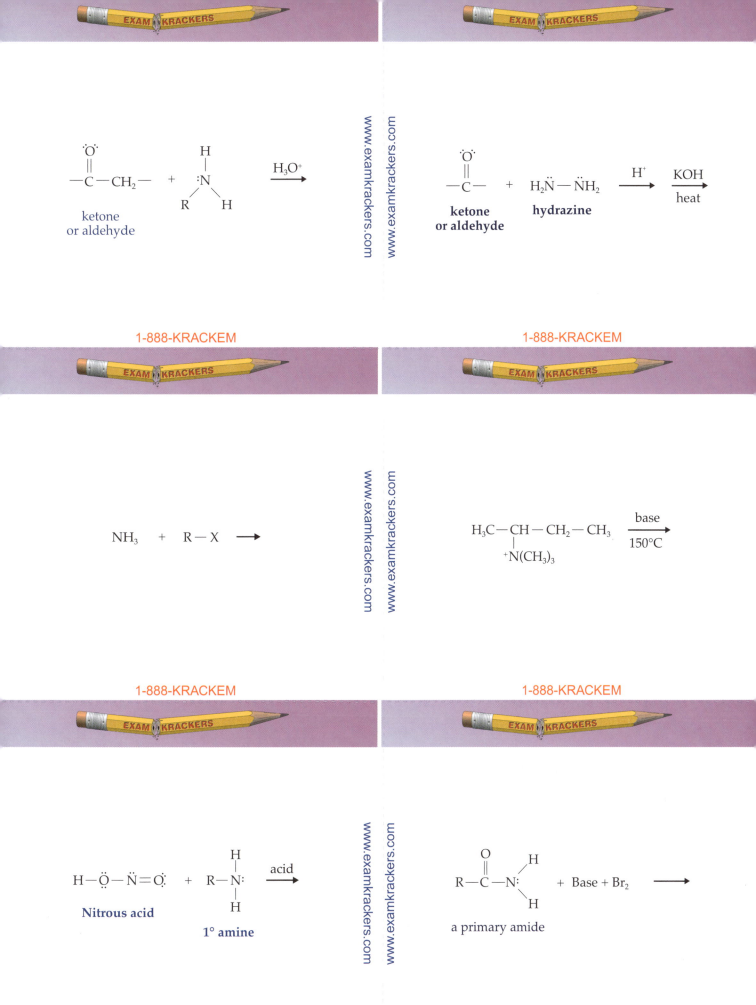

www.examkrackers.com
www.examkrackers.com
www.examkrackers.com
www.examkrackers.com

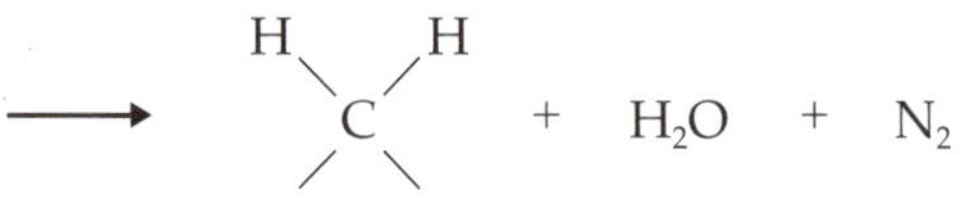

$$\longrightarrow \quad \overset{H}{\underset{}{\,}} \overset{}{C} \overset{H}{\underset{}{\,}} \quad + \quad H_2O \quad + \quad N_2$$

**Desired
Product**

The Wolff-Kishner
Reduction
Page 71

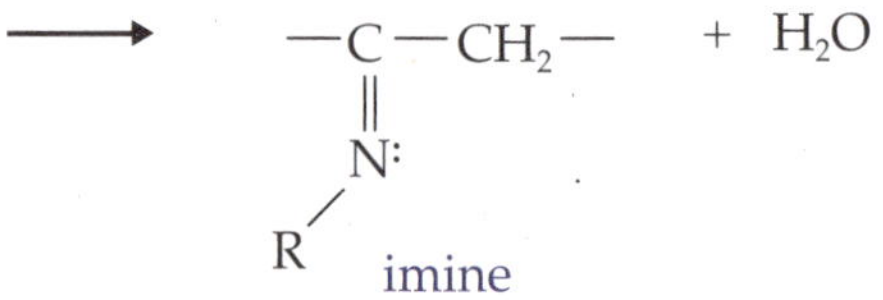

$$\longrightarrow \quad -C=CH_2- \quad + \quad H_2O$$
$$\underset{R}{\overset{\parallel}{N:}}$$
imine

Nucleophilic addition
Page 70

$$H_2C=CH-CH_2-CH_3$$
Hofmann product
(major product)

$$\xrightarrow[150°C]{base} \quad + \quad CH_3-CH=CH-CH_3$$
Saytzeff product
(minor product)

$$+ :N(CH_3)_3 + H_2O$$

The Hofmann Elimination
Page 72

$$\longrightarrow \quad RNH_2 \quad + \quad HX$$

Alkylation of an amine
Page 72

$$\longrightarrow \quad R-NH_2 + CO_2 + OH^-$$

a primary amine

The Hofmann Degradation
Page 74

$$\longrightarrow \quad R-\overset{+}{N}\equiv N: \quad + \quad H_2\ddot{O}:$$

**Diazonium
ion**

Diazotization of an Amine
Page 73